MR THOMAS ■ KATHY B[URKE]

'Kathy Burke's first full-length pla[y] exciting new talent. Taking us bac[k to the] 50s, the tale of Mr Thomas . . . d[...] comedy of kitchen-sink manners t[o ...]ster comment on social stereotyping and . . . sexual impulse.' *Time Out.*

THE AWAKENING ■ JULIAN GARNER

'Set on a remote Norwegian island between the wars . . . we find a child-murderer and rapist, sent to live with a local female farmer who brings him to a kind of tranquillity and forgiveness . . . a new playwright of real promise.' Sheridan Morley. 'He makes his point . . . with an understanding of inner pain that is shock-simple and brutal, but it has a delicacy and sensitiveness too.' *Sunday Times.*

SUGAR HILL BLUES ■ KEVIN HOOD

'Set in 1949, it is an intriguing, original piece which promises much for the future . . . Bernie, a likeable Geordie bricklayer and amateur tenor saxophonist, is working his passage across the Atlantic to meet his hero, the blind black jazz man, Lewis.' *Daily Telegraph.* 'An arresting piece which manages to seem neither derivative nor self-indulgent.' *The Times.*

BOLD GIRLS ■ RONA MUNRO

'Another weekend in west Belfast . . . Nora, Marie and Cassie's men are gone – one passed on, one killed and one in the Maze. A nightmare, of course, and yet an ideal setting for some thoughts on femininity, love and liberation . . . A bold new play.' *Belfast Telegraph.* 'At moments funny, at moments touching and always thoughtful . . .' *Scotsman.* Joint winner of the 1991 Susan Smith Blackburn Award.

INFIDELITIES ■ RICHARD ZAJDLIC

'Richard Zajdlic's prizewinning tragedy about the suspicions and jealousies that mar the relationships of young marrieds is a compelling, potent drama with a lot of shouting, a hint of marital violence and a wholly unexpected denouement . . . There is every reason to agree with the judges who voted this the winner of the 1990 West London Playwriting Competition'. *Time Out.*

in the same series

First Run
Selected and introduced by Kate Harwood
  Prickly Heat by Simon Donald
  Inventing a New Colour by Paul Godfrey
  Low Level Panic by Clare McIntyre
  Leave Taking by Winsome Pinnock
  A Handful of Stars by Billy Roche

First Run 2
Selected and introduced by Kate Harwood
  Ines de Castro by John Clifford
  Back Street Mammy by Trish Cooke
  Sleeping Nightie by Victoria Hardie
  Una Pooka by Michael Harding
  Loose Ends by Stuart Hepburn
  Valued Friends by Stephen Jeffreys

FIRST RUN 3

■ NEW PLAYS BY NEW WRITERS

MR THOMAS ■ KATHY BURKE

THE AWAKENING ■ JULIAN GARNER

SUGAR HILL BLUES ■ KEVIN HOOD

BOLD GIRLS ■ RONA MUNRO

INFIDELITIES ■ RICHARD ZAJDLIC

SELECTED AND INTRODUCED BY
■ MATTHEW LLOYD

NICK HERN BOOKS, LONDON

A Nick Hern Book

First Run 3 first published in 1991 as an original paperback by
Nick Hern Books, a Random Century Company, 20 Vauxhall
Bridge Road, London SW1V 2SA

Mr Thomas copyright © 1991 by Kathy Burke
The Awakening copyright © 1991 by Julian Garner
Sugar Hill Blues copyright © 1991 by Kevin Hood
Bold Girls copyright © 1991 by Rona Munro
Infidelities copyright © 1991 by Richard Zajdlic

Introduction copyright © 1991 by Matthew Lloyd

Set in Baskerville by BookEns Ltd, Baldock, Herts.
Printed by TJ Press, Padstow.

British Cataloguing in Publication Data

First run 3
I. Lloyd, Matthew
822.914

ISBN 1 85459 059 6

Contents

Introduction

Mr Thomas   page 1

The Awakening   59

Sugar Hill Blues   109

Bold Girls   183

Infidelities   259

Introduction

This is the third volume of new plays in the *First Run* series, and
like its predecessors it appears at a time when contemporary
writing for the stage is dimly regarded, and when 'the dearth of
new writing talent' has become a favourite catchphrase of the
critics. The impact of the five plays presented here is bound to be
a positive one – they are so resourceful in their playwriting craft,
yet so often surprising in their imaginative reach as well. And it is
the essence of a *First Run* volume to strike the optimistic note of
discovery. The authors are still in the early stages of their writing
careers, after all, and the printed plays hold the promise of even
better things to come. But the received opinion is nonetheless that
new voices like these are just isolated signs of life and that the
modern British play is in a seriously moribund state. As the
decade came to a close, many people regretted the failure of the
last ten years to throw up any major dramatists apart from Doug
Lucie and Nick Dear (in Richard Eyre's view) or Timberlake
Wertenbaker (in Michael Billington's).

Like Kate Harwood, who introduced the first two editions of
First Run, I think we need to look at how valid that opinion is and
what sort of context these five new writers were working in.

The gloomy view is still supported by some imposing and by
now very boring facts. Theatre practitioners are sick of the sound
of their own voices reciting the litany of financial statistics that
prove – so clearly and irrefutably – how seriously underfunded
they are. And new writing concerns find themselves banging on
even more tediously than the rest, because lack of money
undermines the promotion of new plays in special ways that are
both flagrant and insidious.

The most flagrant is of course that there are fewer productions
of new writing. There are smaller programmes of work than ever
in those theatres that are primarily dedicated to premiering the
untried script. In the eighteen months covered by this volume –
from October '89 to March '91 – the London listings frequently
looked skimpy because many venues were simply forced to go
dark for long periods (the Barbican, the Young Vic, the Theatre

Upstairs, the Soho Theatre, the Albany Empire and –
permanently – the Half Moon have all been out of action, and
were very severely missed). And there is now a greater reluctance
in regional venues to promote contemporary drama generally,
because it is thought of as a financial risk (though it was good to
see the arrival of a new theatre, the West Yorkshire Playhouse,
with a more enthusiastic commitment to new writing).

The insidious effects of underfunding are just as damaging,
even though they may only be apparent to those on the inside of
the production process. At Hampstead Theatre, for example,
worries over pounds and pence have begun to invade all levels of
the creative work, and it's harder and harder to keep them at bay.
When your production budget allows for an average cast of six
actors per show, it can easily begin to twist your responses as a
reader of scripts, however scrupulously you try to take the same
impartial mind to the ten-hander that you take to the two-hander.

The net result is that many cherished projects take longer to
realise, creative energies are diverted into fund-raising schemes,
and artistic ideals can only be pursued in fits and starts. But my
own experience as a literary manager has been that when the
money's there, the plays are waiting to be put on. And there are
always writers that one is eager to work with – even though they
may have to wait until they've made enough money out of more
lucrative television work before they can afford to accept a theatre
commission. In other words, yes, a shortage of cash casts a blight
on new drama, but no, it doesn't follow that a generation of
playwrights can be written off.

The fact is that the background against which the five plays
presented here were produced is variegated in a way that is never
acknowledged by our theatre critics. They would certainly say that
the last year-and-a-half has been a dud period for new talent,
dominated by writers who made their names in the 1970s. Alan
Ayckbourn and Simon Gray had West End plays that were
benignly received and which confirmed their position as
mainstays of the commercial repertoire. The autumn of 1990 also
saw the return en masse of our established political playwrights.
The splash they made was all the noisier because of their
common concern with the new revolutions of Eastern Europe.

At the National, David Edgar's *The Shape of the Table* presented a
fly-on-the-palace-wall treatment of a nominally fictional scenario.
At the RSC, Tariq Ali and Howard Brenton inverted the formula
in *Moscow Gold*, snatching up real political figures and spinning
them through a stylistic merry-go-round of farce, spectacle and

dialectics. For me, it was Caryl Churchill who provided the most eloquent response to the fragmentation of the Communist bloc. Her *Mad Forest*, at the Central School of Speech and Drama, spliced a family drama and ambiguous phantasmagoria with chunks of verbatim reportage, and managed, in its own haphazard way, to evoke the quality of a collective bad dream.

The National was also busy with the work of other familiar writers, producing new pieces by David Hare, Trevor Griffiths and Christopher Hampton, and importing the magisterial new Brian Friel play, *Dancing at Lughnasa*, from Dublin. This body of work sits very comfortably on the stages at the South Bank, and when one looks back now at a play like *Racing Demon*, one is struck by the thematic coherence it shares with Hare's other work, but also by the vitality it draws from a new and unexpected subject matter, the Church of England.

This is a combination of strengths that is only available to a playwright with staying power, and in a way it's easy to understand why other commentators should feel so pessimistic when they ask the question (as they do more and more frequently), 'Where are the Hares and Ayckbourns of tomorrow?' It doesn't seem to me that any satisfying answers are provided by the two new writers – Ben Elton and William Nicholson – who had West End hits in 1990. Even though they both had speedy follow-ups in the Spring of 1991, these were both received less favourably and it remains to be seen whether the commercial style of either playwright has any durable appeal.

This description of current playwriting accords with the normal gloom and doom so far, especially where the need for fresh blood is concerned. But I'd like to lighten things up by suggesting that the conventional pessimism is based too squarely on the idea that a new play must conform to a model of contemporary realistic observation and involve the audience in a more or less explicit moral or political debate. Many of our opinion-forming critics belong roughly to the same generation as the playwrights who have specialised in the development of this model. They bemoan the inability of any writers under the age of 40 to make the model work, or to fuel the momentum that the new writing companies used to possess, but which has now been relinquished to the cause of world drama, the classic revival and the foreign discovery. But the strange fact is that many of our most exciting dramatists have responded very creatively to this interest in classic texts and cultural difference. In a word, the vitality of contemporary writing for the stage is underrated because much of it is exploring new priorities rather than meeting old ones.

This is confirmed by the most memorable moments I had in the theatre in the last eighteen months and by the most impressive pieces of writing that I came across. They all bear out the feeling that the play for today is paradoxically more likely to be set in the past, in some alien time and place that is relocated in shocking proximity to our own.

Tony Harrison's *The Trackers of Oxyrhynchus* mastered the possibilities of the huge Olivier stage with audacious ease. I was enthralled by its wit and spectacle, and the way it extrapolated from a fragmentary Greek satyr play a passionate concern with the origins of high and low art.

Howard Barker's *Scenes from an Execution* at the Almeida exploited a historical perspective too – like all his recent work. The action thrust us into the world of painting and politics in Renaissance Venice and resounded with powerful and moving insights into the position of the artist in society.

And Chris Hannan's *The Baby*, which was produced at the Tron in Glasgow, freely played against its setting in Ancient Rome to suggest Shakespearean or present-day parallels with remarkable results. I was unable to see the show, but when I read the script I was much taken with Hannan's ability to write about ugliness with such delicacy, and about beauty with such severity.

These are not period plays, got up in a spirit of escapism. They are, instead, occasions for dynamic experiments with language in the theatre. Above all they are examples of the current tendency among playwrights to use the past to shed light on the present. Instead of using the theatre to reflect the audience's daily life back at them, the dramatist makes the audience read the traces of their own world in other historical eras. In this way, new writing has begun to provide an experience that is comparable to, rather than in competition with, reinterpretations of classic drama and what has become known as director's theatre.

With these thoughts in mind, the output of those playwrights who did come to the fore in the 1980s begins to take on a certain unanimity – and consequently to look more considerable than is usually allowed. Timberlake Wertenbaker, Frank McGuinness, Deborah Levy, Nick Dear, Stephen Jeffreys and John Clifford have all worked as translators or stage-adaptors of foreign plays, non-dramatic texts or mythological sources. There is a natural continuity between that work and their own plays, which tend to range through history and to telescope seemingly disparate references to culture and literature. We might call the work of these writers, along with that of such authors as Barker and

Harrison, a Theatre of Anachronism, since it makes such creative use of a quality that traditionally carries pejorative connotations.

It's precisely this quality that makes these writers difficult to acknowledge for those critics with the model of contemporary realism uppermost in their minds. But it seems to me quite likely that it's getting harder to use that model with any fail-safe relevance. On the one hand, the saturation-effect of television naturalism seems to push the theatre writer away from observation and towards invention. On the other, the greater pluralism of modern society – multicultural, technological, highly mobile – seems to baffle the existing dramatic formulae. Christopher Hampton has said his plays usually contain a conflict between a moderate and a radical, but these days I frequently read scripts – about, say, blasphemous writers and racial minorities – where it's no longer possible to define either a progressive or conservative point of view.

It's no wonder then that younger exponents of the anachronistic style have been so much in evidence of late. April De Angelis struck sparks off medieval religious dogma in *Crux* (written for Paines Plough). Amani Naphtali produced an ambitious, if overlong, exploration of African heritage in *Song of Songs* (for Double Edge). And Paul Godfrey explored the resonances of two very different kinds of artistic expression, the music of Benjamin Britten (*Once in a While the Odd Thing Happens*) and the sonnets of Shakespeare (*Sweet Sessions*).

The discussion must be widened at this point to include two other productions that stood out in my theatre-going over the last eighteen months – even though neither of them carries a conventional playwriting credit. Gloria's production of *Sarrasine*, by Neil Bartlett and Nick Bloomfield, and *The History of Tears*, devised and directed by Nick Phillipou at RADA, both engaged with classic texts – in the first case, a Balzac story, in the second, Goethe's *Werther*. Tampering with narrative logic and accommodating a mix of genres, each show nonetheless clung to a strong emotional through-line and achieved an unlooked-for compositional rigour. Both pieces also contained passages of highly potent writing, sometimes distilled from working with the performers, sometimes heavily flavoured by the original source – but sharing a close kinship with all those playwrights that I've described as anachronistic. If new writing is in the dock – and it always is these days – it's time for productions like these to be recruited as witnesses for the defence, as part and parcel of a drama that's trying to get in tune with the times. For however much the Theatre of Anachronism might seem to duck a consistent engagement with the here and now, it is easy to see how closely it fits in with all the fashionable precepts of postmodernism. Gloria's *Sarrasine* followed in the footsteps of Roland Barthes' book *S/Z*. A critical theorist would find our new writing for the stage rife with 'intertextuality'. And indeed the Marxist critic Terry Eagleton had his first play, *St Oscar*, produced by Field Day Theatre Company – a rousing and popular piece about Oscar Wilde in which the theatre was used as a vehicle for the radical reinterpretation of one of its own canonical figures.

All this isn't to say that good new plays should all take their cue from encounters with the past and its cultural artefacts. I have continued to spend much of my time as a literary manager advising writers on the realism of their characters, the topical bite of their plots, the currency of their social satire. It is doubtless still true that the best way for a young writer to make an impact is by writing from his or her own experience. I simply feel that large swathes of new writing are ignored or too easily dismissed by critics who are blinkered and set in their ways. They divide things up with journalistic glibness into the old categories of performance art, devised theatre, adaptation and new writing, at a time when these have become inadequate to describe contemporary theatre.

There even seems to be a serious generation gap when one looks at the reception given to those playwrights under the age of 40 who do take on the task of describing the world around them. Terry Johnson and Robert Holman are recent cases in point. Both *Imagine Drowning*, Johnson's piece for Hampstead Theatre, and *Rafts and Dreams*, Holman's play at the Theatre Upstairs, took bold playwriting risks and received mixed notices. Yet they both played to packed houses of young theatre-goers who were keen in both cases to pick up the imaginative gauntlet that had been thrown down.

It was also heartening to see two former *First Run* discoveries, Billy Roche and Clare McIntyre, consolidating their promise with lively second plays. *Poor Beast in the Rain* recreated the nuances of smalltown life in Roche's native Wexford with the same aplomb as his debut two years before. And when the Royal Court produced McIntyre's *My Heart's a Suitcase* in its main auditorium, this quirky play revealed an ability to beguile reviewers as well as audiences.

There were two dark and dangerous comedies that I greatly enjoyed, both with strong regional accents: Robin Glendinning's *Donny Boy*, from Ulster (produced by Manchester Royal Exchange); and *The Evil Doers*, from Glasgow (produced by the

Bush Theatre) – by Chris Hannan again.

At least three exciting stage debuts by writers published elsewhere must be mentioned. Gillian Plowman's shrewdly poised play about four psychiatric patients living in the community, *Me and My Friend*, was one of the last productions at the old Soho Poly. Dermot Bolger's haunting *The Lament for Arthur Cleary* was one of the most authentically original offerings on the Fringe at Edinburgh. And Philip Ridley;s *The Pitchfork Disney*, seen at the Bush Theatre, was a compulsively watchable play studded with daring nightmare images. All three premieres announced the arrival of stylish voices immediately at home in the theatre.

The five playwrights selected for *First Run 3* are also intrinsically theatrical talents. Three of them exploit the possibilities of historical and cultural distance in line with the trend that I've described, and two of them weave their stories effortlessly from the ordinary fabric of the here and now.

All the plays are written for small casts of either four or five performers. This is a sign of the times, and an indication of how careful the playwright of today must be to comply with the demands of impoverished producers. The volume as a whole reads like an object lesson in how to write plays that are cheap to put on – without sacrificing complexity and depth. And the ingenuity is dazzling, but it shouldn't blind us to the withering implications of the general state of affairs. The large ensemble play has practically ceased to evolve, and it's shameful, really, that certain kinds of subject matter (e.g. anything with a crowd scene) should be avoided on our stages for purely economic reasons. It isn't surprising that drama schools like Central, the Guildhall and RADA, where student numbers actually favour large-cast plays, are assuming more importance in the network of new writing organisations as they step into the breach to allow writers to work on a broader canvas.

In common with many previous *First Run* authors, four of these five playwrights have come to writing for the stage after acting on it. The acting profession has of course been the classic breeding-ground for British dramatists from Shakespeare to Osborne and Pinter and onwards. It has always provided us with writers who have a ready-made ear for spoken language, and an instinctive ability to live in other people's shoes and take both sides of an argument. It's good to find this tradition renewing itself so consistently.

Mr Thomas is Kathy Burke's first play. It was produced to great acclaim at the Old Red Lion in Islington, won a *Time Out* award for its author, and was subsequently televised on Channel 4. The

piece inhabits, with uncanny familiarity, a dingy Ortonesque
milieu. The writing evokes the sad repression of its characters
with a beautifully judged grasp of subtext and surface detail. The
dialogue plays grippingly and, for much of the time, quite
hilariously.

The events of *The Awakening* take place in a more rarefied
setting, in the 1930s on the coastline of Norway, a country that
the writer Julian Garner knows well. The piece draws strength
from its compelling austerity and from a feel for physical action
on stage – farmyard chores, enigmatic gestures, the unspoken
threat of violence. It's a controversial piece that demonstrated an
unerring capacity to engage and provoke its audience when
produced at Hampstead Theatre.

Kevin Hood's *Sugar Hill Blues* shuttles between Tyneside and
Harlem at the height of the Bebop era, by way of the after-dinner
lounge on the Queen Mary. Every time the oppositions of race
and class that cut across the play threaten to become schematic,
the drama twists them inside out with scintillating wit and
fervour. The story is told in vividly accented dialogue, and also
through a clever use of live music – requirements that were
superbly met by the Croydon Warehouse production and made
for one of the best nights out of last Summer.

I couldn't put the script of Rona Munro's *Bold Girls* down when
I came across it, and I was disappointed that I'd missed the
touring production by 7:84 Scotland. The play dwells with
unsentimental intimacy and sometimes raucous humour on the
lives of a group of working-class women in West Belfast. It's a
superbly controlled achievement, full of piercing truth and fired
by a special passion and commitment. The drama easily
transcends its immediate concerns and made a very worthy
winner of the prestigious Susan Smith Blackburn Award.

Richard Zajdlic's *Infidelities*, produced at the Tabard in West
London, has certain similarities with *Bold Girls*: it's a taut and
exacting play that involves sexual betrayal and the military
presence in Northern Ireland. The author is cool and non-
judgemental, but he pinpoints all the dangers of machismo and
peer pressure. The narrative technique is wonderfully cunning in
the way it keeps us as the audience right in the crossfire, making
us the impotent go-betweens in a failure of communication,
unable to do anything to avert the impending disaster.

Taken together, these five plays make up a collection of striking
energy and steely temper. Throughout the volume, you'll find
writing that takes pride in its own power to disconcert, its rough
edges and brutal endings. In the end, it is impossible to say

whether new writing as a whole is really in the doldrums, or whether with hindsight we will see that it's begun to tackle the question of its own relevance in new and interesting ways. In any event, the vitality of these five writers, their refusal to be diffident or decorous, is a salutary tonic. I hope they stay true to the robustness that comes so naturally to them.

Matthew Lloyd
March 1991

Acknowledgements: Many people have been helpful in the preparation of this volume. Special thanks are due to Anna Koutelieri, Jenny Topper and Alan Pollock for their kind advice and recommendations.

MR THOMAS ■ KATHY BURKE

KATHY BURKE was brought up in London and attended the Anna Scher Theatre. Since that time she has built a strong reputation for herself as both a comic and a serious actress in a variety of media. She has recently appeared in such productions as *The Boys Next Door* (Edinburgh Festival and Hampstead Theatre), *Amongst Barbarians* (Royal Exchange Theatre, Hampstead Theatre and BBC Television), *A Very Peculiar Practice* (BBC Television) and *Harry Enfield's Television Programme* (Hat Trick/BBC). She began writing some years ago and directed *Mr Thomas*, her own first full-length play, at the Old Red Lion in early 1990, which won a Time Out/01 for London Award. *Mr Thomas* was seen on television in January 1991 in Channel 4's Small Stages season.

For John

Characters

GEORGE, mid to late twenties. Not very healthy looking but has an attractive face. Quiet personality.

WEAVER, late thirties. Small and stocky. Scruffy in appearance, flash and sure of himself. A pain in the bum.

MRS TEBBIT, mid-forties. Dowdy one minute, stunning the next. Frustrated in every way.

GORDON, late forties. Smart dresser, upper-class, the ex-army type.

THOMAS, late forties to early fifties. Small and weak, a nervous wreck. Wears glasses.

The play takes place in one day in a small bedsit in London sometime in the late nineteen fifties.

Mr Thomas was first staged at the Old Red Lion, London on 30 January 1990 with the following cast:

GEORGE	James Clyde
WEAVER	Ray Winstone
GORDON	Oliver Smith
MRS TEBBIT	Anita Graham
MR THOMAS	Ian Jentle

Directed by Kathy Burke
Produced by Simon Brint
Designed by Matthew Duguid and John Pope

TENOVUS SHOPS
14A BRIDGE STREET
HAVERFORDWEST

26/11/2013 000000#093342
14:58   01 CLERK 01

NO SALE

        SA61 2AD

TENOVUS SHOPS
14A BRIDGE STREET
HAVERFORDWEST

26/11/2013 000000#093343
14:58   01 CLERK 01

BOOKS   *1.29

ITEMS   10
CASH   *1.29

        SA61 2AD

ACT ONE

Scene One

Setting: the attic room of a house. A bed in one corner, a battered armchair in another. A sink with a mish-mash of pots, plates and cups. A portable record player and discs scattered around it. Damp-ridden walls, an old lino covers the floor. The curtains are always closed and the room is lit by a large floor lamp. The door to the room is up-stage next to an old wardrobe. The whole room should give off a feeling of despair.

Morning. GEORGE *is asleep on the bed on top of the covers. He has slept in his clothes and they are a crumpled mess. There is a knock on the door.* GEORGE *doesn't move. After a pause another knock, this time louder.*

WEAVER (*off*). George? . . . George? Are you awake?

GEORGE (*stirs slightly and looks up. Mumbles*). What?

WEAVER (*off*). George? Wake up. Come on, I know you're in.

GEORGE (*sits up*). Who is it?

WEAVER (*off*). ME.

GEORGE. Who?

WEAVER (*off*). Stop fucking about George. It's me, Weaver, come on, let me in.

GEORGE. What do you want?

WEAVER. Just let us in, will you. Stop playing silly buggers.

GEORGE. Hold on a minute. (*Gets up, staggers to the door and opens it.*)

WEAVER (*entering*). Fuck me, it's freezing out there. I've just been up the dole, thought I'd pop in and see you as I was in the area. Hope you don't mind.

GEORGE (*goes to the sink and splashes his face with water*). Do you want a cup of tea?

WEAVER. Wouldn't mind.

GEORGE. I ain't got no milk though.

WEAVER. Oh. You got any coffee?

GEORGE. No.

WEAVER. I don't think I'll bother then. I'm not being rude or anything, it's just that I can't stand tea without milk. I can do without it in coffee but I have to have milk in tea even if it's just a splash.

GEORGE. Well I ain't got none, I'm afraid.

WEAVER. No worries. I didn't really fancy one anyway.

GEORGE. I've got a drop of whisky if you'd care for it.

WEAVER. Oh I dunno. Bit early ain't it?

GEORGE. It's twenty-to.

WEAVER. Is it?

GEORGE. I might be a bit slow.

WEAVER. Fuck it. The pubs are open in half an hour so it wouldn't be too out of order would it?

GEORGE (*gets the whisky from the wardrobe and pours out two generous amounts*). Do you want water in it?

WEAVER. Just a splash, don't go mad.

GEORGE. There you go.

WEAVER. Smashing. Just what the doctor ordered.

Pause.

GEORGE. What a night.

WEAVER. Rough was it?

GEORGE (*sits on the bed*). Murder. God knows how I got home.

WEAVER. That bad? I should've been there.

GEORGE. You would've loved it.

WEAVER. I had a gippy tummy. Don't know what was the matter with me. I couldn't walk.

GEORGE. You alright now?

WEAVER. Kosher. I must've had a bug or something.

GEORGE. Well, you missed a good night.

WEAVER. It's always the way, ain't it. Life can be a bit of a bollock like that.

GEORGE. Not to worry. He's bound to have another one soon.

WEAVER. Who was there then?

GEORGE. Just the usual mob, plus a few I'd never met before. Nice people though, friendly.

WEAVER. Any women there?

GEORGE. Quite a few, as it goes.

WEAVER. Any salty ones?

GEORGE. One or two. That bird was there.

WEAVER. What bird?

GEORGE. That bird, you know.

WEAVER. What one?

GEORGE. The one with the teeth.

WEAVER. They've all got teeth, well, most of them have.

GEORGE. Yea but she's got big ones, you know, sort of goofy but not goofy, goofy, if you know what I mean.

WEAVER. What colour hair?

GEORGE. Sort of blondish, oh you know her but I can't remember her name.

WEAVER. Not Gloria?

GEORGE. No, I know Gloria, don't I. She's a bit plump, not fat, just a bit plump, fat arse.

WEAVER. Oh I know who you mean, that's what's-her-name, Janet.

GEORGE. Janet, that's it. She asked me where you were.

WEAVER. Yea? What did you say?

GEORGE. I said you were at home with a bad tummy; she looked a bit put out.

WEAVER. Did she? Oh that's good. I quite like her.

GEORGE. She left with some bloke, though.

WEAVER. Did she? Who?

GEORGE. I don't know, one of Derek's mates.

WEAVER. What, was she with him then?

GEORGE. Well she didn't come with him, just left with him.

WEAVER. Yea, she's a bit loose like that.

GEORGE. Is she?

WEAVER. Yea. Puts it about a bit. Nice girl though.

GEORGE. She didn't look like she'd put it about.

WEAVER. Well she's not a slag or anything, she don't just go
   with anyone. I only know a couple of geezers that have had
   her.

GEORGE. Have you?

WEAVER. What?

GEORGE *(shyly)*. You know.

WEAVER. Yea, once or twice.

GEORGE. You sly bugger.

WEAVER. What?

GEORGE. You never told me.

WEAVER. Well I don't have to tell you do I?

GEORGE. No but . . .

WEAVER. I don't think I told anybody. I don't see why I should
   have to. I hate it when blokes mouth off about the birds they
   pull and all the ins and outs as to what they do with them. I
   respect women, I do. I mean you've got to respect them or they
   won't respect us.

GEORGE. Yea, I suppose you're right.

WEAVER. I mean you never tell me about the birds you pull.

GEORGE. Well, no. I don't think it's something you should talk
   about.

WEAVER. Well that's my point, ain't it. You still ask me questions
   though, don't you.

GEORGE. Yea I know . . . I shouldn't . . . It's not right. Sorry Weaver.

WEAVER. No, don't apologise George. You're my mate, you never have to say sorry to me, I was just making a point, that's all.

Pause.

Wish I'd gone last night, I'd like to see Janet again. Still, I'm bound to bump into her sometime.

GEORGE. Well she did say she'd pop in the Crown one night.

WEAVER. Did she? When?

GEORGE. She didn't say.

WEAVER. Well that's a bugger, ain't it.

GEORGE. What is?

WEAVER. Well she could've said when. I mean, I might not be there.

GEORGE. Might not be there when?

WEAVER. When she pops in. The night she decides to pop into the Crown I might be somewhere else.

GEORGE. But you're always in the Crown. You don't go anywhere else.

WEAVER. I'm not always in there. I wasn't there last night.

GEORGE. That's because you had a gippy tummy.

WEAVER. I know, but I still don't go there every night. We often go to the Swan for a change, don't we.

GEORGE. Only now and then. We're usually in the Crown.

WEAVER. I know that, that's not the point though is it? I mean, one night we might decide to go down the Swan, for a change sort of thing, and Janet might go down the Crown thinking I'd be in there because *you*, soppy bollocks, told her I'm in there all the time and forgot to mention the fact that every now and then we pop in the Swan.

GEORGE. Oh I see what you mean now.

WEAVER. See really, she should have told you a certain night so I could make sure I was in there. You see George, some women just take it for granted that you're gonna be around when it's convenient for them. They don't think most of them. They're just all hair and legs.

GEORGE. I sort of get your point.

WEAVER. And what if she decided to pop in and I was with another bird, she wouldn't like that, would she?

GEORGE. No, I don't suppose she would.

WEAVER. So you can see what I'm getting at then?

GEORGE. Oh yea.

Pause.

WEAVER. It's a bit cheeky when you think about it. Still, it's her loss . . . fat fucker! You got any more scotch going?

GEORGE. Do you want some?

WEAVER. If you don't mind, if you've got any spare. I wouldn't want you to think I was poncing.

GEORGE (*pours out more drink*). Don't be silly. What's mine is yours. You're my mate.

WEAVER. You're a good bloke, George. No doubt about it, you're a little diamond.

GEORGE. Leave it out.

WEAVER. Don't be embarrassed. I mean it. A man couldn't ask for a finer friend.

GEORGE. Well it works both ways, you know.

WEAVER. You've got a point there. That's a bloody good point George. I mean, I think you're a good bloke and I know you think I'm a good bloke, so we get on. We're sort of compatible, ain't we?

GEORGE. That's one way of looking at it.

WEAVER. No mate. It's the only way to look at it. It may sound daft but it's as if we were made for each other. I don't mean in the way that men and women are made for each other, I mean in the way that men and men are made for each other, do you see what I mean?

GEORGE. Sort of.

WEAVER. How old are you?

GEORGE. Twenty-seven.

WEAVER. Is that all?

GEORGE. Yea. Why, how old did you think I was?

WEAVER. Don't know, never really thought about it before, didn't think you was as young as that though. Still, you learn something new every day don't you? Anyway, back to my point. Now you've lived for twenty-seven years right?

GEORGE. Right.

WEAVER. Now in those twenty-seven years you must have had mates come and go, right?

GEORGE. Right.

WEAVER. Now me, I've lived for thirty-six years . . .

GEORGE. Are you thirty-six?

WEAVER. Yea, surprising, ain't it. Now I've certainly seen a lot of mates come and go. Some have been alright and some have been right-bastards, but you George, and I can say this in all honesty, you have been the best mate I've ever had. You see, the main base of a friendship is built on trust and I know I can trust you. I've told you a lot of things about myself and about other people and I've always known you wouldn't breathe a word of it to anyone.

GEORGE. Of course I wouldn't. It's only right, isn't it. I'd never betray someone else's confidence.

WEAVER. That's why you're my mate.

GEORGE. I trust you as well, you know.

WEAVER. Of course you do.

GEORGE. I've told you loads of things I wouldn't dream of telling anyone else.

WEAVER. That's right. I've got a lot on you, ain't I George.

Pause.

This is the life, ain't it. Look at us aye, not a care in the world. I feel sorry for those poor buggers who have to go to work every day.

GEORGE. Silly ain't they.

WEAVER. No. I wouldn't call them silly George; I think 'sad' is a more appropriate word. They don't know how to relax, see. Everything is one big rush to them, even when they're on their holidays. I've studied them down in Southend, I often study people, it's the intelligent man's pastime. What they do is they rush out of bed before all the hot water goes, then they rush down to breakfast before some fat bastard from Wigan eats the last of the bacon, then they rush down to the beach, rush back to the digs for dinner, rush out to the dance-halls to have a quick jive before they have to rush back again in case the landlady locks them out all night. It's a fucking joke! Give me this life any time. Every day's a holiday ain't it. I mean, I know we ain't got as much money as them, but who needs it, that's what I'd like to know.

GEORGE. Well if you ever do go short you know you can always come to me for a bob or two, and vice versa I suppose.

WEAVER. Exactly. You've just taken the words right out of my mouth.

Pause.

Yep, it's all a waste of time, work and families and that, all one big waste of space.

GEORGE. I wouldn't mind a couple of kids one day; I know it sounds silly but I've got a bit of a soft spot for them.

WEAVER. Yea, but to have kids you need a wife, don't you George.

GEORGE. Well I wouldn't mind getting married one day either.

WEAVER. Oh leave it out, I know for a fact you're not the marrying kind.

GEORGE. Ain't I?

WEAVER. Of course you ain't, you like your freedom too much, don't you.

GEORGE. Well I do now, but I might change my mind in a couple of years and want to settle down.

WEAVER. You've got to get a job if you want to settle down.

GEORGE. But what I'm saying is, I might change. I mean, I

know that right now the last thing I want is a job and a wife
and that, but you don't know what you want in the future. I
mean, a few years ago I wanted to be a bloody singer in a band
but I don't want to be one now, do I?

WEAVER. Alright, I get your drift and you're right, people do
change and so do their attitudes.

GEORGE. I'm right, ain't I?

WEAVER. I just said you was.

Pause.

Can you sing then?

GEORGE. What?

WEAVER. Well you just said you wanted to be a singer; does that
mean you can sing then?

GEORGE. Well a bit. I'm not brilliant but I can keep in tune.

WEAVER. Give us a burst then.

GEORGE. What?

WEAVER. Go on, sing me a song.

GEORGE (*laughs*). Leave it out.

WEAVER. Go on.

GEORGE. No.

WEAVER. Why not?

GEORGE. I ain't singing you a song.

WEAVER. Oh go on, don't be shy.

GEORGE. No.

WEAVER. Why not?

GEORGE. I don't want to.

WEAVER. What's the matter, I'm your mate, ain't I?

GEORGE. I know you are but I'm not gonna sing to you; wish
I'd never said it now.

WEAVER. Oh go on George, I'm the only one here, I won't
laugh.

GEORGE. I can't just sing a song just like that can I? I mean, I haven't sung in years, and besides, I can't do it without a piano.

WEAVER. What, you play the piano as well?

GEORGE. A bit.

WEAVER. Fuck me! He's full of surprises, ain't he.

GEORGE. It's no big deal.

WEAVER. Alright. If you don't want to sing, I won't force you. I'm not that way inclined, but will you do me a favour, next time we go down the Swan will you give me a little tune?

GEORGE. Have they got a piano in there then?

WEAVER. 'Course they have; ain't you seen it?

GEORGE. No, we're always in the Crown.

WEAVER. Well they have! So you have to give us a little tune one night.

GEORGE. We'll see.

WEAVER. Just a little bash on the keyboards. No singing. Just a little bash.

GEORGE. I'll see next time we go in there.

WEAVER. That's the spirit. I do love a good sing-song round the piano. You don't find it much these days, it's all that rock around the clock shit, does my fucking head in.

GEORGE. Gordon said he might pop round but he's probably forgotten about it after Derek's party last night.

WEAVER. Bad was he?

GEORGE. Off his head.

WEAVER. I should've been there.

GEORGE. You missed a good piss-up.

WEAVER. Still, nothing I can do about it now.

GEORGE. You'll just have to wait for the next one.

WEAVER. I'll be waiting all year before that tight sod throws another bash.

GEORGE. Well I'd have one but this place is too small.

WEAVER. It's not too small.

GEORGE. It's too small for a party, I can only get about four people in here.

WEAVER. Leave it out. You could fit ten in here if you put your mind to it.

GEORGE. I couldn't have one anyway, my landlady wouldn't like it.

WEAVER. You could have a small gathering though.

GEORGE. Eh?

WEAVER. A small gathering. You know, just a couple of people for a quiet drink and a bite to eat. A sort of dinner party.

GEORGE. I couldn't have a dinner party in here, it's a dump.

WEAVER. Well I don't mean a dinner party exactly, just a couple of people, a few bottles of beer and some tit-bits. Sounds quite cosy to me.

GEORGE. Yea but you know what that lot like. I can't just have one or two up here, they'd think I was being out of order.

WEAVER. Well it doesn't have to be that lot, does it?

GEORGE. How do you mean?

WEAVER. Well, it could just be you, me and a couple of birds.

GEORGE. What birds?

WEAVER. I don't know . . . Janet and her mate.

GEORGE. What mate?

WEAVER. Any mate. You're not fussy are you?

GEORGE. No, I couldn't have any women up here, she wouldn't allow it.

WEAVER. You've had birds up here before ain't you?

GEORGE. I haven't as it goes . . . See, if I meet a bird I go back to her place, don't I.

WEAVER. Oh, I see. Well I'm sure she wouldn't notice if we slipped them up quietly.

GEORGE. I don't know . . .

WEAVER. Where's your spirit of adventure? It'd be a laugh.

GEORGE. I'll have to think about it.

WEAVER. I think it's a great idea, can't wait.

GEORGE. I said I'd need to think about it.

WEAVER. That's alright, you have a good think. No need to rush into it, you can't hurry these things can you, they need planning.

Pause.

She loves a good sorting that Janet. Get any more scotch?

Blackout.

Scene Two

Later that day. WEAVER *is slumped on the bed asleep.* GEORGE *is sitting in the armchair.* GORDON *enters with two mugs of tea and shuts the door.*

GORDON. There you are George, get that down you.

GEORGE. Cheers Gordon, thanks for bringing the milk.

GORDON. Pleasure. How long has he been here?

GEORGE. Couple of hours. He's been asleep for ages.

GORDON. Don't you mind?

GEORGE. Well I was hoping to clean this place up a bit, but it can wait.

GORDON. You should wake him up and ask him to leave, he'll be there all day otherwise.

GEORGE. I'll give him a bit longer. He's had quite a lot to drink.

GORDON. He can't hold it, he thinks he can but he can't. He either falls asleep or throws up, sometimes both. I won't have him in my flat.

GEORGE. Why not?

GORDON. Because once he's in you can never get him out.

GEORGE. He'll go when I ask him.

GORDON. I wouldn't count on it.

GEORGE. He will, I know he will.

GORDON. Oh well, it's your problem.

Pause.

GEORGE. Did you feel rough this morning?

GORDON. Not really, no.

GEORGE. You put away a bit.

GORDON. I'm just lucky I suppose, but then I always remember to drink a pint of water before I go to bed.

GEORGE. Good night wasn't it.

GORDON. Most pleasant. (*Looks at* WEAVER.) And why wasn't he there?

GEORGE. Didn't feel well, couldn't manage it.

GORDON. He must have been bad. I've never known the mighty Weaver to miss a free piss-up before.

GEORGE. He's alright now though.

GORDON. Yes, he looks it.

Pause.

So. Are you coming to see this band with me then?

GEORGE. What band?

GORDON. The one I told you about last night, don't you remember?

GEORGE. I can hardly remember anything about last night.

GORDON. Well, this friend of mine, Pete his name is, I used to drink with him years ago, well he plays the trumpet in a jazz band. I bumped into him the other day and he gave me a couple of free tickets for tonight.

GEORGE. Where is it?

GORDON. A little club that's just opened at the Angel. They're open till two, the drinks are quite cheap, so it should be a good night.

GEORGE. How much is it to get in?

GORDON. I've just told you, I've got two free tickets.

GEORGE. Oh that's handy.

GORDON. Do you want to come then?

GEORGE. Might as well, I've got no other plans.

GORDON. Good George, good, you won't regret it. He's a wonderful trumpeter and I also thought it was jolly decent of him to give me these tickets, especially as I haven't seen him for so long.

GEORGE. Why ain't you taking Marion?

GORDON. She's gone to her parents for the weekend. Besides, we're always together, it's nice to have a break from each other now and then.

GEORGE. Do you think you'll ever get hitched?

GORDON. I'd like to one day but she's not that keen. She seems to think we're fine as we are. She's right I suppose.

GEORGE. She's a lovely lady, isn't she.

GORDON. Smashing.

GEORGE. Everyone likes her.

GORDON. Well she's so warm and understanding. Never nags, never moans, always there when I need her, and she likes a drink.

GEORGE (laughs). Not half.

GORDON. But she never loses control of herself, that's what I like. You know George, I can't stand some of those women in the Crown who start shouting and screaming after a couple of drinks, either that or they disappear into the Ladies for half an hour.

GEORGE. I've always wondered what they do in there.

GORDON. They cry.

GEORGE. Do they?

GORDON. Oh yes. It's the gin, it sparks off the emotions. They sit there and start pondering on all the awful things that have happened to them, usually it's men, and they start to cry about it. They feel a lot better afterwards, then turn the other way and start laughing at the slightest thing; I find it most infuriating.

GEORGE. I never noticed that before. It's quite funny really. I mean, it's strange how blokes don't act like that.

GORDON. Oh but they do. We're just better at hiding it. Men aren't supposed to show their feelings, it's not the 'done' thing.

Pause.

Have you ever wanted to scream, George?

GEORGE. I don't know what you mean.

GORDON. Have you ever sat in this room, on your own, feeling as though the whole world was against you and just wanted to scream?

GEORGE. I don't know, sort of I suppose.

GORDON. But have you ever done it?

GEORGE. No, no, I haven't.

GORDON. Why not?

GEORGE. I don't know, I'd feel silly.

GORDON. But why feel silly when you're the only one in the room? Nobody's going to hear you, are they? It's such a relief to get it out of your system. I do it all the time.

GEORGE. Well, I'll have to try it the next time I get the hump. (*Changing the subject.*) So, what time are we going to this club then?

GORDON. I could pick you up if you like. We'll get a taxi: the tube is such a bore. Nine o'clock should be fine.

GEORGE. We could get a bus.

GORDON. Oh no, we'd have to get two and we'd be waiting for ever. A taxi is a much better idea.

GEORGE. Well I haven't got much money, you see.

GORDON. Don't worry, I'll pay.

GEORGE. Oh no I couldn't . . .

GORDON. I'd be getting a taxi if I went on my own, so it makes very little difference.

GEORGE. If you're sure.

GORDON. Of course I am.

Pause.

You know, I'm rather looking forward to this.

GEORGE. It'll make a nice change, anyway.

Pause.

GORDON. Right. Well, I'll be off then. (*Gets up.*)

GEORGE. Oh, you off then?

GORDON. Better make tracks, yes.

GEORGE. O.K. then. (*Gets up.*) I'll see you tonight then.

GORDON. Nine to half-past, yes? (*Looks at* WEAVER.) Will you be able to manage him?

GEORGE. Oh yea, I'll wake him up in a minute and give him a cup of tea. Thanks again for the milk.

GORDON. Think nothing of it.

Pause.

Right. I'll see you later then.

GEORGE. See you later.

Pause.

GORDON. Cheerio. (*Exits.*)

GEORGE. Bye. (*Shuts the door.*)

Pause.

WEAVER. He's such a wanker that bloke.

GEORGE. Oh. You awake?

WEAVER. No.

GEORGE. Have a good kip?

WEAVER. I was sleeping like a baby 'til he starts going on. He does my head in.

GEORGE. He's alright.

WEAVER. He's an old toss-pot. Goes on about fuck-all most of the time.

GEORGE. Do you want a cup of tea?

WEAVER. No, you're alright. (*Sits up. Pause.*) You know he's a queer-boy don't you?

GEORGE. No he isn't.

WEAVER. He is, you know.

GEORGE. He can't be, he goes out with Marion.

WEAVER. Just because he's got a woman doesn't mean he's not into men as well. Come to think of it a lot of 'em have a bird on their arm as a sort of cover-up.

GEORGE. Well I don't believe you.

WEAVER. Fair enough, but don't come running to me when he starts lifting your shirt.

GEORGE. Oh shut up.

Pause.

WEAVER. You going then?

GEORGE. Going where?

WEAVER. This club, with him?

GEORGE. Yea, sounds like it could be good.

WEAVER. Can I come?

GEORGE. I don't know.

WEAVER. What do you mean by that?

GEORGE. Well he's only got two tickets.

WEAVER. That's alright, I'll pay me own way in and come down with you two in the taxi.

GEORGE. Well it's not up to me, is it.

WEAVER. Gordon won't mind.

GEORGE. How do you know?

WEAVER. He likes me.

GEORGE. Does he?

WEAVER. Yea, he thinks I'm a laugh, he's always telling me what a laugh I am. He'll be dead chuffed when he knows I'm coming.

GEORGE. Well you can ask him then, 'cos I ain't.

WEAVER. There's no need to ask him is there? I'll just stay here, get cleaned up and wait for him with you.

GEORGE. I don't know Weaver . . .

WEAVER. What's the matter with you? He won't mind, I know he won't. Anyway, he can't stop me going can he? He don't own the fucking place. I'll even go there on my own and meet you in there.

GEORGE. Alright.

WEAVER. It's only a poxy jazz club, anyone would think he had tickets to see the Queen fart the way you're going on.

GEORGE. I said alright Weaver, just forget it.

WEAVER. I just want you to see how silly you're being. Anyway, I would've thought you'd want me to be there. Can't leave you on your own with him, can we?

GEORGE. Oh don't talk soft.

WEAVER. It's because his dick's so small, that's why he's a poof.

GEORGE. What are you going on about?

WEAVER. It's a well-known fact that poofs are the way they are because they've got small dicks. They can't satisfy women you see and I happen to know that Gordon's got the smallest dick in the world.

GEORGE. Well I've seen it and it don't look small to me.

WEAVER. He's got two balls and an helmet.

GEORGE. Oh stop talking crap Weaver! You do my bloody head in sometimes. Gordon is supposed to be one of your mates so I think it's really unfair that you talk about him like that. Now let's just drop it.

Pause.

WEAVER. Can I borrow a shirt?

GEORGE. Can't you go home and get one?

WEAVER. I only need a fresh shirt, no point in going all the way home just for a fresh shirt is there?

GEORGE. I'll see what I can find.

WEAVER. Clean shirt, quick splash of water on my face and bosh, I'm ready.

There is a knock on the door.

TEBBIT (*off*). George, are you in?

GEORGE. It's my landlady. Sit up properly and fix that bed up.

WEAVER. Alright, alright, don't get jumpy.

GEORGE (*shouts*). Is that you Mrs Tebbit?

TEBBIT (*off*). Yes. Can I come in?

GEORGE. Hold on a mo'. (*Opens the door and lets her in.*)

TEBBIT. Oh sorry to disturb you George. I didn't know you still had company. Afternoon Mr Weaver.

WEAVER. Afternoon Mrs Tebbit. Rotten day, ain't it?

TEBBIT. Lovely for ducks though.

WEAVER. Yea, it would be if it was raining.

GEORGE. What can I do for you then?

TEBBIT. This letter came for you.

GEORGE. Oh, thank you.

TEBBIT. It's post-marked Brighton, so it must be from your sister.

GEORGE. Yes it is, I can tell by the writing.

TEBBIT. Nice getting letters, isn't it?

GEORGE. Lovely.

TEBBIT. I like getting letters. Much nicer than talking on the phone. I'm not very good at writing them though.

GEORGE. No, me neither.

WEAVER. I'm quite a good letter writer myself.

TEBBIT. That's probably why I don't get many.

WEAVER. Oh that's a shame.

TEBBIT. Still, it's my own fault, shouldn't moan. Anyway, I just thought I'd better bring it up to you.

GEORGE. Well that's very kind of you, thank you very much.

TEBBIT. It's my pleasure George. Well. I'd better get back to my business, I've got this cabbage on the boil. Sorry to disturb you.

GEORGE. That's alright, you pop up any time you feel the need.

TEBBIT. I'll see you later then.

WEAVER. Take care.

TEBBIT. I'll try. (*Exits.*)

WEAVER. Not a bad old sort is it?

GEORGE (*sits and opens the letter*). Yea, she's alright.

Pause.

WEAVER. Can I have a bath?

GEORGE. What?

WEAVER. Would it be alright if I had a bath?

GEORGE. Not really, no.

WEAVER. Oh. Alright then.

GEORGE. It's not up to me you see. If it was my bath I'd say yes, but we have to share it you see . . .

WEAVER. That's alright, I understand.

GEORGE. Sorry.

WEAVER. Don't worry about it. Read your letter. (*He gets up and wanders around the room. Goes to the wardrobe, opens it, rummages inside, then holds out a shirt.*) Can I wear this?

GEORGE. What?

WEAVER. This shirt, can I wear it tonight?

GEORGE. If you like.

WEAVER. You sure you don't want to wear it?

GEORGE. I'm wearing the blue one.

WEAVER. What blue one?

GEORGE. That one there, near your left hand.

WEAVER (*takes out the shirt*). Oh yea, that's nice ain't it. So you don't mind if I have this one then?

GEORGE. 'Course not.

WEAVER. Cheers, that'll go nice with me slacks.

There is a knock on the door.

TEBBIT (*off*). George?

GEORGE (*to* WEAVER). Open the door.

WEAVER. Yes Mrs Tebbit.

TEBBIT. Oh thank you Mr Weaver. I'm ever so sorry to disturb you again George.

GEORGE. That's alright. What can I do for you?

TEBBIT. I knew there was something I wanted to ask you but it went right out of my head before. You must think I'm a bit of a pain.

GEORGE. Don't be silly. Would you care to sit down?

TEBBIT. No thank you, it won't take a minute. (*She sits in the chair.*) The thing is, I'm a bit worried about Mr Thomas.

GEORGE. Mr Thomas?

TEBBIT. Yes, you know, the gentleman who lives in the room below you.

GEORGE. Oh I know, yes?

TEBBIT. Well the thing is, I haven't seen him since last night and he's not in his room because I've knocked.

GEORGE. Have you looked inside?

TEBBIT. Well yes I have. I know I shouldn't but I was worried you see. Anyway, he's not there.

WEAVER. Perhaps he's done a bunk.

TEBBIT. Oh no, he wouldn't do that. His rent's all paid up. He likes to pay monthly because that's how his work pays him and he's still got two weeks of this month left.

GEORGE. Perhaps he's gone on a little holiday.

TEBBIT. That's what I thought at first, but all his clothes are still there. The only thing that's missing is the suit he wears for work. I do his washing for him you see, just as a sideline, he gives me a couple of bob for it.

WEAVER. Oh that's handy.

TEBBIT. I was hoping that you might have seen him, George.

GEORGE. I don't see him that much anyway.

TEBBIT. Yes. He's a very private person.

GEORGE. I never see him use the cooker either.

TEBBIT. That's because he likes to eat out. He always has his dinner in a restaurant.

WEAVER. Well it's alright for some, ain't it?

GEORGE. I can't help you, I'm afraid.

TEBBIT. I know this may sound dramatic but do you think I should inform the police?

WEAVER. What for?

TEBBIT. To tell them he's gone missing.

WEAVER. Well he's not been gone long and he is a grown man. You never know, he might have pulled a bird and stayed with her for the night.

TEBBIT. I couldn't see him doing that, he's not the type. He's very religious you see, he reads the Bible before he has his hot milk.

WEAVER. Even religious men get the urge.

GEORGE. He could be right, you know.

TEBBIT. I don't think so . . .

WEAVER. He's a human, ain't he?

TEBBIT. But he's not the type!

WEAVER. Let me tell you something, darling. No matter how a man may appear on the outside we're all the same on the inside. We all have the same thoughts and we're all after the same thing. I'm right ain't I George?

GEORGE. Well . . .

WEAVER. I bet that's where he is. Don't worry about it.

TEBBIT. I know I shouldn't but I can't help it. He's such a nice man, I'd hate to think something had happened to him.

WEAVER. Nothing's happened to him. You care too much about others, that's your problem.

TEBBIT. I do yes, it's in my water.

GEORGE. Look. Give it another couple of days and if he doesn't
show up by then, call the police.

TEBBIT. I suppose I am being a little hasty.

WEAVER. Of course you are. I'll tell you one thing though, I
wish I had a lovely lady like you worrying about me.

TEBBIT. Oh Mr Weaver, you are kind.

WEAVER. It's the truth.

TEBBIT. You do say the nicest things, doesn't he say the nicest
things, George?

GEORGE. He does that. He's a right charmer.

WEAVER. I've just got respect for people that's all.

TEBBIT (*gets up*). Well thanks, anyway. Sorry to bother you again.

WEAVER. It's no bother, stop being a silly-billy. As George said,
you come up any time, it's your house, ain't it.

TEBBIT. You are kind.

WEAVER. Not at all.

TEBBIT. If Mr Thomas doesn't come back you're quite welcome
to have his room, it's very cheap.

WEAVER. That's very nice of you, I'll keep it in mind.

TEBBIT. Cheerio then. (*Exits.*)

WEAVER. What a lovely lady. Attractive too . . . if you look
properly.

   Blackout.

Scene Three

That evening. WEAVER *is combing his hair in front of the mirror.*
GORDON *is in the armchair.*

WEAVER. We wasn't expecting you till nine see, that's why we
ain't ready yet.

GORDON. That's alright, my fault.

WEAVER. So you don't mind me coming then?

GORDON. Not at all. I've only got the two tickets though.

WEAVER. That's O.K. I'll pay my own way in.

GORDON. Fine.

WEAVER. And Brenda.

GORDON. I'm sorry?

WEAVER. I'll pay for Brenda as well.

GORDON. Who is Brenda?

WEAVER. Oh sorry . . . I didn't tell you did I? I've asked
   George's landlady along as well. I hope you don't mind.

GORDON. Well, no . . .

WEAVER. She's a bit down you see. Got a few problems with one
   of the tenants. I thought a night out might cheer her up. She
   was quite chuffed when I asked her.

GORDON. I'm sure she was.

WEAVER. Ever met her?

GORDON. A couple of times.

WEAVER. She's a lovely woman, you know. There's a really nice
   gentleness about her, do you know what I mean? She seems
   quite lonely though you'd never think it, puts on a brave face
   and all that. Between you and me Gordon, I could see myself
   getting quite fond of her. She's my kind of woman you see, I
   sussed that this afternoon. I'd never really noticed it before but
   she's quite sexy. I think she's got it in her to be a right little
   raver.

GORDON. How interesting.

WEAVER. Funny how you spot these things ain't it? Still, she
   could do with a night out.

GORDON. It was most thoughtful of you to ask her.

WEAVER. Yea, I'm good like that.

Pause.

Do you like this shirt?

GORDON. Oh yes, it's very nice.

WEAVER. George lent it to me. Do you think the colour suits me?

GORDON. Very becoming.

WEAVER. I've never seen him wear it though, have you? He probably don't like it. I might as well ask him if I can keep it, do you think he'd mind?

GORDON. No harm in trying, I suppose.

WEAVER. I'll ask him later. No point in him keeping it if he don't wear it is there?

Pause.

I like your shoes.

GORDON. Do you?

WEAVER. Lovely.

GORDON. Thank you.

WEAVER. New, are they?

GORDON. I bought them yesterday.

WEAVER. Expensive?

GORDON. Not very.

WEAVER. The stitching looks good, important that.

GORDON. Very.

WEAVER. Did you get them from Brownings?

GORDON. As a matter of fact I did.

WEAVER. Thought so; that's a good shop. Yep, that's a very good pair of shoes you've got there.

GORDON. Thank you.

GEORGE *enters, looking very smart.*

WEAVER. Here he is. Oh don't he look dapper!

GEORGE. Sorry I took so long.

GORDON. Not to worry, I'm early.

WEAVER. Have you seen Gordon's new shoes?

GEORGE. Yea I saw them last night. Blimey, they've got a bit scuffed haven't they?

GORDON. I went for a walk during the party and fell in a bloody ditch.

WEAVER (*laughs under breath*). Silly cunt.

GORDON. What time is it?

GEORGE. About quarter past eight.

GORDON. Gosh, I am early.

GEORGE. We can have a drink here before we go.

WEAVER. Good idea. Shall I go downstairs and see if Brenda's ready?

GEORGE. Might as well. See if she wants a drink too.

WEAVER. I'll do that then. Do I look alright?

GEORGE. You look fine.

WEAVER. Right then. Back in a minute. (*Exits.*)

GORDON. Well. This is a right bugger-up.

GEORGE. What is?

GORDON. Oh come on George, you know very well what I mean. Why did you ask Weaver to come?

GEORGE. I didn't ask him. He sort of invited himself.

GORDON. How did he find out about it then?

GEORGE. He heard us talking. He was awake.

GORDON. The sneaky little bastard.

GEORGE. It doesn't matter does it?

GORDON. Of course it matters! This is a respectable club with respectable people. You know what he's like when he's had a few drinks; there's no telling what he might get up to.

GEORGE. He'll be alright. He'll have Mrs Tebbit with him so he'll be on his best behaviour, I know he will. He wants to impress her, doesn't he.

GORDON. I still think he's got a nerve.

GEORGE. It was a bit cheeky, but there was nothing I could do about it.

GORDON. I know. I'm not blaming you George, but I do think you should be a little harder with him; don't let him get his own way so much.

GEORGE. Sorry.

GORDON. Well there's nothing we can do about it now.

Pause.

God, I hate that man.

GEORGE. Do you? He thinks you like him.

GORDON. Well he would, wouldn't he. He's a nasty piece of work George, believe me.

GEORGE. He's not that bad, you've just never seen the nice side of him.

GORDON. I don't believe he has one.

GEORGE. You should give him a chance, you know.

GORDON. Why do you always stand up for him?

GEORGE. Well he's my mate, isn't he. He's never done me any harm.

GORDON. Give it time.

GEORGE. Look. I'm sorry you've got the hump about him coming, but, like I said, there was nothing I could do about it. Anyway, it might be quite a laugh with him and Mrs Tebbit. I couldn't believe it when he asked her along. She looked right chuffed about it as well.

GORDON. So I believe.

GEORGE. It was good of him though and she's not a bad sort. She's a bit worried about one of the blokes that lives here.

GORDON. Yes, the weasel did mention it.

GEORGE. A night out will take her mind off things.

Pause.

GORDON. May I have that drink now please?

GEORGE. Oh yea, sorry. Vodka alright?

GORDON. Fine.

GEORGE (*gets the drink, mugs, etc.*). Do you want tonic in it?

GORDON. Please.

GEORGE. There you go.

GORDON. Oh, thank you.

Pause.

Look. I'm sorry for being such an old stick-in-the-mud, but you do understand don't you?

GEORGE. Course. Let's just forget about it and have a good time.

GORDON. You're right, as always. It's the best thing to do.

WEAVER (*enters*). She'll be up in a minute, just getting her bag.

GEORGE. Do you want a drink?

WEAVER. Wouldn't mind. She don't half look tasty.

GEORGE. Yea?

WEAVER. A right little cracker. I was quite surprised. I knew she had it in her though. You'd better pour her out one of them; she'll be here in a minute.

GEORGE. Righty-oh. (*Hands* WEAVER *a drink.*)

WEAVER. Cheers Georgy-boy. I need this. I know it sounds soppy but I think I'm a little bit nervous. I want to impress her I suppose.

GORDON. You'll have to be on your best behaviour then.

WEAVER. Oh yea. I'm gonna take it easy with the old booze alright.

GORDON. Good idea.

WEAVER. Besides, I might get a result later and I don't want anything letting me down do I? (*Laughs crudely.*)

There is a knock on the door. GEORGE *opens it.* TEBBIT *walks in looking very different from the first time we see her. She looks stunning.*

TEBBIT. Evening George.

GEORGE. Blimey, you look nice.

TEBBIT. Thank you.

WEAVER. What did I tell you, bit of alright ain't she?

TEBBIT (*loving it*). Mr Weaver!

WEAVER. You sit down in that chair you little sex-pot.

TEBBIT (*sits*). Oh isn't he terrible, George.

GEORGE (*hands her a drink in an old tin mug*). It's a vodka and tonic, I hope you like it. Now, you've met Mr Davis before haven't you.

TEBBIT. A couple of times, yes.

GORDON (*shakes her hand*). Pleased to meet you again.

TEBBIT. And you Mr Davis.

GORDON. Please, call me Gordon.

TEBBIT. And I'm Brenda.

Pause.

GORDON. I hope you don't mind my saying, and I'm sure we're all agreed, but that really is the most lovely dress.

TEBBIT. Oh thank you Gordon. I've had it for quite a few years now but luckily I've managed to retain my figure. I don't get the chance to wear it that often. Tonight is quite a treat.

GORDON. I was most delighted to hear that you and Weaver were to be joining us. It should be a lovely evening.

TEBBIT. You know someone in the band, I believe.

GORDON. Yes, the trumpet player.

TEBBIT. Is he good?

GORDON. First class. He's a very old friend.

TEBBIT. Will we get to meet him?

GORDON. Of course. He'll have a drink with us when he's finished his spot.

TEBBIT. Oh how exciting! I've never met a proper musician before.

WEAVER. I've got a mate who plays the drums.

GEORGE. Have you? You never told me.

WEAVER. Well I don't like to brag about it do I! He's over in America at the moment making quite a name for himself. I'll have to introduce you to him Brenda, if he comes back for a holiday or something.

TEBBIT. Oh. That would be lovely.

Pause.

GORDON. Have you lived here long, Brenda?

TEBBIT. All my life. The house belonged to my parents; they took in boarders as well. When they passed on I decided to keep it going. I'm not trained to do anything else anyway.

GORDON. And what about your husband?

TEBBIT. Husband?

GORDON. Well you are Mrs Tebbit not Miss.

TEBBIT. Oh I see. No, I just call myself Mrs to gain respect. I was engaged once but he was killed in action during the war.

GORDON. Oh I am sorry.

WEAVER. So am I.

TEBBIT. At least here I'm always surrounded by people, I'm never alone.

WEAVER. Well that's one good thing, there's nothing worse than being on your tod.

TEBBIT. I do regret not marrying and having children. I would've liked to have someone to pass the house on to, if you see what I mean.

WEAVER. There's still plenty of time for that, I mean you're not old or anything are you?

TEBBIT. You are kind, Weaver, but I'm quite a bit older than I look.

WEAVER. How old are you then?

TEBBIT. That's not the sort of question you should ask a lady.

WEAVER. Whoops, beg your pardon.

TEBBIT. Well, not on the first date anyway.

WEAVER. Can I ask you something else then? Would you ever let one of your tenants have a party?

TEBBIT. How do you mean?

WEAVER. Well not a party party but a little drink-up sort of thing, a little gathering.

TEBBIT. Well George is having one now and I'm one of the guests, so I'd be wrong to object.

WEAVER. There you are George, I told you. He didn't think you'd allow it.

TEBBIT. Well I'd need to be told about it in advance. Are you thinking of having one then?

GEORGE. No. We were just talking about it, that's all.

WEAVER. He worries too much you see, cares too much about other people.

TEBBIT. Well I would say that's a good quality to have.

WEAVER. Oh so would I. He's a good bloke is George, I'm always telling him that.

TEBBIT. He's lovely.

WEAVER. Smashing.

GORDON. Oh look, you're embarrassing him.

GEORGE. Oh I don't mind, it's quite nice really.

WEAVER. That's the spirit Georgy-boy.

Pause.

Right then. I think we should hit the road.

GORDON. Good idea.

TEBBIT. How are we getting there?

WEAVER. Taxi.

TEBBIT. Oh how grand.

WEAVER. Only the best for you, my lovely.

GORDON. I shall be paying for it though.

WEAVER. Right and all, you're the one with the free tickets, I've got to pay for me and her to get into the gaff!

There is a knock on the door.

GORDON. Did somebody knock?

GEORGE. I think so.

TEBBIT. Are you expecting anyone else?

GEORGE. No.

Another knock.

WEAVER. Well you'd better see who it is then, mate.

GEORGE. Yea. Sorry.

GEORGE *opens the door. A man covered in dirt and dried blood stands in the doorway for a few seconds before falling on the floor into the room.*

TEBBIT. Fuck me! It's Mr Thomas!

Blackout.

ACT TWO

Scene One

Later that night. GEORGE *is in the armchair drinking vodka. After a few moments* TEBBIT *enters.*

GEORGE. How is he?

TEBBIT. Not too bad. He's gone to sleep.

GEORGE. Has he told you anything?

TEBBIT. Not yet. It's terrible not knowing.

GEORGE. We should call the police.

TEBBIT. That's what I keep telling him but he doesn't want me to. I can hardly go against his wishes can I?

GEORGE. I suppose not.

TEBBIT. Anyway, he might feel differently in the morning; he might want me to fetch them then. He's a very proud man you see, he likes to keep himself clean and tidy. He was very embarrassed about us all seeing him in that state.

GEORGE. That's silly, it's not his fault, is it.

TEBBIT. I know but some men are funny like that.

Pause.

He'd messed his trousers.

GEORGE. Oh dear.

TEBBIT. Poor thing. He didn't know where to look.

GEORGE. Did you clean him up then?

TEBBIT. Yes.

GEORGE. That was good of you.

TEBBIT. I didn't mind. I couldn't really leave him like he was, could I?

GEORGE. No, I suppose not. It was still good of you, though.

TEBBIT. I don't mind doing my bit.

GEORGE. Would you like a drink?

TEBBIT. I don't think I should, I've had a couple already.

GEORGE. Go on, you deserve one.

TEBBIT. I'm not used to it, you see.

GEORGE. I insist, it'll calm you down.

TEBBIT. I suppose I am a bit shaky. Go on then, just a small one, mind.

GEORGE. That's the spirit. (*Gets up and pours a drink.*)

TEBBIT. I'm sorry you missed seeing the band.

GEORGE. Well you missed it too.

TEBBIT. It's not the same thing though, is it.

GEORGE. I couldn't leave you alone with Mr Thomas. It was my duty to stay with you, what with being one of your tenants and that.

TEBBIT. At least the tickets won't go to waste. I do like your friends but I'm glad they're out of the way.

GEORGE. Not much help were they?

TEBBIT. Well some men are like that George, the sight of blood makes them go funny. I'm lucky to have such a strong tummy; yours must be quite strong too.

GEORGE (*starts to giggle*). Oh dear.

TEBBIT. What?

GEORGE. Nothing.

TEBBIT. What you laughing at?

GEORGE. I was just wondering how Gordon and Weaver are getting on.

TEBBIT. How do you mean?

GEORGE. They can't stand each other.

TEBBIT. Really?

GEORGE. Yea, they hate each other. They've never got on, they pretend they do, but they don't.

TEBBIT. How funny, I thought they were really good friends.

GEORGE. Well now you know.

TEBBIT. They both like you though, don't they?

GEORGE. I think so.

TEBBIT. Oh they do. Gordon thinks the world of you.

GEORGE. I don't know why, I'm nothing special.

TEBBIT. Well that's just it, you're not a threat.

GEORGE. What do you mean?

TEBBIT. Well, you're not flashy like Weaver and you're not a ladies' man like Gordon.

GEORGE. I don't know how to take that.

TEBBIT. Take it as a compliment, it's meant as one. You're a lovely man George, the sooner you realise that the better.

GEORGE. I think I'm boring.

TEBBIT. You're not boring.

GEORGE. I bore myself sometimes. I've never done anything with my life, don't suppose I ever will.

TEBBIT. You've got friends, haven't you?

GEORGE. A few, yes.

TEBBIT. Well that's an achievement in itself. It's not easy making friends you know. I haven't got any.

GEORGE. I don't believe that, you must have.

TEBBIT. Don't get me wrong, I've got acquaintances, I've got lots of them but I haven't got what you'd call a real friend, you know, someone who comes round for a cup of tea and a natter. I used to have one. Her name was Betty. We were mates at school together and all that. We had a bit of a tiff about twelve years ago. She got married, moved to Wales and I haven't seen or heard from her since.

GEORGE. That's a shame. What did you row about?

TEBBIT. A fella. He was one of the tenants. He'd only been here a couple of months and he took a fancy to me, if you see what I mean. Well, I wasn't interested at first because my fiancé had only been laid to rest for a short while so it would've looked bad if I'd started walking out with other men so soon after.

GEORGE. Yes, it would a bit.

TEBBIT. Anyway, I told Betty that I liked him but wanted to leave it for a while before I started seeing him. She told him I didn't like him at all so he started taking her out instead. I thought it was terrible of her to do such a thing so I stopped talking to her. I know it's silly now, but when you're young you take these things so seriously don't you. There hasn't been anyone else since then. I went out with the man who reads the meter a couple of times, but we wasn't well matched. Weaver is the first man I've had a date with in five years.

GEORGE. Blimey.

TEBBIT. I don't mean to sound big-headed or anything but I know that quite a few of the men who have stayed here have had their eye on me but they never do anything about it. I'm sure they think I'm some kind of old bag because I'm a landlady.

GEORGE. It could be that they don't think you're interested in them. You are a very attractive lady, if you don't mind me saying so.

TEBBIT. That's a lovely thing to say. I've been quite spoilt tonight with all the flattery that's been chucked about. I won't be able to get my head out of the door.

GEORGE. It hasn't been much of a date for you has it?

TEBBIT. I don't mind. I'm glad I was here when Mr Thomas came back. Anyway, I'm quite enjoying myself, having this little drink with you.

GEORGE. So am I. I don't know why we haven't done it before.

TEBBIT. We should do it again.

GEORGE. Oh yes, we should.

TEBBIT. Or you could come down to my flat one night and I could cook you a meal, I haven't used my roasting-pan in years.

GEORGE. That would be lovely.

TEBBIT. You could bring your lady friend as well, that's if you've got one.

GEORGE. No, no I haven't.

TEBBIT. I thought not. You're too young to tie yourself down. Enjoy yourself while you're young. I wish I had.

GEORGE. I would like to have someone, you know, a sort of steady, but I'm not much good with girls.

TEBBIT. I don't believe that, you're alright with me, ain't you?

GEORGE. Yea but that's different, I know you.

TEBBIT. Not that well.

GEORGE. But I know who you are, sort of thing. See, I don't think most women take me seriously, I'm just someone to confide in, I'm a good listener you see. I was really hooked on this woman Marion for a while. We used to have really good chats. I think I sort of fell in love with her, but she goes out with Gordon. I used to hate listening to him talking about her, but I'm alright about it now. Got over it I suppose.

TEBBIT. Did she know how you felt about her?

GEORGE. I don't think so. I never told her anyway, never told anyone, not even Weaver, and I tell him most things.

TEBBIT. I'm flattered.

GEORGE. What for?

TEBBIT. Well you just told me a secret, that means you trust me. Oh I've come over all warm.

GEORGE. Oh. That's nice.

Pause.

TEBBIT. Can I have a look through your collection?

GEORGE. I beg your pardon?

TEBBIT. Your records. Can I see what you've got?

GEORGE. Oh of course. They're a bit old I'm afraid, can't remember the last time I bought one.

TEBBIT. Blimey, they are old ain't they. (*Holds up a record.*) Oh I really like this one. Can I put it on?

GEORGE. What is it? Oh yea, I like that one. It is a bit old isn't it, must be one of Weavers. Here, I'll put it on for you.

TEBBIT *sits down and* GEORGE *starts cleaning the record, etc.*

GEORGE. Here, I'll tell you what. Why don't we have a little dance?

TEBBIT. For someone who isn't good with girls, you're doing alright.

GEORGE. Yea but you're . . .

TEBBIT. I know, I'm different. Oh why not. We would've had one at the club wouldn't we?

GEORGE. I don't know about that, Weaver probably wouldn't let anyone else go near you.

TEBBIT. Well he isn't here now so we might as well. I might not be very good mind, I haven't danced with anyone in years.

GEORGE. That's alright. Neither have I.

The record starts. They both stand self-consciously, then put their arms around each other. They move well together. TEBBIT *starts to run her fingers through* GEORGE's *hair. He looks scared but is also enjoying it. After a few seconds* THOMAS *enters in his pyjamas with a make-shift bandage on his head.* GEORGE *quickly switches off the record player.*

THOMAS. Oh I'm so sorry, I didn't mean to disturb you, I was just wondering if I might have a cup of tea?

Blackout.

Scene Two

THOMAS *is in the armchair and* GEORGE *is on the end of the bed. An embarrassed silence. After a few moments* TEBBIT *enters with a cup of tea.*

TEBBIT. There you are Mr Thomas, that should make you feel better.

THOMAS. Thank you Brenda, you are kind.

TEBBIT. I thought you was asleep.

THOMAS. I couldn't. Too many thoughts swimming around in my head.

TEBBIT. Oh. I see.

Pause.

GEORGE. What happened?

THOMAS. I'd really rather not talk about it. I hope you don't think I'm being rude.

GEORGE. 'Course not. You just sit there and drink your tea.

THOMAS. Thank you.

TEBBIT. I must say I was quite worried about you, Mr Thomas. If you wasn't back here by tomorrow I would've had the police in.

THOMAS. Oh please you mustn't do that, I really don't want to get them involved.

TEBBIT. Why ever not?

THOMAS. I just don't, that's all.

TEBBIT. Well, it's up to you I suppose. I'm not going to force you into anything you don't want to do.

THOMAS. Who were those two gentlemen who were here earlier?

TEBBIT. They're friends of George, we were all on our way out when you dropped in.

THOMAS. Where are they now?

GEORGE. Gone on to a club. They had a couple of free tickets you see, seemed a pity to waste them.

THOMAS. But you helped me downstairs didn't you?

GEORGE. Yes, me and Gordon.

TEBBIT. And I cleaned you up.

THOMAS. Yes, I remember that. Thank you.

TEBBIT. My pleasure.

THOMAS. I'm so sorry. I've ruined your evening.

TEBBIT. Oh don't be silly. I'm just glad you're back here safe and sound. This place wouldn't be the same without you, would it George?

GEORGE. Well I don't know really . . .

TEBBIT. You're always so polite and you keep up with your rent payments. I don't know what I'd do without you, really I don't.

THOMAS *starts to cry.*

TEBBIT. Mr Thomas! Whatever is the matter?

THOMAS. I'm sorry, I'm so sorry.

TEBBIT (*goes over and puts her arm around him*). There, there. It can't be that bad. What are you crying for?

THOMAS. I don't know, I just feel like letting it all out, I'm so sorry.

TEBBIT. Don't keep saying sorry all the time, you're not doing anyone any harm are you?

THOMAS. I just feel such a fool that's all.

TEBBIT. Well don't. If you feel like having a little cry you do that. We don't mind, do we George?

GEORGE. 'Course not. You carry on.

TEBBIT. See. No point in bottling it all up is there? (*She rocks him.*) You let it all out. Don't mind us, it'll do you good.

GEORGE. Would you like a drop of vodka?

THOMAS. No, no thank you.

TEBBIT. What about brandy? That might help.

GEORGE. I ain't got any brandy.

TEBBIT. You could pop down the off-licence and get some, I'll pay. Would you like some Cyril, it'd do you good?

THOMAS. I don't want you to go to any trouble.

TEBBIT. George doesn't mind, do you George?

GEORGE. 'Course not. It's only down the road, won't take me a minute.

THOMAS. Well it would be nice, I suppose.

TEBBIT. There, that's what I wanted to hear. (*Gets her bag.*) Here's some money George, just get a normal bottle, nothing fancy.

GEORGE. Righty-oh.

TEBBIT. And here's the key to my flat. On your way back pop in and get a glass out of the cabinet in my front room. Can't ask him to drink out of a mug, being in that state.

GEORGE. Right. I'll be back in a minute then. (*Whispering*.) Will you be alright with him?

TEBBIT. 'Course I will. Don't take too long, though.

GEORGE. See you in a minute then. (*Exits*.)

TEBBIT. He's a good boy, isn't he.

THOMAS. Yes.

TEBBIT. You'll feel better with a drop of brandy in you. It always helps in times like these. (*She wanders around the room, goes to the wardrobe and starts to rummage through* GEORGE's *belongings*.) Do you want to tell your Aunty Brenda what happened?

THOMAS. Not really.

TEBBIT. It might help.

THOMAS. I doubt it.

TEBBIT. Come on Cyril. I'm your friend, ain't I?

THOMAS. Of course you are.

TEBBIT. And you trust me, don't you?

THOMAS. Of course I do.

TEBBIT. I wouldn't tell anyone.

THOMAS. I know you wouldn't.

TEBBIT. And we've always got on.

THOMAS. Always.

TEBBIT. So tell me what happened.

THOMAS. I don't want to.

TEBBIT. Why not?

THOMAS. I just don't.

TEBBIT. That's a feeble excuse.

THOMAS. It's not meant to be an excuse.

TEBBIT. So tell me.

THOMAS. I can't.

TEBBIT. You mean you won't.

THOMAS. No, I want to but I can't. You wouldn't like it.

TEBBIT. Why wouldn't I?

THOMAS. Because it's not very pleasant.

TEBBIT. I can take it.

THOMAS. I don't think so.

TEBBIT. Try me.

THOMAS. Please! I can't talk about it yet. It's too soon.

TEBBIT (*sits on the bed*). Funny, I've never thought of you as being weak.

THOMAS. What do you mean?

TEBBIT. I always thought you were strong, could face up to things. Seems I got the wrong impression.

THOMAS. I am strong Brenda, very strong, it's just . . .

TEBBIT. What?

THOMAS. I'm scared you won't like me any more.

TEBBIT. Now why ever should I feel like that?

THOMAS (*crying*). Oh Brenda! I feel so humiliated, so confused. I feel as though I don't want to go on any more!

TEBBIT. Now come on. That's enough of that. I won't have that sort of talk, not in my house, it's not proper. Look. What happened? Did you attack someone? Take advantage of a lady in distress?

THOMAS. Of course not. I'd never hurt anyone. Surely you know that?

TEBBIT. Well of course I do love, but I mean, what am I to think? I didn't mean to offend you.

THOMAS. I know, I know.

TEBBIT. So what happened then?

Pause.

THOMAS. You see, it was my own fault. I provoked the attack

. . . I was the one who has hurt, but it was my own fault. That's why I can't go to the police.

TEBBIT. But surely if you was the victim . . .

THOMAS. No, it's the circumstances. Under the circumstances I can't do anything about it. It was probably God punishing me.

TEBBIT. I hate to say this Cyril but I think I'm a bit more confused than you are.

THOMAS. Oh this is all wrong! I should never have told you.

TEBBIT. But you haven't told me anything. I don't know what the hell you're going on about. I wish you'd make yourself clearer Cyril, this is bloody frustrating for me you know!

THOMAS. Please, don't shout.

TEBBIT. Sorry. I lost control of myself then. Don't know what came over me, I'm usually so patient.

THOMAS. I know you are. You should know the truth, you've been so kind to me and I know I can trust you.

TEBBIT. Please, you just take your time. I'm only here to listen. I'll understand.

THOMAS. You see Brenda, I'm not like other men . . .

TEBBIT. I know. You're lovely, I wish there was more like you.

THOMAS. That's very kind of you but that's not what I mean. You see . . . I 'go' with other men . . . I 'go' with them and last night I 'went' with one and he beat me up.

TEBBIT. Oh dear.

THOMAS. I . . . I'm 'that' way you see and I've always been 'that' way and I do 'it' with other men.

TEBBIT. Oh dear.

THOMAS. I know you must be shocked, I know you probably think I'm dirty or something, but I can't help the way I am.

TEBBIT. Oh dear, oh dear.

THOMAS. If you want me to move out I'll do it. I mean, I would understand if you didn't want me to live here any more.

Pause.

I'm not ashamed of myself, of being the way I am, I used to be but I'm not any more. I'm just ashamed of you seeing me in this state, this is more unbearable than being beaten up. I've always looked up to you, Brenda, but if you want me to go I will . . . Now, please be honest with me, for your sake as well as mine.

TEBBIT. Of course I don't want you to go. I am shocked, I'll admit that, I'd be a liar if I said otherwise, but I don't want you to go.

Pause.

Oh you poor man. You poor, poor man. What you must have been through.

THOMAS. I've been to hell and back.

TEBBIT. Oh I can imagine.

THOMAS. You do understand don't you?

TEBBIT. Well, as much as I possibly can.

THOMAS. I knew you would, I should never have doubted you.

TEBBIT. Well, I don't blame you for being apprehensive. There are some who wouldn't have taken it so well.

THOMAS. You've hit the nail on the head there.

TEBBIT. But what I don't understand is why? Why did that man beat you up?

THOMAS. Well at first I thought he was yet another queer-basher.

TEBBIT. I beg your pardon?

THOMAS. A queer-basher. They wait to be picked up by men like me and then they beat us up because of the way we are.

TEBBIT. Really? I don't believe you.

THOMAS. Oh it's quite true, I can assure you.

TEBBIT. But that's terrible.

THOMAS. I know, but it happens all the time.

TEBBIT. Well you learn something new every day. I don't get out much you see.

THOMAS. Anyway he wasn't one of them. You see, I recognised him, I thought I knew him from somewhere and I told him. That was a mistake, I can see that now. See with him, it's not only the police finding out. He wouldn't want anyone to find out because he'd be frightened, you know, frightened that they would think he wasn't a 'real' man.

TEBBIT. I see.

THOMAS. That man obviously thought I'd tell someone so he tried to kill me.

TEBBIT. Kill you?!

THOMAS. Oh he definitely tried to kill me. He hit me over the head with a brick.

TEBBIT. Oh dear.

THOMAS. I wouldn't have told anyone, I'm not the sort, but he must have thought otherwise.

TEBBIT. But you must go to the police, he might do it to someone else.

THOMAS. No I won't do that, I can't do that. I'm perfectly alright, he didn't hit me as hard as he thought. The cut's not that deep, I won't even need a stitch in it. My ribs hurt where he kicked me, but I don't think anything's broken. I'm just bruised a little, that's all.

TEBBIT. Oh Mr Thomas, you are brave, I must say.

THOMAS. He won't do it again, I know he won't. He was just *scared* that's all, *scared out of his mind.*

TEBBIT. Where did you know him from?

THOMAS. Oh just around. You know, around and about.

TEBBIT. Do you know him well?

THOMAS. No, I'd just seen him around, I knew his face.

TEBBIT. I see.

Pause.

THOMAS. Thank you Brenda.

TEBBIT. What for?

THOMAS. For everything.

TEBBIT. Go away you old soft-pot. It was my pleasure.

THOMAS. You know, you really are quite wonderful, I feel I . . .

GEORGE (*enters and is rather out of breath*). There, didn't take long did I?

TEBBIT. You must have ran all the way.

GEORGE. I did. You feeling any better?

THOMAS. Much better thank you George.

GEORGE. Glad to hear it. I got the brandy.

TEBBIT. Good boy. (*She pours some out for* THOMAS.) There you are Cyril, that should make you feel better.

THOMAS. Thank you. Are you going to join me?

TEBBIT. Might as well. Do you want some George?

GEORGE. Wouldn't say no. That's if you don't mind.

TEBBIT. Of course I don't, silly bugger.

GEORGE. Right then. (*Goes through the process of pouring the drinks, then hands one to* TEBBIT.)

TEBBIT (*after a long embarrassed silence*). Well this is cosy isn't it?

THOMAS. Very. I feel much better now, more relaxed.

TEBBIT. Good. It helps to talk.

GEORGE. Had a chat about it, did you?

TEBBIT. Yes, Mr Thomas got it off his chest.

GEORGE. Are you going to the police then?

TEBBIT. No. Mr Thomas and I decided it would be best to leave it.

THOMAS. I just want to try and forget about it, George.

GEORGE. Oh.

TEBBIT. He just needs to clear the whole thing from his mind.

GEORGE. Oh well. You know best.

TEBBIT. I've just had a thought, George. I think it would be a good idea if Cyril slept up here tonight so that you could keep an eye on him.

THOMAS. Oh no Brenda, there's really no need . . .

GEORGE. I don't mind.

THOMAS. No really, I don't think it's necessary . . .

TEBBIT. Don't be silly. I think it would be much better if someone kept a close watch on you, just in case you have a funny turn in the night. It could affect you later you know, being hit on your head.

THOMAS. But it's quite unfair to ask George to do such a thing.

GEORGE. I don't mind, it could be fun. I've never looked after anyone before. I can sit in the chair and read my book. I never sleep at night anyway, only ever drop off when the birds start singing. They're fresh sheets as well, I only washed them the other day.

THOMAS. Well, I don't know . . .

GEORGE. Go on Mr Thomas.

THOMAS. No, please, Cyril.

GEORGE. Cyril. Go on, you won't be any trouble and Brenda's right: you could go a bit funny later on, you never know.

THOMAS. Well, if you're sure you don't mind.

GEORGE. Of course I don't.

THOMAS. I suppose it would be for the best.

TEBBIT. Of course it is.

THOMAS. Oh alright then. Just for tonight though, I shall be alright by tomorrow. Thank you George. Thank you very much indeed.

GEORGE. Think nothing of it.

TEBBIT. It's his pleasure, isn't it George?

GEORGE. Yes, it's my pleasure Cyril.

THOMAS. Thank you.

GEORGE. You're welcome.

Pause.

TEBBIT. Well, at least one good thing has come out of this; we've all got to know each other a bit better.

GEORGE. That's true.

TEBBIT. They do say a crisis brings people closer together. Just goes to show there's a lot of truth in that doesn't it, George?

GEORGE. Yea.

THOMAS. Do you know, at the last place I lived there were six of us all in the same house and I never knew any of their names. Two years I stayed there. I remember the house was always very quiet. I used to walk about on my tiptoes day and night. It wasn't because I had to, I just felt I should. Strange isn't it?

TEBBIT. Very. I don't know how you could stick it.

THOMAS. It wasn't that bad, just a bit lonely at times, that's all.

TEBBIT. Still, you're amongst friends now.

THOMAS. Yes, this is much more pleasant. (*Flinches and rubs his side.*) Oh dear.

TEBBIT. Are you alright Cyril?

THOMAS. Just a slight pain in my side.

TEBBIT. Come on. It's time you were in bed.

THOMAS. Oh no. I'm fine, honestly.

TEBBIT. No you're not, you're in pain. It would be much better for you if you got into bed.

THOMAS. But I'm enjoying our little chat.

TEBBIT. Just because you're getting into bed it doesn't mean you have to keep your mouth shut does it? Come on George, help me get him sorted.

GEORGE. Righty-oh. (*They go through the process of getting* THOMAS *into bed.*) It's quite comfy but there's a spring sticking out somewhere near the bottom, so you watch your feet.

TEBBIT. Is there?

GEORGE. Yea.

TEBBIT. How long has it been like that?

GEORGE. Just a couple of weeks.

TEBBIT. Why didn't you tell me about it?

GEORGE. I didn't think it was important.

TEBBIT. Well I think the comfort of my residents is very important. You should have reported it to me the moment it started poking through the material. Remind me in the morning to order a new mattress from the Co-op. Now, are you comfy Cyril?

THOMAS. I'm as snug as a bug in a rug.

TEBBIT. Oh I am pleased.

GEORGE. I always thought it was slug.

TEBBIT. I beg your pardon, George?

GEORGE. I always thought it was snug as a slug in a rug, but it's not is it, it's bug.

TEBBIT. Well of course it's bug, how can a slug look snug? (*Laughs.*) Honestly Cyril, these young people.

GEORGE. Well I know now, don't I.

TEBBIT. You are silly George.

GEORGE (*grins*). I know.

TEBBIT (*sits*). Could you get me another brandy please?

GEORGE. 'Course. Do you want one Cyril?

THOMAS. Not for me, thank you.

GEORGE. Can I have another one?

TEBBIT. Of course you can, no need to ask.

GEORGE. Cheers. (*Pours out the drinks, then sits on the floor.*)

TEBBIT. You alright Cyril?

THOMAS. Perfect.

TEBBIT. You look very contented. Doesn't he look contented, George?

GEORGE. Very.

THOMAS. 'Weary with toil, I haste me to my bed,
The dear repose for limbs with travel tired;
But then begins a journey in my head,
To work my mind, when body's work's expir'd.' Shakespeare.

TEBBIT. Oh how very cultured.

GEORGE. I can never understand him.

TEBBIT. Well I don't think you have to really, it just sounds pretty, doesn't it.

THOMAS. I want you to know that I'm going to close my eyes for a few moments. I'm not going to sleep, I just want to rest my eyes, so please carry on chatting.

TEBBIT. Are you sure?

THOMAS. Quite sure. It's very soothing listening to you talk.

TEBBIT. I'm not going to stay much longer anyway, I'm quite worn out. I've never known an evening like it.

GEORGE. It's been a long day hasn't it?

TEBBIT. Very.

Pause.

How's your sister keeping?

GEORGE. Oh, she's fine thank you.

TEBBIT. Has she got any children?

GEORGE. No. I don't think they want any yet.

TEBBIT. Want to wait a while do they?

GEORGE. I think so, yes.

Pause.

TEBBIT. I like Brighton.

GEORGE. So do I.

TEBBIT. Nice, isn't it?

GEORGE. Lovely.

TEBBIT. I think I like Hastings better though, on account of the castle.

GEORGE. I've never been to Hastings.

TEBBIT. Oh you should try and go sometime, it's lovely.

GEORGE. Maybe we could go together, have a day out.

TEBBIT. Yes. We could go by train and fetch a picnic.

GEORGE. I'd like that.

TEBBIT. Of course it's much better to go for a couple of days. You can take everything in at a more relaxing pace.

GEORGE. Yea, I suppose you could.

TEBBIT. Book into a nice little hotel overlooking the sea. I've always wanted to do that.

GEORGE. We should do it then, in the summer.

TEBBIT. I haven't had a holiday since 1952.

GEORGE. It'd do you good then.

TEBBIT. We could get a double room.

GEORGE. Could we?

TEBBIT Oh yea, it'd be cheaper than two singles.

GEORGE. I suppose it would.

TEBBIT. Have a nice big double bed to frolick about on. (*She goes and checks on* MR THOMAS.) Cyril? Cyril? Aaahh, he's fast asleep, poor love.

GEORGE. He dropped off quick.

TEBBIT. So would you if you'd been hit on the head with a brick. (*Sits.*)

Pause.

GEORGE. You're a very sophisticated woman, Brenda.

TEBBIT. Oh George, you do say the nicest things.

GEORGE. I mean it.

TEBBIT. I really can't understand why you haven't got a girl-friend, you've got such lovely qualities.

GEORGE. That's because I feel comfortable with you, I can be myself.

TEBBIT. Maybe you see me as a mother figure.

GEORGE. I don't think so.

TEBBIT. What do you see me as then?

GEORGE. I don't know, a lady I suppose, a woman.

TEBBIT. Oh you smooth talker you. Come over here and give us a kiss.

GEORGE. Pardon?

TEBBIT. Don't you want to?

GEORGE. Wouldn't you mind?

TEBBIT. I've been wanting one all night.

GEORGE. What, off me?

TEBBIT. Well I don't want my lipstick smudged by four-eyes over there do I? Come on George, what are you frightened of?

GEORGE. I'm not frightened.

TEBBIT. Come over here then.

GEORGE (*makes his way over to her on his knees*). What if Mr Thomas wakes up?

TEBBIT. He'll be asleep for hours yet. (GEORGE *is kneeling in front of her and she runs her fingers through his hair.*) You're very sexual you know, George.

GEORGE. Am I?

TEBBIT. Oh yes. There's definitely something of the Humphrey Bogart in you.

GEORGE. Really?

TEBBIT. And in my younger days I was told I was like a taller Lauren Bacall. I'm also a bit more filled out than her but I don't like to brag.

She grabs him and kisses him quite violently. After a few seconds, we hear a loud knock coming from the front door downstairs.

GEORGE. What was that?

TEBBIT (*pissed-off*). Well what do you think it was?

GEORGE. Sounds like someone knocking on the front door.

TEBBIT. Ten out of ten.

More knocks.

GEORGE. Shall I answer it?

TEBBIT. You'd better, otherwise Mr Thomas might wake up.

GEORGE (*gets up*). Right.

TEBBIT. And whoever it is, try and get rid of them, I was just beginning to enjoy myself.

GEORGE. Yea, so was I. (*Exits*.)

TEBBIT goes over to THOMAS, *takes his glasses off and puts them on the side-table. She goes to the mirror, checks her hair, then pours herself another brandy. We hear some commotion outside then* GEORGE *enters holding up a very drunk* WEAVER.

WEAVER. Georgy-porgy pudding and pie . . .

TEBBIT. Bloody hell!

WEAVER. Hello Brenda, my darling.

TEBBIT. What are you doing here?

WEAVER (*falls into the chair*). Me and Gordon thought we'd come and visit you, make up for your lost evening. I brought some gin.

TEBBIT. Is Gordon here as well?

GEORGE. He's collapsed in the passage downstairs.

TEBBIT. Collapsed?

GEORGE. Well he sort of went all floppy, then slid down the wall. I think he's had a few too many.

WEAVER. He's had the same amount as me, he just can't hold it, the fucking idiot.

TEBBIT. We'll have less of that talk, thank you very much.

WEAVER. Sorry darling I forgot you was here.

GEORGE. What are we gonna do about Gordon?

TEBBIT. Well, we can't just leave him down there, you'll have to help him upstairs.

GEORGE. I can't manage him on my own and Weaver's not much help at the moment.

WEAVER. I'm quite capable of carrying that skinny tit up a flight of stairs.

TEBBIT. You stay where you are, me and George'll get him.

WEAVER (*notes* THOMAS). Who's that?

TEBBIT. That is Mr Thomas.

WEAVER. What, that bloke from earlier?

TEBBIT. Yes.

WEAVER. What's he doing in George's bed? You three been playing naughty games?

GEORGE. Don't be stupid.

TEBBIT. We thought it best that he stayed up here for the night so that George could keep an eye on him.

WEAVER. Did he tell you what happened to him?

TEBBIT. Partly, yes.

WEAVER. What did he say?

TEBBIT. I really don't think that's any of your business.

WEAVER. Did he tell you anything George?

TEBBIT. Mr Thomas spoke to me in private.

WEAVER. Is he going to the police?

TEBBIT. At the moment he doesn't want to but I'm hoping to change his mind.

WEAVER. I wouldn't take any notice of what he told you. He looks a bit shifty to me.

TEBBIT. I can assure you he is not shifty.

WEAVER. Well what did he tell you then?

TEBBIT. Please Mr Weaver . . .

WEAVER. I mean, does he know who did it to him, because if he does I'm quite willing to sort them out for him. It's out of order ain't it, he's only a little bloke.

TEBBIT. That's very kind of you but Mr Thomas only knew the culprit by sight. Now we can't stand here chatting all night, we'd better go and fetch Gordon. Weaver, would you keep an eye on Mr Thomas for me, he had a knock on his head you see, so he might have a funny turn.

WEAVER. Certainly. I may be pissed out of my brain but I'm in total control of me whereabouts.

TEBBIT. Right. Come on George, let's do our duty.

GEORGE. We won't be a minute. (*They both exit.*)

WEAVER *looks at* THOMAS. *He gets up and goes over to him. He gives him a little dig and* THOMAS *stirs.* WEAVER *then gets a pillow from the bed and puts it over* THOMAS's *head. As he is suffocating* THOMAS *there are kicks and struggles from under the bedclothes.* WEAVER *finds this sexually exciting and starts to make fuck noises. There are a few more kicks until* THOMAS *is dead. After a few seconds* WEAVER *stops and puts the pillow back in its original place. He walks away, spots something is wrong, picks up the eye-glasses and puts them back on* THOMAS. *He takes a bottle of gin from his pocket, drinks from it then sits back in the chair. After a few moments* GEORGE *and* TEBBIT *return carrying* GORDON.

GORDON (*very drunk*). I can assure you I'm perfectly alright.

TEBBIT. Weaver, would you mind if we put Mr Davis in the chair?

WEAVER (*gets up*). Be my guest. I don't mind sitting on the floor, there's no boils on my bum.

GORDON (*falls into chair*). I'm so sorry Mrs Tebbit, I don't make a habit of this sort of thing.

TEBBIT. I'm sure you don't, you've just had a few too many that's all.

WEAVER. Bollocks! He's always pissed him, ain't he George?

GEORGE. Not always, no.

WEAVER. Yes he is. He can't hold it. He only had four whiskys and that was it, splattered.

TEBBIT. I'm really not interested.

GEORGE. You shouldn't have come back here you know, not at this time of night.

WEAVER. Brenda don't mind, do you Brenda?

TEBBIT. I do actually, but there's not a lot I can do about it now.

WEAVER (*gets up*). Oh well, if that's how you feel, I'll be off.

GEORGE. Don't be silly.

WEAVER. No, no, I insist. You're quite right Brenda, I took a liberty and I'm sorry. I'm quite capable of getting myself home, unlike Bette Davis there. I think you should put him up for the night but I'm fine, ain't I.

TEBBIT. Well if you're sure you don't mind. I mean it's bad enough that George has to look after Mr Thomas.

WEAVER. Oh yea, of course.

GEORGE. I wonder if he's alright. (*Goes over to* THOMAS.)

WEAVER. He's fine, I just looked at him, sleeping like a baby he is.

GEORGE. He's still got his glasses on.

TEBBIT. That's funny . . .

GEORGE. Shall I take them off him?

TEBBIT. You'd better, otherwise he might turn over in the night and hurt himself.

WEAVER. Maybe he always wears them in bed to see his dreams better.

TEBBIT. Oh Weaver, you are funny.

GEORGE (*lifts* THOMAS's *head and removes the glasses*). Blimey, he's out for the count.

TEBBIT (*smooths the blankets*). He's in another world.

WEAVER. Yea well, don't fiddle about with him you'll wake him up.

TEBBIT. He's right George, come away now. Oh dear, it looks like Mr Davis has dropped off as well.

WEAVER. Well I'm on my way, so you've no worries there.

TEBBIT. You can stay if you like, you can have Mr Thomas's bed.

WEAVER. No, you're alright. I could do with the walk, it might sober me up. Will you be alright with Gordon, George?

GEORGE. How do you mean?

WEAVER. Well you know, in case he has one of his turns.

GEORGE. What turns?

WEAVER. Ain't you ever seen him throw a wobbly?

GEORGE. No.

WEAVER. Oh. Perhaps he only does it with me, I don't think he likes me very much.

TEBBIT. Why, what does he do?

WEAVER. Nothing much, just gets a bit violent, that's all. It's mainly talk though, I've never actually seen him hit anyone. He can never remember anything about it the next day, he sort of blacks out.

TEBBIT. Oh dear, I don't like the sound of that.

WEAVER. I'm sure he'll be alright though. Look at him, he's out for the night.

TEBBIT. I hope so.

WEAVER. Now don't you worry yourself about it. He won't get up to anything, he's in no state to.

GEORGE. Blimey, you learn something new every day. Mind you, only this morning he was going on about how he screams all the time. He sits on his own in his flat and screams.

TEBBIT. Poor thing, he don't sound right in the head.

WEAVER. If you want me to stay, I will.

TEBBIT. No, you get off home to bed.

WEAVER. Wish I'd never said anything now. I don't want you to worry.

GEORGE. We're not worried; he won't do anything. I'm glad you told us about him though.

WEAVER. Right, I'll be off. Oh, (*Takes the gin out of his pocket.*) you might as well have this, I bought it for you anyway.

TEBBIT. Thank you, Weaver.

WEAVER. I took a couple of swigs, just to keep the cold out on the way over.

TEBBIT. That's perfectly alright.

WEAVER. I'll pop up in the morning, just to see if everything's alright.

GEORGE. Yea. See you then.

TEBBIT. Mind how you go now.

WEAVER. Right. Cheerio then. (*Exits.*)

GEORGE (*gets an overcoat and covers* GORDON). Ain't that funny about old Gordon, he just don't seem the type.

TEBBIT. You can't judge a book by its cover, George.

GEORGE. That's true.

Pause.

TEBBIT. Well, I think I'd better be getting to my bed now.

GEORGE. Oh. Right.

TEBBIT. It's a pity about this evening, we were just beginning to get to know each other better.

GEORGE. Yea. I know.

Pause.

TEBBIT. Would you be a gentleman and walk me to my room?

GEORGE. I'd be delighted.

TEBBIT. And you might like to come in for a nightcap, I've got the gin.

GEORGE. I can't stay too long though, can I.

TEBBIT. Oh no, you've got patients to look after.

GEORGE. Right then.

TEBBIT. Right then. (*They exit and close the door.*)

The sound of the door closing wakes GORDON. *He looks around confused. He looks at the bed and staggers out of the chair. He sits on the end of the bed and takes off his shoes. He moves* THOMAS *across the bed.*

GORDON. Come on old chap, make way for the rest of the troops. (*Gets in the bed not facing* THOMAS.) I hope you don't mind, but there's enough room for three in here, never mind two.

Pause.

You know, I do so hate sleeping in a chair don't you? It's most unpleasant. You wake up as stiff as a corpse in the morning.

Blackout.

THE AWAKENING ■ JULIAN GARNER

JULIAN GARNER was born in 1956 and brought up in South East London. He studied theatre at Dartington College of Arts, and *Small Ads*, his first full-length play, was presented at the Young Vic Studio in 1978 whilst he was still a student. *Cyril's Little Moments of Weakness and Strength* followed in 1980 at the Bristol Old Vic and the following year *Golden Leaf Strut* appeared at the Bush Theatre before going on to further productions both in England and Scandinavia. From 1981–89 he made his home in Norway, during which time his plays were produced throughout Scandinavia including the premieres of *Yesterday Now*, *Days Become So Long* and *Black Bulls* at Trøndelag Teater, Trondheim; *Noah's Rejects* at Den Nationale Scene, Bergen; *A Travelogue of There and Back*, a play for one woman at Nationaltheatret, Oslo and *Hunger and Pearls*, a children's play for Studio Teater in Trondheim, which was also presented in Helsinki and on tour in Finland. *Guardian Angels* was commissioned for the main house at Belgrade Theatre, Coventry and produced there in 1987. In 1989 he returned to England to live, writing *The Awakening* for Hampstead Theatre, where he is currently Thames Television Writer in Residence. In 1990 he translated the Danish play *Fair Kirsten* for Radio 3 and his own radio play *Thinking of You* was broadcast on Radio 3 in December 1990. He is currently working on new plays for Hampstead Theatre and Belgrade Theatre, Coventry, and a new English version of Ibsen's *Pillars of Society* for Arena Stage, Washington D.C. *Black Bulls* (an earlier version of *The Awakening*) won the Henrik Ibsen prize for Best Norwegian Play in 1989.

Special thanks to Rita Abrahamsen, Lasse Kolsrud and Janne Kokkin who participated in the original workshops at Trøndelag Teater, Norway.

Characters

AGNES, a Salvation Army officer, 40 years old and active prison
  reformer
JOHANNES, mid-20s prisoner serving a life sentence. A slight
  mental handicap renders him 'tuppence short of a shilling'
IVERSEN, late 30s, a prison warder
UNN, mid-20s, has the sole running of the island farm she owns
  with her brother

Norway, between the wars.

A prison cell
An island farm
A church

Running time: 1 hour 45 minutes

The Awakening was first staged at the Hampstead Theatre, London on 19 April 1990 with the following cast:

SERGEANT AGNES	Linda Bassett
JOHANNES	Con O'Neill
IVERSEN	Paul Copley
UNN	Gabrielle Reidy

Directed by John Dove
Designed by Michael Taylor
Lighting by Christopher Toulmin
Music by Ilona Sekacz and John Leonard

ACT ONE

Scene One

AGNES. In the beginning was Johannes.

JOHANNES is asleep in his cell.

In a bare cell, on the isolation wing of the prison I visited weekly.

JOHANNES wakes.

Each morning, he would awake, disturbed to find himself aroused.

Goes out.

JOHANNES (*quotes from memory*). 'Hear my prayer, O God; attend unto my prayer.
From the end of the earth will I cry unto thee, when my heart is overwhelmed: lead me to the rock that is higher than I.
For thou hast been a shelter for me, and a strong tower from the enemy.
I will abide in thy tabernacle forever: I will trust in the covert of thy wings.
For thou, O God, hast heard my vows: thou hast given me the heritage of those that fear thy name . . . ' (*Psalm 61.*)

His erection does not subside. Finds his bible. Reads with difficulty.

'O God, in the multitude of thy mercy hear me, in the truth of thy salvation.
Deliver me out of the mire, and let me not sink; let me be delivered from those that hate me, and out of the deep waters.
Let not the waterflood overflow me, neither let the deep swallow me up, and let not the pit shut her mouth upon me. (*Increasingly desperate.*) Hear me, O Lord; for thy loving kindness is good; turn unto me according to the multitude of thy tender mercies.

And hide not thy face from thy servant; for I am in need, hear me speedily . . .' (*Psalm 69.*)

The erection is still with him. From a kneeling position, he throws himself forward onto his stomach. Cries out in pain. Afterwards he is calm. He folds his blanket. IVERSEN, a prison officer, comes in with a plate of food and a mug of water.

IVERSEN. Breakfast.

JOHANNES (*dresses. Regards   IVERSEN*). Are you new here, sir?

IVERSEN. Yes.

JOHANNES (*presents himself formally*). Johannes Kristoffer Zachariassen.

IVERSEN. Just eat your breakfast.

JOHANNES (*kneels*). 'For what we are about to receive, may the Lord make us truly thankful, Amen.'

Sits at the table. Pause.

Herr Hagerseter never watches. Neither does Herr Hoff. They leave my plate and come back when I've eaten.

IVERSEN. I'm not Herr Hagerseter. Neither am I Herr Hoff. Just eat.

JOHANNES (*eats*). It's very good, this food.

IVERSEN. Good.

JOHANNES (*drinks*). And the water. (*Pause.*) God's very generous, isn't he, sir?

IVERSEN. Is he?

JOHANNES. He provides for us. Our food and drink. And clothes and shoes and socks. And chairs and tables and beds and blankets and windows and doors and ` . . .

IVERSEN. I suppose he does.

JOHANNES. God is kind. He loves us all. Even the ants and spiders, even worms. Insects don't say prayers, nor do animals, nor birds. But God forgives them, because they have such small brains and can't think, like we can.

IVERSEN. How long have you been here?

JOHANNES. Sir?

IVERSEN. How long have you been in solitary?

JOHANNES. Captain Agnes says I shouldn't count the days . . .

IVERSEN. Days? Years, you mean. You've been here two years. (*Pause.*) Are you at peace?

JOHANNES (*not understanding*). I . . . have to be here . . .

IVERSEN. I didn't ask that. Are you at peace? (*Pause.*) Why are you kept separate from the other prisoners? (*Pause.*) I'm glad it's not me kept locked up in here. Two years! How can you stand it? (*Pause.*) What have you done? It must've been something evil. Was it? Johannes Krist? That's what they call you, isn't it? Johannes Krist, the man with the bible? The man with his prayers and his hymns and his weekly visits from Aunt Sally Anne. Johannes Krist?

JOHANNES. Yes, sir . . .

IVERSEN. Johannes Loon suits you better. Isn't that what you're known as where you come from, out there in the world; Johannes Loon?

JOHANNES (*scared*). Yes, sir . . .

IVERSEN. How do I know? A little girl told me. I met her in the woods. She was lying under a bush. Ever so still, she lay. But she told me all about you, who you were, what you'd done to her. She was a pretty little girl. Her name was Anne Lise. She was eight years old.

JOHANNES. I've finished now, sir.

IVERSEN. Finished?

JOHANNES. You can take my plate.

IVERSEN. But you've not finished. You've hardly started. Aren't you going to eat your bread and cheese? No? Try and eat some at least, it's good cheese, and bread, it's good for you, it's full of goodness.

He crams food into JOHANNES's *mouth.*

It's a shame to waste this good food, that God has provided. When you think of all the starving people in the world who'd give their right arm for food like this, and here you are, just throwing it away.

Throws food about the cell. JOHANNES *starts to cry.*

If you don't shut up, I'll give you something to cry about. Do you hear? I'll really give you something to cry about!

JOHANNES *forces himself to stop crying.*

Pick up the food you've thrown on the floor.

JOHANNES *crawls around, picking up the food.*

What about your other appetite?

JOHANNES. S-sir?

IVERSEN. Your hard appetite? Have you lost that, as well? You know what I mean don't you, Johannes Loon?

Grabs JOHANNES *by the crutch.* JOHANNES *screams.*

Remember now why you need protection from the other prisoners? Remember? Why you're in danger outside this cell? Inside it as well, Johannes Krist, or Loon, or whatever you call yourself!

IVERSEN *beats* JOHANNES *mercilessly, seems to lose control. He doesn't stop when* JOHANNES *loses consciousness. What stops him is* AGNES *banging on the door.*

AGNES. What's going on in there?! Johannes? Guard! Guard! Open up, open up! Do you hear me in there?!

She comes in. Sees JOHANNES *lying by the wall.*

IVERSEN. He attacked me, Ma'am. Was violent. It was self defence.

AGNES *inspects* JOHANNES *more closely.* IVERSEN *edges towards the door.*

AGNES. Stay where you are!

JOHANNES *comes round, whimpering.*

It's alright, Johannes, it's me, it's Captain Agnes. Don't speak, rest now. I'm here, I won't let him touch you. It's alright, Johannes, lie still, still. (*He is quiet. To* IVERSEN.) Well?

IVERSEN. It's like I said, he went wild, flew at me. I had to defend myself. He's a murderer, after all.

AGNES. How do you know what he is?

IVERSEN. Well . . . .

AGNES. Records on this wing are strictly confidential, you know that as well as I do.

IVERSEN. Yes. Still, rumours, Ma'am . . .

AGNES. It's your job to be deaf to rumours! A rule it took me three years to have introduced. (*Pause.*) Show me your wounds.

IVERSEN. Ma'am?

AGNES. He attacked you, didn't he? A dangerous murderer, he must have left his mark?

IVERSEN. Well . . .

AGNES. How dare you lie to me! I know this boy, I know him well. You'd have me believe he'd attack a guard, and a man of your size into the bargain? You expect me to believe such a story?! (*Pause.*) Have you nothing to say? Well!?

IVERSEN. It's no more than he deserves!

AGNES. I beg your pardon?

IVERSEN. He's a murderer! Murdered a little girl . . .

AGNES. That's enough!

IVERSEN. Not just murdered her, had his way with her first . . .

AGNES (*shouts him down*). YOUR CRIME IS NOT EXCUSED BY HIS! (*Pause.*) You're new here, aren't you? What's your name?

IVERSEN. What's it to you?

AGNES (*pause*). It would be unwise to think of me as just another busybody, another do-gooder getting in the way. I have influence in this place.
When I began my mission here, this wing was known as 'The Zoo'. The inmates were treated worse than animals, tortured and starved, trussed up for weeks on end, used as punchbags by such morons as yourself . . .

IVERSEN. Iversen. My name's . . . Iversen.

AGNES. 'Two men went up into the temple to pray; the one a Pharisee, the other a publican.
And the Pharisee prayed thus with himself, God, I thank thee that I am not as other men are, or even as this publican.
And the publican, standing afar off, would not lift so much as his eyes unto heaven, but smote upon his breast saying, God be merciful to me a sinner.

I tell you, this man went down to his house justified rather than the other: for everyone that exalteth himself shall be abased: and he that humbleth himself shall be exalted.' (*Luke 18: 9–14.*)

IVERSEN *pushes past her and goes out.* AGNES *shouts after him.*

I'LL HAVE YOU DISMISSED FOR THIS!

JOHANNES. Captain Agnes! Captain Agnes!

AGNES. I'm here, Johannes.

JOHANNES. God doesn't love me!

AGNES. Of course He does . . .

JOHANNES. No, no! He doesn't love me!

AGNES. God loves all his children, Johannes.

JOHANNES. Not me! Not me!

AGNES. Christ died on the cross that our sins might be forgiven.

JOHANNES. I'll never be forgiven! Never. Never. Never. Never. Never. Never . . .

AGNES (*restrains him*). 'The Lord hath not dealt with us after our sins, nor rewarded us after our iniquities.
For as the heaven is high above the earth, so great is his mercy towards those that fear him.
As far as east is from west, so far has he removed our transgressions from us . . .' (*Psalm 103.*)

JOHANNES *is quiet.*

Scene Two

Farmhouse kitchen. AGNES *and* JOHANNES *have just arrived,* JOHANNES *wearing civilian clothes and carrying a suitcase.* UNN *has paused from ironing laundry at the table.*

AGNES. Hello Unn.

UNN. Agnes.

AGNES. How good it is to see you again.

UNN *eyes* JOHANNES, *warily.*

This is Johannes.

JOHANNES. Johannes Kristoffer Zachariassen.

UNN. Hello, I'm Unn.

AGNES. I'm sorry if we're later than expected. The bus developed a mechanical fault and we were delayed two hours whilst it was repaired. Then when we arrived, the ferryman was out. And then we walked over Gull Spike from the jetty. I wanted Johannes to see the whole island, to get an impression of his new home. It's a clear night, we could see out as far as the lighthouse and the church on the mainland. I'd forgotten how stiff a climb it was. (*To* JOHANNES.) At your age I'd run up there without a thought, often with Unn on my shoulders. Now, I feel like I've climbed Mount Sinai, with all my sins, not a child, on my back!

JOHANNES is standing awkwardly, his legs apart. UNN has noticed, now AGNES does too.

What is it, Johannes?

JOHANNES (*ashamed*). Please, Captain Agnes, I . . . I couldn't help it. I just . . . I . . .

Before AGNES can react, UNN takes a towel from the pile of fresh laundry and gives it to JOHANNES.

UNN. Have you a change of clothes?

JOHANNES. Yes, Ma'am.

UNN. I'll show you to your room. You can wash there and change.

JOHANNES. Forgive me, Captain Agnes.

UNN. This way.

JOHANNES follows UNN out. Eventually, AGNES takes off her coat and carries on with the ironing UNN has left off. UNN comes in.

AGNES. This was my job. I've no time for it now, nor the energy; my work takes all I have of both. Besides my visiting, I sit on a number of boards and committees. There are meetings, funds to be raised, all manner of business to attend. My days are full. Sometimes, I'm so tired at night I fall asleep in a chair and don't wake up until morning.

She finishes the shirt, holds it up.

Is this Erik's?

UNN. Yes.

AGNES. He's grown.

UNN *takes the shirt, folds it and puts it in the basket. Continues ironing.*
AGNES *is unsure how to handle* UNN's *unexpected sullenness.*

Are you well, Unn?

UNN. I don't complain.

AGNES. And your brother?

UNN. He's alright.

AGNES. You can't imagine how I've looked forward to this. I
showed Johannes our names on the Spike. They were still clear,
as if it were yesterday we'd carved them. Nothing's changed:
the path down, the farmyard, kitchen, the smell of ironing.
There have been some hard times during the past ten years; my
memories of this place and the people here have often helped
me through them.

UNN. I hope he knows how to wash himself.

AGNES. Johannes?

UNN. He'd shit all down his legs.

AGNES. He didn't say . . .

UNN. It happened on the boat, he said.

AGNES. We had to carry him on board, the sea so disturbed him.
It was the first time he'd seen it, you understand. Poor
Johannes. He so wanted to make a good impression.

UNN *says nothing, continues ironing.*

He's a good boy, Unn. He'll work hard, I know. Of course,
he'll take a while to settle. Two years in solitary will have taken
their toll. But I know from experience how well he responds to
kindness. Above all, he's a good Christian.

UNN. So long as he works better than he sails, I don't care what
he is. I run a farm, not a mission.

Exits with iron. Enters with another, hot off the range. Continues ironing.

AGNES. Unn.

UNN. What?

AGNES (*pause*). Have I made a mistake?

UNN. What mistake?

AGNES. When I approached the Prison Board, I made plain my dislike for a system where the likes of Johannes provide slave labour for the nation's farms. To be honest, it's a practice I'd like to see abandoned. But I was convinced on this particular farm he'd find not just a place of toil but a Christian home.

UNN. Why should you think that?

AGNES. For two years, he has lived in a cell not twice the size of this table. Alone. With nothing to occupy him, no one to speak to, nothing even to look at but the walls. For two years there has been nothing soft or warm or kind in that boy's life.

UNN. So?

AGNES. Unn, he needs kindness.

UNN. Don't we all.

AGNES (*watches her ironing*). Do you know my clearest memory of you? You found a seagull on the beach, with a damaged wing.

UNN. Did I?

AGNES. You brought it home and kept it in a box in your room. All winter you nursed it back to health. And when your brother teased you – all this fuss over a bird – do you remember your answer? 'Are not five sparrows sold for two farthings and not one of them is forgotten before God?' You were barely seven years old, yet that was the answer you gave.

UNN. And that made you proud, did it?

AGNES. Yes, it did.

UNN. It proved I'd learned my lessons right?

AGNES. Were they such bad lessons?

UNN. And what lesson was I supposed to learn when you suddenly just upped and left?

AGNES *is taken aback, but before she can say anything,* JOHANNES *comes in.*

JOHANNES. I'm clean now, Captain Agnes.

UNN. Did you pour the water out?

JOHANNES. Yes Ma'am, like you said.

UNN. And your dirty clothes?

JOHANNES. I put them in the bucket, Ma'am like you . . .

UNN. And the window?

JOHANNES. Ma'am?

UNN. Did you open it?

JOHANNES. No, Ma'am . . .

UNN. Well, it's you that has to sleep with the smell, not me.

AGNES. Unn, please . . .

Beat. UNN *goes out, comes in immediately with a bowl, gives it to* JOHANNES.

UNN. Take this to the barn. There's a door under the ramp, the nesting boxes are to the right as you go in. There won't be many eggs. The hens are laying some place I've not had the chance to find yet. Bring whatever's in the boxes. And be careful not to break any, they're your supper.

JOHANNES. Yes, Ma'am. (*Hesitates.*)

UNN. What are you waiting for?

AGNES. Go on, Johannes.

JOHANNES *goes out. Long silence.*

UNN. If I woke up at night, it was you I called for, you I wanted.

AGNES. I told you why I had to leave.

UNN. If there was one day in eight years you weren't here, that's all there was. For eight years you were my mother, and suddenly you weren't there any more.

AGNES. It was my job . . .

UNN. You deserted me.

AGNES. I was not your mother, Unn . . .

UNN. Then who was?!

AGNES (*pause*). I was fifteen years old when your mother died. Your father needed a house-keeper, someone to cook and wash. It was to be for a few months, but it became eight years. We were close, I know, but . . .

UNN. I don't want your explanations.

AGNES. I couldn't stay forever, Unn.

UNN suddenly throws all the ironing things into the laundry basket. As she exits with it, AGNES *reaches out to touch her.*

UNN. No! You're here to deliver the loony, no other reason.

Goes out. Comes in with a jug of milk and three cups.

AGNES. Unn . . .

UNN. Are you hungry?

AGNES. We must . . .

UNN. Excuse me.

She pushes past AGNES *to get to the table, takes cutlery, etc., from the drawer and lays the table for three. She goes out, comes in with a loaf of bread on a board. Cuts it into slices at the table.*

AGNES *(eventually, businesslike)*. Where's your brother?

UNN. Not here.

AGNES. Where is he?

UNN shrugs.

Will he be back soon?

UNN. Don't know.

AGNES. What do you mean?

UNN. I don't know where he is, nor when he'll be back.

AGNES. I have to speak to him. *(Pause.)* He will be here before I leave tomorrow?

UNN. Shouldn't think so. Erik's a fisherman. If he's here two months of the year, I'm lucky.

AGNES *(beat)*. What?

UNN. He won't be back before May.

AGNES *(shaken)*. You're here alone?

UNN. I can sign any papers.

AGNES. Papers . . . ?

UNN. If there are any papers, I'll sign them.

AGNES. No . . .

UNN. You wrote to me as well, didn't you? My name was also on the envelope. And it was me wrote back to you, saying we'd take him in.

AGNES. I must take him back.

UNN. What . . . ?

AGNES. Johannes, I must . . .

UNN. Take him back?

AGNES. I'm sorry. We'll stay the night, if we may, and leave first thing in the morning.

UNN. I run this farm, not Erik!

AGNES. I'm sorry . . .

UNN. Since my father died.

AGNES. I can't . . .

UNN. Erik got the boat, I the farm. There's nothing I don't do. Cut hay; muck out; deliver calves; slaughter cattle, if I have to. Whatever needs doing, I do it. And you think I can't manage a loony?

AGNES. Don't call him that!

UNN. . . . ?

AGNES. I can't leave him here. I can't. A man must be responsible. The law's quite clear.

UNN. A man?

AGNES. There's nothing to be done. If I'd known . . .

UNN. There's loonies, or whatever you call them, all along this coast – more than one on some islands – and most of the men are away all the time . . .

AGNES. No, it's impossible. I must take him back.

UNN (*beat*). I need help. Your letter was a Godsend.

AGNES. I'm sorry . . .

UNN (*shrugs*). Take him, then. I'll write to the authorities myself. There are plenty more where he came from.

JOHANNES *comes in. He has made his jacket into a makeshift bag which is full of eggs.* UNN *and* AGNES *stare at him in amazement.*

UNN. Where did you get all those?

JOHANNES. I found them, Ma'am.

UNN. Where?

JOHANNES. It was dark. I was afraid. There were so many sounds. I felt in all the boxes. There weren't any eggs in the boxes. There weren't any hens in them, either. Then I heard – cluck-cluck-cluck. A hen! But I couldn't see her. Then she came out through a little gap under a door. And I could hear other hens on the other side of the door. Cluck-cluck-cluck, they said, Cluck-cluck-cluck-cluck-cluck! I opened the door. There were some cows in there, big black cows.

UNN. You went into the bulls?

JOHANNES. I could hear them, chewing and breathing and moving. And the hens! Lying in the straw, near the black cows. And when they saw me they got up, the hens, and ran away! Cluck-cluck-cluck-cluck-cluck, they said! And there were lots of eggs, where they'd be laying in the straw. Lots and lots and lots of eggs!

UNN *stares at* JOHANNES. *Then she goes out, returning immediately with a much larger bowl. She puts the eggs into the bowl, all the time shooting strange glances at* JOHANNES. AGNES *stands apart, watching. When all the eggs are in the bowl,* UNN *pours a glass of milk.*

UNN. Drink that. I'll make you some supper.

She goes out.

Scene Three

The kitchen. AGNES *sitting at the table in the darkness. Very gradually, throughout the scene, it grows lighter.* UNN *comes in still in night clothes, her hair unkempt.*

UNN. Agnes.

AGNES (*starts. Sees* UNN). Forgive me. I couldn't sleep.

UNN. It's early.

AGNES. Yes.

Pause.

UNN. I'll make some coffee.

She goes out.

AGNES. So quiet it is here. I'd forgotten. In the town it's never still, people shout on the streets even at night. There's never any peace.

It grows lighter. AGNES doesn't move. UNN comes in with cups and a coffee kettle. She is now dressed, her hair combed. She pours coffee. They sit for a while, sipping coffee. It grows lighter.

The first time I visited him at the prison, he was washing himself. Scrubbing with a coarse brush and disinfectant. His arms were red and in places he's removed the skin. He was trying to make himself clean.

UNN watches her.

I've taught him the bible. I've tried to help him recognise the presence of God in his heart. A loving God, a forgiving God. And sometimes he would smile and say, yes, he understood, and he felt hope and happiness. At other times, nothing I could say would diminish the hopelessness of that room. 'God doesn't love me', he would say. 'I'll never be forgiven. I'll never be forgiven.'

Looks at UNN.

I wanted him to have a chance to make a life for himself. He has repented his sin. Has sought after God and been forgiven. I don't believe he'll ever be a danger to anyone, ever again. If I didn't believe that, how could I have argued so vigorously on his behalf?

It grows lighter still as they look at each other for a long time. Then UNN goes out. JOHANNES comes in, dressed, with his suitcase. AGNES does not look at him, she is deep in her own thoughts. He sits down. UNN enters with a bowl of porridge for JOHANNES.

JOHANNES (*prays*). 'For what I am about to receive, may the Lord make me truly thankful.'

He eats.

AGNES. If I were a man, my name should be Thomas!

She gets up and goes out into the farmyard. UNN *and* JOHANNES *exchange glances. It is still getting lighter.*

(To herself.) 'But Thomas said unto them, Except I shall see in his hands the print of the nails, and put my finger into the print of the nails, I will not believe . . .
And Jesus said to Thomas, Reach hither thy finger and behold my hands . . .
Thomas, because thou hast seen me, thou hast believed: blessed are they that have not seen, and yet have believed.' *(John 20: 24–29.)*

Seagulls circle overhead, moaning. She looks up at them. Suddenly, goes back into the kitchen.

(To JOHANNES.) You must read your bible every day.

JOHANNES. Captain Agnes?

AGNES. You must say your prayers.

JOHANNES *(confused).* When I get up and when I go to bed, and before and after meals.

AGNES. You must put your trust in the Lord, Johannes.

JOHANNES. Yes, Captain Agnes.

AGNES. You shall love God, but you shall fear him, too.

JOHANNES. Fear him?

AGNES. Fear him and obey his commandments.

JOHANNES. Yes, Captain Agnes.

AGNES. Repeat the Ten Commandments.

JOHANNES. Captain Agnes?

AGNES. Let me hear you.

JOHANNES. 'Thou shalt have no other gods before me.
Thou shalt not worship any graven image.
Thou shalt not take the name of the Lord thy God in vain.
Thou shalt remember the Sabbath and keep it holy.
Thou shalt honour thy father and mother.
Thou shalt not . . . kill.
Thou shalt not commit adultery.
Thou shalt not steal.

Thou shalt not bear false witness.
Thou shalt not covet thy neighbour's house, nor his wife, nor his manservant, nor his maidservant, nor his ox, nor his ass, nor anything that is thy neighbour's!'

AGNES. 'For God so loved the world that he gave his only begotten son, that whosoever believeth in him . . . should not perish but have everlasting life.'

JOHANNES *looks at her*.

ACT TWO

Scene One

Farmyard. UNN *splitting logs.* JOHANNES *watches her.*

UNN. You try.

   JOHANNES *takes the axe. Places a log on the block and attempts to split it.*

UNN. No. *(Takes the axe.)* Watch me. *(She splits the log.)* Let it fall.

JOHANNES. Fall.

UNN. Let the axe do the work.

JOHANNES. Axe do the work.

UNN. Try again.

JOHANNES. Try again. Axe. Wood. Axe do the work.

UNN. Let it fall.

JOHANNES. Let it fall. *(Manages to split the log.)*

UNN. And again.

JOHANNES. And again. Axe. Wood. Let it fall. Axe do the work. Let it fall.

UNN. Then stack the split logs over there. See where I've started. *(Points off.)*

JOHANNES. Yes, Ma'am.

UNN. Stack them neatly.

JOHANNES. Yes, Ma'am.

UNN. Can you manage that?

JOHANNES. Yes, Ma'am.

UNN *goes into the kitchen.*

On the table is a bag of flour, salt, a dish of fermenting yeast, a mixing bowl, wooden spoon and a clean dish cloth. She begins mixing the ingredients to a dough.

Eventually she notices that JOHANNES *is splitting one log at a time, adding it to the woodpile before going onto the next. She goes out into the farmyard.*

UNN. What are you doing?

JOHANNES. . . . ?

UNN. Not one at a time. Fill the basket first, then stack them.

JOHANNES. Yes, Ma'am.

UNN. You'll take all year, otherwise.

She goes back into the kitchen and continues mixing the dough.

JOHANNES *retrieves the logs he's already stacked from the woodpile, putting them into the basket. Then continues splitting the logs.*

After a while he tires. He puts down the axe, sits on the chopping block and takes out his bible. Struggles to understand each section of the text before proceeding to the next.

JOHANNES (*reads, inexpertly*). 'Wherewithal shall a young man cleanse his way? by taking heed thereto according to thy word. Blessed are the undefiled in the way, who walk in the Law of the Lord.
Blessed are they that keepeth his testimonies and that seeketh him with a whole heart.
With my whole heart have I sought thee: O let me not wander from thy commandments . . .' (*Psalm 119.*)

UNN *comes out.*

UNN. What do you think you're doing?

JOHANNES. Reading, Ma'am.

UNN. Reading?

JOHANNES. I was tired, Ma'am.

UNN. Tired? How can you be tired – you've only just started!

She snatches the bible. He grabs the axe.

UNN *backs off. Pause.*

Until half that pile's split and stacked there'll be no supper for
you – understood?

He glares at her.

Is that understood?

She goes back into the kitchen, taking the bible with her. JOHANNES
continues to work, taking out his anger on the logs.

JOHANNES. Let it fall. And let it fall. And let it fall. And let it
fall . . . (*Etc.*)

UNN *takes a sheath-knife from the drawer and straps it to her belt.*

Scene Two

JOHANNES *polishing a pair of boots. He works with great thoroughness,*
humming the tune of Psalm 23 quietly to himself. A neat row of shoes, some
four or five pairs in all, all immaculate. UNN *sits nearby, a basket of*
clothes beside her, mending a hole in a pair of trousers.

JOHANNES *finishes the boots and places them carefully with the others.*

JOHANNES. Please Ma'am . . .

UNN. Yes?

JOHANNES. I've finished, Ma'am.

UNN. Put them back in the cupboard.

JOHANNES *picks up the shoes and boots and goes out with them.*
Comes back in.

Pause. UNN *notices him staring at her feet.*

UNN. What is it?

JOHANNES. Should I clean yours, too?

UNN *takes off her shoes.* JOHANNES *takes them and goes to work.*
UNN *discovers a hole in one of her socks. She removes this also, threads*
a bodkin and begins darning.

JOHANNES *keeps glancing at* UNN's *bare foot and lower leg.*
Eventually, she realises and tucks it out of sight.

JOHANNES *gives himself utterly to the task of shoe-polishing, humming*
the same tune under his breath.

Scene Three

Kitchen. Night. Outside, a strong wind blowing.

UNN comes in with a water-jug and basin, soap, flannel and towel. Puts them on table, pours water into the basin. Takes off her apron and blouse. Washes her face and neck.

A sound in the house makes her start.

UNN. Hello? . . . Johannes . . . Johannes, is that you? . . . Hello? . . .

She dries her face. Begins to take off her vest, but stops. Changes her mind. She washes her torso without removing the vest.

She washes fast, as if all the time anxious that JOHANNES might come in.

Johannes . . . ?

Scene Four

JOHANNES chopping wood, his axemanship improved beyond recognition, his shirt and jumper discarded and his face alight with satisfaction.

JOHANNES (*as he works, sings*). 'The Lord is my shepherd; I shall not want.
He maketh me to lie down in green pastures; he leadeth me beside still waters.
He restoreth my soul; he leadeth me in the paths of righteousness for his name's sake.
Yeah, though I walk through the valley of the shadow of death I shall fear no evil: for thou art with me: thy rod and thy staff, they comfort me.
Thou preparest a table before me in the presence of mine enemies: thou annointest my head with oil; my cup runneth over.
Surely goodness and mercy will follow me all the days of my life and I will dwell in the house of the Lord forever.' (*Psalm 23.*)

He takes the full basket and heads for the woodpile. Almost collides with UNN as she comes on carrying three or four fish in a pail and a fishing net over her shoulder.

UNN (*embarrassed*). Put on your shirt, at once!

JOHANNES *puts on his shirt.*

And your jumper.

He does so.

You'll catch your death.

JOHANNES. Please Ma'am, it was hot.

UNN. You work too fast. It's not a race.

JOHANNES. No, Ma'am.

Awkward pause.

JOHANNES *goes off with the wood-basket. He sings Psalm 23 again, as he stacks the logs.* UNN *watches him, off.*

She hangs the net between pegs in the wall, begins checking it for holes. JOHANNES *comes in.*

JOHANNES (*inspecting the fish*). Cod; hake; and . . . Cod, hake and . . . er . . .

UNN. Whiting.

JOHANNES. Whiting. Whiting. (*He watches* UNN.) Please Ma'am, I think I can do that.

UNN. What?

JOHANNES. I've watched you before.

UNN (*pause*). Let's see, then.

JOHANNES *takes over. He works surprisingly competently.*

UNN. Not too fast.

JOHANNES. No, Ma'am.

UNN (*watches him a while*). I caught it on the rocks, so there'll be some holes, I expect. If you find any you must call me.

She takes the fish into the kitchen. She stands quite still by the table. Again, she feels her cheeks.

JOHANNES *stares at the net, perplexed. After a while he goes into the kitchen.*

UNN (*immediately begins to 'clean' the fish*). What is it?

JOHANNES. Erm . . .

UNN. Well?

JOHANNES. It's the net, Ma'am . . .

UNN. Have you found a hole?

JOHANNES. Yes.

They go out into the farmyard. UNN inspects the net.

UNN. Where?

JOHANNES. Erm . . .

UNN. I don't see any holes.

JOHANNES. Erm . . .

UNN (*realises what's confusing him*). You thought . . . ? These aren't holes! A hole is where there is a break in the net.

JOHANNES. Oh.

UNN laughs. JOHANNES continues to hang the net.

UNN (*eventually*). Johannes.

JOHANNES. Yes Ma'am.

UNN. Are you thirsty? Would you like something to drink?

JOHANNES looks at her.

Come.

They go into the kitchen. UNN gives him a glass of milk, he drinks. UNN takes out the bible from the drawer of the table and gives it to JOHANNES. He reads to himself. UNN 'cleans' the fish.

UNN (*eventually*). Have you ever seen Spring on a farm, Johannes?

JOHANNES. No, Ma'am.

UNN. Just wait until you see the animals when we let them out. Especially the bulls. They're scared at first; we have to lead them out. It's so long since they saw daylight. But once they're used to it, you have to keep your distance, then! They kick their legs and bellow and jump about. Like fat men at a barn dance, who've had too much to drink!

JOHANNES laughs. Pause.

I think we must try to take you fishing again.

JOHANNES *rushes out into the farmyard, begins chopping wood.* UNN *follows.*

It's nothing to be afraid of. The boat's steady as a rock and you're never more than a stone's throw from the shore. Johannes, you have to take over the fishing, sooner or later. April's a hard month.

She takes his hands.

Remember the first time you used an axe, how blistered your hands were? But they soon hardened up, didn't they, and now you can chop wood all day, if you like, your hands are used to it. It's the same with your stomach. It'll soon get used to a few waves.

Pause. Lets go his hands.

You can be out with me, tonight. I'll show you how to set the nets. If you're still sick after a week you can stop. But you must try it for a week, at least.

JOHANNES. Yes, Ma'am.

UNN *goes into the kitchen.* JOHANNES *stares at his hands.* UNN *stares at hers. Goes back out.*

UNN. Johannes . . .

JOHANNES. Yes, Ma'am?

UNN. Don't call me Ma'am. Agnes used to call my mother 'Ma'am'. Call me Unn.

JOHANNES. Unn?

UNN. Yes.

JOHANNES. Unn.

UNN *goes back into the kitchen.*

JOHANNES (*to himself*). Unn . . . Unn . . . Unn . . .

UNN *continues cleaning the fish.* JOHANNES *splits logs.*

JOHANNES (*on each swing of the axe*). Unn . . . Unn . . .

UNN (*cuts her finger*). Ow! (*Sucks her finger.*)

JOHANNES (*As he works*). Unn . . . Unn . . . Unn . . .

UNN *smiles to herself.*

Scene Five

Night. JOHANNES *has fallen asleep at the kitchen table, his bible open in front of him.*

UNN *comes in and sees him. Goes out, comes back in with a blanket. Drapes it round his shoulders. Goes out.*

JOHANNES *wakes. Notices the blanket. Randomly selects a new place in the bible and reads, slowly and deliberately.*

JOHANNES. 'Thy navel is like a round goblet, wherein no mingled wine is wanting: Thy belly is like a heap of wheat set about with lilies.
Thy two breasts are like . . . (*Pause. Rubs his eyes.*)
Thy two breasts are like two fawns . . . (*Pause.*)
Thy two breasts . . .

Moves quickly away from the table.

Captain Agnes!

Stands for a few moments, uncertain what to do. Approaches the table, cautiously.

(*Reads.*) 'This thy stature is like to a palm tree, and thy breasts to clusters of grapes . . . (*Pause.*)
Thy breasts to clusters of grapes . . .
(*Louder.*) Thy breasts to clusters of grapes . . .'

He takes the bible. Goes out, across the farmyard and into the barn.

(*Joyous.*) 'Thy breasts are like to clusters of grapes! Thy breasts are like to clusters of grapes! Thy grapes are like to clusters of . . . Thy breasts are like to . . .

He masturbates.

Thy breasts are like clusters of . . . grapes. Thy breasts are like . . . Are like . . . Thy breasts . . .

Reaches orgasm. Lies still, hugging the bible to his chest.

Scene Six

Kitchen. JOHANNES *is sitting at the table, watching* UNN *kneading dough for bread. His bible is open in front of him.*

JOHANNES. Am I a good fisherman, Unn?

UNN. You will be, one day.

JOHANNES. I helped you didn't I?

UNN. Yes, you did.

JOHANNES. If I hadn't had my wits about me, that cod
would've slipped out of the boat and we'd have lost him,
wouldn't we?

UNN. Yes, we would.

JOHANNES. I grabbed him just in time.

UNN. You did very well.

JOHANNES. Are you pleased with me, Unn?

UNN. You know I am.

JOHANNES (*pause*). I like fishing.

UNN. Do you?

JOHANNES. I like it very much.

UNN. That's good.

JOHANNES. I'll be a good fisherman one day, won't I, Unn?

UNN. I'm sure of it.

JOHANNES (*reads*). 'And when they had this done, they enclosed
a great multitude of fishes, and their nets were breaking . . . '
'But Simon Peter, when he saw it, fell down at Jesus knees
saying, Depart from me; for I am a sinful man, O Lord . . . '
'And Jesus said unto Simon, Fear not; for henceforth thou shalt
catch men.' (*Luke 5*)

(*Eventually.*) Unn.

UNN. Yes, Johannes?

JOHANNES. When Jesus said to Simon Peter, 'From henceforth
thou shalt catch men', what did he mean?

UNN. That he would catch men instead of fish.

JOHANNES. But what had they done wrong?

UNN. Who?

JOHANNES. The men, that should be caught?

UNN. It's a symbol, Johannes, Men are like fish; Simon will be the fisherman, catching them in his net, which is Christianity.

JOHANNES. Saving them, you mean?

UNN. That's what Jesus meant.

JOHANNES (*pause*). I'm a fish!

UNN. What?

JOHANNES. And Captain Agnes is the fisherman who caught me in her net! Captain Agnes saved my soul, by showing me the way to Christ.

UNN. Did she?

JOHANNES. She was very kind to me. Every week, she came to teach me how to say my prayers and read me stories from the bible, and help me understand their real meanings. She always brought me something nice, some apples or some sugar or chocolate. Once she brought me some grapes. She went to town, early, specially to buy them for me. Oh, they were good! A big bag, I ate them all myself, more than a hundred grapes! I offered some to Captain Agnes but she'd already had something to eat, she said.

UNN. Didn't you have any other visitors?

JOHANNES. What?

UNN. Your family, your father and mother?

JOHANNES. No. (*Pause.*) I wasn't sick, was I, Unn?

UNN. What?

JOHANNES. On the boat.

UNN. No, you weren't.

JOHANNES. I was, nearly.

UNN. Were you?

JOHANNES. I wanted to be sick, but I wasn't.

UNN. No.

JOHANNES (*pause*). We caught five fishes, didn't we, Unn?

UNN. Yes Johannes, we caught five fishes.

JOHANNES. Hake and cod and . . . Hake and cod and . . .

UNN. Whiting.

JOHANNES. Two whiting. That's five fishes in all. That's a lot, isn't it, Unn?

UNN. No. It's not bad, but it's not a lot.

JOHANNES. Five fishes isn't bad.

UNN. No.

JOHANNES (*pause*). I wish Captain Agnes had seen me, carrying them up from the boat. She'd have been proud of me, wouldn't she, Unn? Wouldn't Captain Agnes have been proud of me?

UNN. I expect she would, yes . . .

JOHANNES. I expect she would. Because I'm almost like a son to her.

UNN. What?

JOHANNES. That's what she said, once; that I was almost like a son to her.

UNN. Did she say that?

JOHANNES. Yes.

UNN *is very still.*

Unn? . . . Unn? . . . Unn? . . .

UNN. It's nothing, Johannes. Nothing. (*Continues kneading.*)

JOHANNES *takes a piece of dough.*

JOHANNES (*kneading also. Eventually*). Jesus was very clever, wasn't he, Unn?

UNN. What?

JOHANNES. The way he cured the sick and raised the dead, and forgave people their sins.

UNN. Yes.

JOHANNES. But he couldn't cure people unless they had faith, could he? He could only cure those that believe in God.

UNN. Yes, that's right.

She takes the piece of dough JOHANNES *is kneading. He goes back to his bible.*

JOHANNES. Here, it says here – 'Thy faith hath made thee whole . . .'

UNN. Haven't you anything better to do than read the bible half the night?! Haven't you?

JOHANNES. Erm . . .

UNN. If not you can polish the copper, instead, you know where the cloths are. Well, what are you waiting for?!

JOHANNES. Captain Agnes said . . .

UNN. Can't you forget about 'Captain' Agnes? She's forgotten you.

JOHANNES. . . . ?

UNN. If you're like a son to her, then I was a daughter. Every day for eight years she was here, then she disappeared for ten! Until she needed a favour doing. She's forgotten you like she forgot me. (*Calmer.*) She's a fisher of men, Johannes. You're in the net; her mind's on other fishes now. It doesn't matter. You'll get used to her not being there, it's nothing to be frightened of. No more than the dark, or the sea.

JOHANNES stares at her. She reaches out to touch him. He leaps up and runs out.

Johannes . . . !

She follows him.

He runs into the barn. Shadows: sounds of the animals in their stalls, pulling at their chains, breathing. UNN *stays outside.*

Johannes . . . Johannes, you must come out.

JOHANNES. No!

UNN. It's not safe with the bulls. Come back to the house. You can read to me, if you like. I didn't mean what I said. Johannes.

JOHANNES. I won't come out!

UNN (*comes into the barn*). You shouldn't stand so close to the bulls, Johannes. They can be dangerous.

JOHANNES. So can I!

UNN. They might attack.

JOHANNES. So might I!

UNN. Shhhh, don't shout so loud.

JOHANNES. Don't come so close to me! You shouldn't come so close!

UNN. Johannes.

She lays a hand on him to calm him.

JOHANNES (*pulls away*). Don't touch me!

UNN. We don't need Agnes. Let her forget us if she wants, we don't need her, Johannes.

JOHANNES. Depart from me, for I am a sinful man!

UNN. We've all sinned, Johannes.

JOHANNES. But I've sinned so terribly!

UNN. Shhhh . . .

JOHANNES. I'll never be forgiven!

UNN. Of course you'll be forgiven . . .

JOHANNES. No! No! Never!

UNN. You are forgiven. I forgive you.

JOHANNES. You don't know what I've done!

UNN. It doesn't matter. I forgive you, anyway.

She moves closer to him, touches him. At first he is tense, but then responds. Eventually, they hold each other close.

ACT THREE

Scene One

*Kitchen. Outside it is raining heavily. UNN lies on her back on the table,
asleep. She is wearing a summer dress and no shoes. After a while, she
wakes; lies peacefully for a few moments staring at the ceiling, then realises
that it is raining. Leaps up from the table and runs out with the empty
laundry basket. Returns shortly, soaked through, the basket full of sheets. She
rigs up a clothes line; takes off her dress and hangs it on it. Leaves the room.*

*AGNES comes in. She has a bag with her and an umbrella. Puts the open
umbrella to one side to drain. UNN comes in in dry clothes.*

UNN. Hello Agnes.

AGNES. Forgive me arriving unannounced. I hope it isn't
inconvenient?

UNN. Sit down, I'll fetch some coffee.

AGNES sits. UNN brings coffee.

If it's bitter, I'll make fresh. It's stood a while.

AGNES. Thank you.

UNN (*hanging sheets on the line*). I woke up and it was raining.
They've been outside all day.

AGNES. We were half way across the sound and the sky just
opened.

UNN. We need it, it's been a dry summer.

AGNES (*pause*). I'm sorry I haven't been, earlier. I'm setting up a
shelter for the homeless.

They come in from the districts looking for work, but the town
can barely employ its own folk, and they end up sleeping under
bridges and in parks. I have managed to persuade a leading

citizen to place a building at my disposal, a disused wharf. It's inadequate, but it's a start.

UNN. How's the coffee?

AGNES (*drinks*). It's fine.

UNN. Johannes is doing the nets. He'll not be long.

AGNES (*notices the sheets are embroidered at the edges*). Aren't those the best sheets?

UNN. I found them in a cupboard in the loft.

AGNES. Your mother only used them for special occasions.

UNN. My mother's dead.

AGNES (*pause*). Your hair's wet, Unn. You'll catch cold if you don't dry it.

UNN *looks at her a moment. Then dries her hair quickly and brushes it. Pours herself coffee, sits across the table from* AGNES. *Pause.*

UNN. You look tired.

AGNES. From the journey. You look well.

UNN. Won't you have some cake?

AGNES. How is Johannes?

UNN. Well. (*Pause.*)

AGNES. He works hard?

UNN. Yes. (*Pause.*)

AGNES. Did he take long to settle in?

UNN. Not long.

AGNES *takes a bite of cake.*

How is it?

AGNES. Good.

UNN. Johannes made it. He learns fast; I never have to tell him anything more than once. He cuts hay, feeds the animals, bakes bread and cakes, polishes copper, gathers eggs. Is there anything he doesn't do? The fishing's his job, now, I don't interfere. And he chops wood like a demon. (*Laughs.*) Sorry, but angels don't chop wood, do they?

AGNES. You're satisfied, then?

UNN. Satisfied? Yes, I'm satisfied.

AGNES. It's stopped raining.

UNN. Yes.

They drink coffee, in silence, AGNES *clearly building up to something. Finally.*

AGNES. I'm glad to have found you alone. I hoped we'd have a chance to talk, I've thought a lot about what was said. About when I left. You were a child. I thought I'd explained it adequately to you. I realise, now, how confused you must have been. For eight years, I'd cared for you . . .

UNN. It doesn't matter, now.

AGNES. I didn't want to leave you. I loved you. But what life was there here for me?

UNN. I understand . . .

AGNES. I'd seen what marriage had done to my mother. And yours. I didn't want that, I wanted a different life. I wanted to serve God. I couldn't stay here. (*Pause.*) I'm sorry, Unn. I'm sorry. Forgive me. I'm sorry.

UNN (*drinks, grimaces*). Midwives' coffee. Johannes will be back any moment and want fresh.

She goes out with the coffee kettle. JOHANNES *bursts in, soaked through, with an armful of wild flowers.*

JOHANNES. They're all for you, Unn!

Stops dead when he sees AGNES.

AGNES. Hello, Johannes.

UNN *comes in.*

UNN. Captain Agnes has come to see you, Johannes.

AGNES. How are you?

He glances uneasily at UNN.

You look well. You've caught the sun, and put on weight, I think. Life here must agree with you. You're good at chopping wood, I hear. I had some of your cake, it was excellent. Unn tells me you're working hard. She's very satisfied with you,

Johannes. I knew you wouldn't let me down. I'm very proud of you. (*Unnerved by his lack of response.*) I've brought you some clothes. A couple of shirts, a jacket, some trousers. I didn't know if you'd want them.

She puts them on the table.

UNN (*prompting*). Johannes.

JOHANNES. Thank you, Ma'am.

AGNES. And a special treat. (*Takes out a small bunch of grapes.*) Grapes.

JOHANNES *laughs.* UNN *smiles.* AGNES *is puzzled then embarrassed by this.* UNN *takes the flowers from* JOHANNES.

UNN. We'll get these in water straight away. Fill as many jugs as you can find with water, and bring them here.

JOHANNES *goes out, sniggering.*

(*To* AGNES.) Forgive us, a private joke.

Picks up a towel.

He must dry his hair.

She goes out with the towel. Suppressed giggling heard off. UNN *comes in. Begins sorting flowers.*

Have you ever seen so many? He'll have been to one of the other islands for these; this one's picked clean. He's always bringing me flowers.

AGNES. What did you say to him?

UNN. . . . ?

AGNES. Did you have to turn him against me? (*Upset.*) Of all my people, it was Johannes I felt most able to help. In some small way, I felt I had helped ease the burden of his torment. To bring some light into his life . . .

Silence. JOHANNES *comes in with a number of jugs and vases and jars filled with water, on a tray. Puts it on the table. Helps* UNN *with the flowers. He giggles.*

UNN (*warning*). Johannes.

JOHANNES. Sorry.

But he cannot suppress his laughter. UNN *has filled a jar with flowers.*

UNN. Take this up to our room.

JOHANNES. Where shall I put it?

UNN. Anywhere.

He goes out, giggling. AGNES stares at UNN.

AGNES. Our room?

UNN. Yes.

AGNES (*shocked*). Unn . . .

UNN. What? I know what he's done, if that's what you mean. He told me.

AGNES. What did he tell you?

UNN. Huh?

AGNES. What did he . . . ?

UNN. Don't you believe me? A little girl, wasn't it? He told me everything. We've no secrets. I'm carrying his child. You don't have to look so shocked. I'm happy about it, why shouldn't you be?

AGNES. It's not true!

UNN. We've shared a bed all summer.

AGNES hastily gathers her things.

Are you going?

AGNES. Yes, I . . .

UNN. But you've only just arrived.

AGNES. Goodbye . . .

UNN. You don't have to go.

AGNES (*searching for words*). I . . .

A roll of thunder. AGNES runs out. UNN goes to the door and looks out. Eventually, she continues putting the flowers into the jugs, etc. The colours are vivid against the white backdrop of the sheets.

After a while, JOHANNES comes in. He registers AGNES's absence, but makes no comment. He sits at the table, reading his bible. Outside, the rain begins to fall in a steady downpour. JOHANNES listens to it a few moments, then starts reading aloud.

JOHANNES (*quite fluently*). 'How fair and how pleasant art thou,
O love, for delights!
This thy stature is like to a palm tree, And thy breasts to
clusters of grapes . . .'
'I said, I will climb up into the palm tree, I will take hold of
the branches thereof:
Let thy breasts be as clusters of the vine, and the smell of thy
breath like apples;
And thy mouth like the best wine, that goeth down smoothly
for my beloved, gliding through the lips of those that are
asleep.'

Pause. He looks at UNN, *who continues arranging the flowers,
throughout.*

(*Reads.*) 'Come, my beloved, let us go forth into the field;
Let us lodge in the villages.
Let us get up early in the vineyards;
Let us see whether the vine hath budded, and it's blossom be
open.
And the pomegranates be in flower:
There I will give thee my love.
The mandrakes give forth fragrance,
And at our doors are all manner of precious fruits, new and
old, which I have laid up for thee, O my beloved.' (*Song of Songs
7:6–13.*)

UNN. Johannes! Your clothes are wet. You'll catch your death!
Hang them on the line, I'll fetch you some dry ones.

She goes out. JOHANNES *hesitates, then strips off all his clothes and
begins hanging them on the line. He doesn't hear* UNN *come in. She
stands with his dry clothes, watching him hanging up his wet ones.*

Scene Two

*Church. Chairs. Crucifix on the wall – a highly realistic rendering, the face
twisted in pain, blood pouring from wounds in hands, feet and side, a
vicious crown of thorns on the head. It is night and outside it is still raining.*

AGNES *bursts in. She is wet, and breathless from running. Her distress
and agitation are palpable. Kneels at the altar.*

AGNES. What have I done? Oh God, I don't know what I've done. What shall I do?

A sudden sound in the darkness pulls her up short. She peers into the shadows.

Hello . . . Who's there? . . . Is anybody there? . . . Hello?

A figure becomes apparent.

Forgive me if I disturbed you. I thought I was alone. You must forgive me.

The figure doesn't move.

My name is Agnes Bauer. My father was Fridtjof Bauer, he was lay preacher here. In my day, this church was deserted, except for the Sabbath. Though it's fifteen years since I lived here. I've been visiting friends and missed the evening bus. I didn't wish to bother them, so late. I thought I'd shelter here the night and take the bus in the morning. (*Pause.*) Who are you? Why don't you answer me?

The figure laughs.

(*Frightened.*) Who are you? Don't come near me. Do you hear? Stay away from me. Stay away!

The figure moves into the light. It is IVERSEN.

You . . . ?

IVERSEN. Forgive me. I didn't mean to frighten you.

AGNES. You frightened me very badly.

IVERSEN (*laughs*). I don't know why I laugh.

He is dishevelled, unshaven and his clothes are creased and dirty. He has a bottle of altar wine in his hand. He drinks from it.

Too sweet for blood. Even his. 'Suffer the little children to come unto me.' No bite to it. 'Sugar and spice and all things nice, that's what little girls are made of.' Your health, Captain Agnes! (*Drinks.*)

AGNES. What are you doing here, Herr Iversen?

IVERSEN. Huh . . . ?

AGNES. What are you doing here?

IVERSEN. Been travelling all day. Arrived too late to find a room. 'No room at the inn!.' Where else was I to go? I've got to sleep somewhere, too. Though it's cold here, bitter. Why's a church always such a cold place? I never knew a warm church. Cold as graves. Even on a warm day, an hour in a church and you're chilled to the marrow. At the end of a funeral, you're all dead, ready for the hole in the ground, the worms to eat you up. Feed the worms to feed the birds. Bang! Bang! Put them in a pie, serve it hot with gravy!

He takes a handful of communion wafers from his pocket and crams them into his mouth.

His flesh, eh? Dry old stuff, found it in the cupboard. No nourishment in it. Where's the loaves and fishes kept? I've searched high and low; not a fish or a loaf to be found. Just his flakings, wouldn't keep the fat on a baby. You have to feed a baby well. It won't grow, otherwise, won't live. Feed it, keep it washed and clean, warm. Sing it to sleep; send it to school. Church. What else can you do? Not much. Love it. It'll kill you with worry, anyway. (*Drinks.*) Kids'd like this. They like sweet things. 'Suffer the little children . . . .' Forgive me looking this way. A beard might suit me, but not the stink. I'm unemployed, homeless. Sleep where I can. Under bridges, in barns. Churches, when they're not locked. Surprising how many are, these days. It's hard to keep up an appearance. You don't bother, after a bit. Don't make any difference. You can look how you want, they won't give you a job without an address. And 'God's House', won't do. Not respectable enough! Why's it so bloody cold in here?!

He takes the candlesticks from the altar and stands them on the floor. Tries to light them, but his hands are so cold, he can't get the match lit.

Damn these things!

Kicks the candlesticks across the room.

Forgive me, O Lord, for I know not what I do! (*Laughs.*)

AGNES. What do you want, Herr Iversen?

He looks at her.

What do you want?

IVERSEN (*eventually*). Been following you. Found out where you lived. Been sleeping most nights in a doorway, across the road from your house. Just keeping an eye. 'An eye for an eye, a tooth for a tooth.' Just keeping an eye and a tooth! You should keep your curtains pulled at night, Captain. Never know who's out there, watching you get undressed, eh? Or following you around on your walkabouts, dealing out your kind words and your charity. Soup and sandwiches to the down-and-outs, hymns and prayers. Got to keep them going, eh? Can't let them give up the ghost. Might be a riot at the Pearly Gates, all those people trying to get in. Beware the Devil at your back. That's what my father taught me. Keep a wary eye, careful who you trust. Beware the bite behind the smile. Tried to teach my kiddy. Never take sweets from strangers. Revenge is sweet.

AGNES. It wasn't I had you dismissed, Herr Iversen. You brought it upon yourself. If I'd not arrived when I did, you might have killed that boy! What choice had I, but to report you to the Governor?

IVERSEN *moves away from her.*

However guilty a man's found to be, of whatever crime, he's still a human being, with the right to be treated as one!

IVERSEN. Shut up.

AGNES. Three years it took for the authorities to embrace this basic Christian principle!

IVERSEN. I said . . .

AGNES (*bitter*). Three years, persuading politicians, canvassing businessmen and other influential people. Most of them should be in prison themselves! But you mustn't make waves, mustn't upset anybody. It's controversial, to suggest treating prisoners as human beings. One small, painful, humiliating step at a time, is all we can take! It's like emptying the ocean with your bare hands! Was I supposed to allow you to undo all I'd achieved with one morning's handiwork?

IVERSEN *kicks a chair across the room.*

You're a man capable of violence, I know. But I warn you, Herr Iversen, I shall defend myself as best I can.

IVERSEN. Stop calling me that, it's not my name! Justvold's my name, Egil Justvold.

AGNES. But . . . ?

IVERSEN. I'm Anne Lise Justvold's father. Was. I was her father. She was my daughter.

He gazes at the crucifix.

AGNES. Herr Justvold, I . . .

IVERSEN. Don't talk to me! I won't have you talk to me. One more word out of you and you'll be sorry you were born. (*Gazes at the crucifix.*) How can that save us? 'God so loved the world, he gave his only begotten son . . . ' How can nailing your son to a tree have anything to do with love? Do you see any love in that? Where's love? I don't see it. All I see is that God was no father. To do that to his child? His only begotten son? How could a father do that?

AGNES. He didn't – we did. God didn't put Jesus on the cross, Herr Justvold, we did. And we do it still, every day, again and again, nail him up, every day. We do harm. We make mistakes, cause pain to others. Sometimes the hurt is only small and we can put it right. Other times, it's as if you've brought all the pain and sorrow into the world by yourself. I don't know how to put it right. Herr Justvold, what Johannes did is the worst thing anyone can do, there is nothing worse. But how do we put it right? Johannes has repented. He can't do anymore. And Jesus said . . .

IVERSEN (*low*). No quotes.

AGNES. Herr Justvold, you have been done a great wrong. One that cannot be put right. But Jesus told us . . .

IVERSEN. No quotes, I said!

AGNES. All I know is, nothing will bring her back. Revenge won't bring her back. Revenge does no good, it never did and it never will. It won't give you your daughter back. I know you're in pain, Herr Justvold . . .

IVERSEN. How can you know? How? (*Shakes her.*) You don't know what I feel! You know nothing, that's what you know! You know nothing! Nothing! Nothing!

He shakes her and shakes her, then pushes her to the floor. She bangs her head as she goes down. IVERSEN *takes the huge lectern bible, stands over* AGNES, *ripping pages out of it and throwing them at her.*

This is all you know! Words, lies, shit! Wipe your arse on it! It's all it's worth! All you're worth! Hypocrite! Bloody hypocrite!

He throws the bible at her and storms out of the church.

AGNES, *very distressed, and concussed from her fall. She tries to rise, but cannot.*

Scene Three

Darkness. Suddenly, a huge door in the back wall opens, letting in a fan of daylight. **JOHANNES** *stands silhouetted in the doorway. Yawns, stretches his arms out the sides in a brief image of the cross. Comes into the barn, peering into the shadows, searching for eggs.*

JOHANNES. Cluck-cluck-cluck-cluck-cluck-cluck. Cluck-cluck-cluck-cluck-cluck. Cluck-cluck-cluck-cluck-cluck. (*Etc.*)

He hears the hens in another section of the barn. Goes off.

UNN (*off; approaching*). Johannes . . . Johannes . . . Johannes . . . Johannes . . .

She comes to the door, wearing just a night dress. Comes into the barn, cautiously.

Are you in here? . . . Johannes . . . Johannes, where are you?

JOHANNES (*off*). Here!

UNN exits in the direction of his call. **JOHANNES** *comes on and crouches in the shadows.*

UNN (*off*). I can't see you.

JOHANNES giggles.

UNN comes back in, straining to see in the darkness. As she passes **JOHANNES** *he touches her on the shoulder. She squeals in alarm.*

JOHANNES. Can you see me now? (*Laughs.*)

UNN. That wasn't funny!

JOHANNES. There's lots of eggs. Lots and lots. I found them.

UNN (*angry*). You frightened me.

JOHANNES. Sorry.

Awkward pause.

UNN. I had a dream. That you'd gone. I was running all through the house, calling out your name, in and out of all the rooms. Then I woke up, and you weren't there. I was frightened.

JOHANNES. Sorry.

UNN kisses him. He responds eagerly, unmindful of the eggs.

UNN *(laughs)*. Careful of the eggs, you'll break them!

He kneels, kissing her stomach, caressing her gently. She strokes his hair.

My father used to go fishing. He'd take the boat and go off for months, sometimes. He'd leave so early, I'd still be asleep, and when I woke up, he'd be gone. *(Pause.)* You won't go off like that again, will you? Not while I'm still asleep. *(Pause.)* I must wash! So must you. I'll take those, shall I?

Makes a 'bag' with her nightdress. Taking the eggs.

Are you hungry?

JOHANNES *caressing her legs and thighs, much aroused.* UNN *stands quite still a few moments. Then his caresses become too intimate, and she moves away from him.*

No, not now.

JOHANNES *freezes. Tense pause.*

Johannes. *(Pause.)* I'm going in now. What would you like for your breakfast? *(Pause.)* Don't be long. *(Going.)*

JOHANNES. Unn . . .

UNN *(stops in the doorway.)* What?

JOHANNES *(struggling to contain his violent emotions)*. You remember when I first came here? With Captain Agnes? You remember that?

UNN. I remember.

JOHANNES. I found the eggs then too, didn't I?

UNN. Yes, you did.

JOHANNES. You sent me out to get the eggs and I went into the bulls. And all the eggs were in there, lots and lots and lots of eggs. In with the bulls. And it was so dark, there were noises, and smells, and the animals. And I was scared!

UNN. Were you?

JOHANNES. But I found them, didn't I? All those eggs. I found them!

UNN. Yes.

JOHANNES. You remember that, Unn?

UNN. I remember it, Johannes.

JOHANNES. I was scared, but I found them!

UNN. Yes.

JOHANNES (*becomes calm*). I'm not scared, now.

UNN. No.

JOHANNES. Not now. I'm not scared. Not now.

He looks at her. Pause.

UNN. I'll go in with these.

She goes out. JOHANNES *remains sitting. Suddenly, the barn door is closed, plunging the stage into darkness.* JOHANNES *starts.*

JOHANNES. Unn? . . . Unn, is that you? . . . Don't frighten me, Unn. Please, don't frighten me . . . You shouldn't frighten me! Don't frighten me! Don't frighten me!

UNN *opens the door and comes in.*

UNN. What is it, Johannes?

JOHANNES (*frightened*). Why did you close the door?!

UNN. I didn't . . .

JOHANNES. You closed it . . . !

UNN. No.

Suddenly, IVERSEN *steps into the light. His face is ashen, numb.*

Who are you? . . . What do you want? . . .

IVERSEN (*stares at* JOHANNES.) 'Suffer the little children to come unto me . . .' Suffer them . . . It means permit. Suffer. Let them. It means let them come. Let the little children . . . It doesn't mean . . . make them suffer . . . hurt them. It doesn't mean . . .

JOHANNES *recognises* IVERSEN. *Cries out in alarm.*

UNN. What . . . ?

JOHANNES. Don't hit me!

IVERSEN. It means . . .

JOHANNES (*retreating*). Please, sir, don't . . . Don't hit me . . . Please! Please . . . (*Backs away, shouting.*) Don't hit me, don't hit me! Don't hit me! . . .

UNN *doesn't know what's happening. Suddenly,* IVERSEN *rushes at* JOHANNES, *grabs hold of him.* JOHANNES *struggles to get free.* UNN *grabs* IVERSEN *from behind, trying to pull him away. A brief struggle.*

Don't hit me! Don't hit me!

IVERSEN. GIVE HER BACK! GIVE HER BACK! Give her back . . . Give her back . . .

He lets go of JOHANNES *and just stands there, crying, all his strength gone.*

UNN *takes* JOHANNES *by the arm and leads him out.* IVERSEN *doesn't seem to notice them leave.*

IVERSEN. Give her back . . . Give her back . . .

Blackout.

Scene Four

In the darkness, sound of people walking along a bare corridor – prison acoustic. A bunch of keys rattling; a key turned in a lock and a metal door opened, then slammed shut, and locked.

An ante-room at the prison. A bench. UNN, *wearing 'best' clothes beneath a dark coat, sits nervously, waiting. A bag on her lap.*

AGNES *comes in.* UNN *rises.*

AGNES. Unn!

UNN. Where is he?

AGNES. Sit down.

UNN. I want to see him!

AGNES. Please, sit down.

UNN. I think I'll stand.

AGNES (*pause*). They phoned me to say you were here. If you were thinking of coming why didn't you write and tell me?

UNN. What's it to you?

AGNES. Do you have anywhere to stay? (*Pause.*) You can stay with me, if you like.

UNN. It's Johannes I've come to see, not you.

AGNES. That won't be possible, I'm afraid.

UNN. He's the father of my child! They can't stop me seeing him.

AGNES. Yes, I'm afraid they can. (*Pause.*) Please, will you sit down. (UNN *sits*.) Would you like some coffee?

UNN. I'd just like to see Johannes.

AGNES *sits on the bench beside* UNN. UNN *moves further along the bench. Pause.*

AGNES. I'm sorry. It's my fault. Everything. I couldn't bear the thought of Johannes back in his cell, so I left him with you. I should have been more mindful of the risks.

UNN. He's back in it now, anyway.

AGNES. Unn, he's a convicted murderer . . .

UNN. You said he'd never be a danger to anyone, ever again.

AGNES (*exasperated*). Unn!

UNN. That's what you said!

AGNES. It's not a question of danger, it's a question of public morality. You're carrying the illegitimate child of a man who first raped and then killed a child of eight! And you wonder why they wouldn't allow you to remain living together as man and wife!

UNN *looks away.*

I know it's hard. But you are in no position to make demands. The prison authorities will never allow you to visit Johannes. Not ever. You must face that fact now. I wish it were different. Believe me.

UNN (*eventually, the fight gone out of her*). Will anyone visit him?

AGNES. Of course . . .

UNN. Will you?

AGNES (*beat*). You're not the only one to emerge from this shamefully, Unn. I no longer work in the prison service.

Awkward silence.

We both have to try and forget Johannes. We must look to the future. The matter is out of our hands, now. We must try to live our own lives. (*Pause.*) Does your brother know about the child?

UNN *shakes her head.*

Would you like me to tell him?

UNN *nods.*

He must allow you to stay on the farm. That's the important thing, now. At least there you can have the child and bring it up in peace. How much worse it would be, if you lived here in town.

UNN *looks away, suddenly frightened by the prospects ahead of her.*

Don't be frightened. I'll talk to him.

IVERSEN, *sitting in a chair, staring at the ground in front of him.*

JOHANNES, *in his cell.*

JOHANNES. 'Hear my prayer, O God; attend unto my prayer. From the end of the earth will I cry unto thee, when my heart is overwhelmed: lead me to the rock that is higher than I. For thou hast been a shelter for me, and a strong tower from the enemy.
I will abide in thy tabernacle forever: I will trust in the covert of thy wings.' (*Psalm 61.*)

AGNES *holds out her hand.* UNN *takes it.*

KEVIN HOOD was born and grew up in Spennymoor, County Durham. He studied Chemistry at the University of Newcastle upon Tyne before taking his PhD at University College, London. After a period of research work at the National Institute of Medical Research, he taught science in London for ten years. His first full-length play, *Beached*, was produced at the Croydon Warehouse Theatre in March 1987 and revived at The Old Red Lion, March 1990. *The Astronomer's Garden,* which was also produced at the Warehouse in 1988 and revived at the Royal Court Theatre Upstairs in October 1989, won the Charringtons Fringe Award for Best Playwright 1989. *Sugar Hill Blues* was produced at the Croydon Warehouse in 1990 before transferring to the Hampstead Theatre. Kevin is currently writing a play for the Royal Court Theatre. His TV work includes episodes for *Grange Hill* and *The Bill* as well as *Work*, a Fourplay for Channel Four TV screened in March 1991 and a play commissioned by the BBC. Currently he is writing a film for Channel Four.

Characters

Notes on voices

LEWIS, a college educated jazz musician with a cool, ironic, self-mocking tone.

ELAINE, a singer with an ear for the streets and a powerful bluesy voice.

JENNIFER, a singer with very little ear, but a very upper class English voice.

BERNIE, a Geordie bricklayer and amateur saxophone player who dreams of being great.

ACCOMPANIST, a professional pianist with a sarcastic, dry and cynical Birmingham accent.

Sugar Hill Blues was first staged at the Warehouse Theatre, Croydon on 16 March 1990. It was commissioned during Kevin Hood's term as Resident Playwright under the Thames TV Theatre Writer's scheme. The same production was subsequently staged at the Hampstead Theatre in July 1990.

LEWIS	Okon Jones
ELAINE	Pauline Black
BERNIE	Simon Slater
JENNIFER	Liza Sadovy
NORMAN	Stefan Bednarczyk

Directed by Ted Craig
Designed by Michael Pavelka
Lighting by Steve O'Brien

ACT ONE

Scene One

LEWIS's *apartment on Sugar Hill, Harlem. In a pool of light at the door,* LEWIS *is ready to leave,* ELAINE *is holding him back.*

ELAINE. Days . . . days you lie by me like meat and then outa nowhere – up, runnin' for the door – but I got here before you, I will always get here before you, Lewis. *(Beat.)* I'm gonna let go now and you gonna stand and talk it *out*.

She lets go. He moves. She grabs him again.

Goddam it – talk! *(Pause.)* Then listen – I am pregnant. And this time I fully intend to stay that way.

She lets go. He doesn't move.

LEWIS. Shit.

ELAINE. Praise the Lord, a week: the man finally spoke.

LEWIS. *Shit*.

LEWIS *goes for the door.*

ELAINE. Ain't so good for you on the streets, honey, you ain't capable. Explain!

LEWIS *(stops)*. I stopped . . .

ELAINE. Middle of your solo.

LEWIS. Because the horn . . . refused me.

ELAINE *(sighs)*. Nice apartment, famous man, you even make money – everything's fine.

LEWIS. Everything's wrong. My music makes no sense, no sense at all. *(Beat.)* I've been in confusion.

ELAINE. Two weeks?

LEWIS. But I figured the way out, Elaine – follow back down to the beginning, to my father.

ELAINE. Follow back down someplace else, honey – the preacherman ain't friendly.

LEWIS. I gotta see him. Take me to the tabernacle.

ELAINE. I got a bad feeling, Lewis.

LEWIS. I want to hear the choir.

Reluctantly she gets his coat, her coat, and leads him out.

My father will be just fine.

Lights change . . .

Scene Two

The soundproof recording booth in a department store. BERNIE waiting with tenor sax. He plays one chorus of a tune, not well. Then speaks into microphone. We hear the regular swish of heavy static.

BERNIE. Not very good I know, but I can do better. I'm speakin' from a place in England you won't have heard of – aw, straight away, the words are gannin' – goin' – gone wrong. You see, worra feel isn't worra end up sayin' somehow, which is why I suppose I'm makin' this record . . . because I've heard all them records of yours . . . and worra feel is there, all there, in them. (*Beat.*) Like, some of it's in Lester, and some in Bird, and some in lotsa them fellas, but all of it's there in the way you play your saxophone.

(*Looks at watch and panics.*) You don't know it right but thousands of miles away you spoke to me. Direct. So I went and chucked it all in, gorra job on the Queen Mary. Can you believe it? I cannat. But you see I know now. Worra mean is . . .

BERNIE *plays again and in the middle of his improvisation, the swish of the static abruptly stops. He opens the door.*

Hey.

SHOPMAN *comes on with a record.* BERNIE *puts away his sax.*

I was in the middle of me improvisation. I had it all timed out exactly. Two minutes for twelve and six.

SHOPMAN (*posh*). There's a notice.

BERNIE. There's always a notice.

SHOPMAN. There most definitely is.

BERNIE. Explainin' why the eyes are bein' robbed out of your head.

SHOPMAN. No. Describing the time as two minutes *approximately*, which has to include one minute and fifty seconds –

BERNIE. Forty.

SHOPMAN. Fifty.

BERNIE. Forty.

SHOPMAN. Fifty.

BERNIE (*beat*). You know what's wrong with this country?

SHOPMAN (*beat*). The Labour Government? Stafford Cripps? Aneurin Bevan?

BERNIE. No that's what's right with it, what's wrong with it is – turn over a stone anywhere and there's always summat like you creepin' underneath.

SHOPMAN (*accent drops*). Your record.

BERNIE *takes it and goes.*

Just what does he think he is? Amateur musicians – they're all fantasists.

The SHOPMAN *crosses the stage, to piano . . . Lights change . . .*

Scene Three

And it is night in the empty for'ard lounge of the Queen Mary.

ACCOMPANIST. Speaking as a pro. And to tell the truth I've just about had it with this gig: accompanist to a post-prandial chanteuse. Look at her. Look at him. Lost souls. Sailing round the Atlantic like albatrosses, looking for someone to get their wings round.

The ACCOMPANIST *plays 'I'll Be Seeing You.'*

JENNIFER *and* BERNIE *dance on . . .* BERNIE *in a cheap, racy suit.* JENNIFER *in expensive, working evening-dress . . . She steps out of the dance and laughs.*

JENNIFER. Darling, how did you ever get past the stewards?

BERNIE. Don't know what you mean.

JENNIFER *laughs.*

BERNIE. So what did I say this time?

JENNIFER. Oh, my dear oick . . .

BERNIE. What's an oick?

JENNIFER. With the *amazing* shoulders. I've heard one or two stories in my time but – what was it – jazz musician?

JENNIFER *does an embarrassing, drunken impersonation of a traditional jazz trombonist.*

ACCOMPANIST (*sighs*). Oh . . .

BERNIE. Not that kind of jazz musician.

JENNIFER. Then what kind of jazz musician?

BERNIE. Ha. I think you're err . . .

She approaches him.

JENNIFER. What?

BERNIE. You know.

JENNIFER. What do I know?

BERNIE. Nothin'.

JENNIFER (*painted on his shirt*). Oh – come . . . *on.*

BERNIE (*beat*). My style's more modern stuff, like. Bebop. Ultra modern.

JENNIFER. Really?

BERNIE. Aye.

JENNIFER. 'Aye'? Your friend . . .

BERNIE. Not exactly me *friend*. More . . . I like the way he plays.

JENNIFER. I see. You mean as one artist might appreciate the work of another artist?

BERNIE. Well, not exactly that either.

JENNIFER. Make up your mind, darling. Is he good?

BERNIE. Good? He's *avante garde*.

JENNIFER. So, you're *au fait* with the *avant garde*!

BERNIE. And you're pissed.

ACCOMPANIST. Not just pissed, pissed again.

JENNIFER. And the men gang up. (*To* BERNIE.) Dance with me darling.

They dance.

You dance very well.

ACCOMPANIST. This it, Jen?

They dance.

JENNIFER (*arms around* BERNIE's *neck*). This is it. I suppose.

ACCOMPANIST. Right then.

Stops playing.

BERNIE. Hey, worrabout us?

ACCOMPANIST. Staff. (*Yawns. Lights up.*) Here we are, for'ard lounge empty at ten o'clock. I do hope it's another funeral.

JENNIFER. Unfortunately not. (*Yawns. Gets out a fag.*) I counted the old dears at tea, they're all there – in body at least.

ACCOMPANIST. Pity, I like a good funeral, makes me feel more alive somehow. So where are they if they're not here?

BERNIE. With the Orchestra.

ACCOMPANIST *moves to light* JENNIFER's *cigarette,* BERNIE *beats him to it. She smiles.*

JENNIFER. Where we would be, if we were good enough.

ACCOMPANIST. I have been with Geraldo, me duck. Reckon you must have been too, after all there's only twenty-five. (*For her ears.*) To get round.

JENNIFER *stares into his eyes.*

JENNIFER. Nasty.

ACCOMPANIST (*nods at* BERNIE). So, what's the attraction this time?

JENNIFER. You wouldn't understand.

BERNIE. How d'he know I was staff?

JENNIFER. Easily enough.

ACCOMPANIST. Tell me.

She breaks from the stare.

JENNIFER. Oicks smell different darling, like goats.

BERNIE. You what?

ACCOMPANIST (*grins*). You're right, that's what she said.

JENNIFER. I didn't mean . . . it's just my way.

ACCOMPANIST. But it's just her way.

She puts her arms round BERNIE's *neck.*

BERNIE. Worrabout him?

JENNIFER. Piss off, Mr Pianist.

ACCOMPANIST *rolls a cigarette.*

ACCOMPANIST. Don't mind me.

JENNIFER. Forget him, he's furniture. What an extraordinary suit.

BERNIE. It's a zoot suit.

JENNIFER. Zoot Suit. (*Strokes the suit.*) And just how much of all this is you then? Find out shall we, if the evening progresses as it – (*Breaks away.*) Oh God.

ACCOMPANIST. Small town boy, Jenny.

JENNIFER (*to* BERNIE). Play for me. For the drunken lady.

BERNIE *backs off. He's had enough.*

Up whose sick you are not good enough to lick.

BERNIE. Disgustin'.

JENNIFER. The voice – like cheap shoes, like the boils on his neck.

BERNIE. I haven't gorrany boils.

JENNIFER. In his braces watching the shirt dry, smoking Woodbines.

BERNIE. I haven't a clue what you're on about.

JENNIFER (*to* ACCOMPANIST). A musician.

ACCOMPANIST. Oh?

JENNIFER. Jazz.

ACCOMPANIST. Oh!

JENNIFER. Play for me, oiky.

BERNIE. I'm a horn player.

JENNIFER. You're a kitchen steward. (*Sniffs his hair.*) Bacon fat. What's it like to wash plates for a living when you are 'a musician'?

BERNIE. Almost as bad as singin' when you haven't gorra voice. (*Finds his hair smells.*) You oughta try writing detective stories.

JENNIFER (*to pianist*). Piss off.

ACCOMPANIST. I like it here. (*Pause.*) But I'm telling you – you're wastin' it.

ACCOMPANIST *goes.*

JENNIFER *sits at the piano. Picks out chords of 'Black Magic'.*

BERNIE. Talkin' to the singer at the bar like in the films – and she's a snotty bitch.

JENNIFER. Take no notice, darling – it's just a reflex.

He moves to go.

It doesn't mean anything.

BERNIE. Naw?

JENNIFER. Being alone too much, you know.

He hesitates.

BERNIE. Aye, I am a kitchen steward, and you oughta respect me for that. I jacked in me trade to do this.

JENNIFER. Trade?

BERNIE. Brickie. Makin' walls. What is it you *make*?

JENNIFER (*beat*). Play.

BERNIE. I keep on tellin' you, I'm a horn player.

JENNIFER (*sings*). In a spin / Loving the spin I'm in.

She turns, kisses him. He does not resist.

BERNIE. We're not the same type. Nothin' like at all.

JENNIFER. Then why stay? (*Beat.*) Drop the dignity, Oicky, I know why. And there's no need to be embarrassed, darling, because it's all there is. That and the morning, and the hangover, and three thousand grey miles of Atlantic. I know.

They kiss.

I've been here before.

BERNIE. The morning – New York, *America*!

JENNIFER. Yes.

She leads him off.

In the morning.

We hear the 'A' from the Queen Mary's fog horn.

Lights change . . .

Scene Four

Night. A Harlem street. Outside the Baptist Tabernacle. ELAINE *and* LEWIS *on slowly, in shock.*

ELAINE. That asshole.

LEWIS. I'm cold.

ELAINE. You said it would be okay. I trusted you.

LEWIS. I mean really cold.

ELAINE. Five below. Radio said.

LEWIS. *Radio* said?

ELAINE. Radio.

LEWIS. Not a person on the radio, but the radio itself, the Bakerlite box –

ELAINE *(fast and angry)*. Sure looked like the radio I was lookin' at when I was hearin' the – 'five below tonight folks'.

LEWIS *(fast and angry)*. Radios cannot talk because they are things. Things need voices to speak.

ELAINE. It was both of us in there, ME TOO! Listen –.

LEWIS. Get me home.

ELAINE. Sometimes . . . I think you think the goddam words are inside your head, all of them. *Just* inside your head.

LEWIS. Screw the psychology, get a cab.

ELAINE tries to hail a cab.

ELAINE. Elaine gets her shit. Elaine gets your shit. Elaine gets all the shit.

Fails to hail a cab.

Damn it!

LEWIS *(mocking)*. Watch your mouth in the shadow of the tabernacle.

She goes back for another cab.

The cab?

ELAINE. White driver.

LEWIS. And the Lord don't bring him to our feet?

ELAINE. Cut it out.

LEWIS. Then we got to sing louder, we ain't singin' loud enough.

ELAINE. Jesus.

LEWIS. The Lord can't hear his people. *(Sings.)* Precious Lord . . . / Take my hand . . . / Lead me on . . . / To the promised land . . .

Turns back and walks into the blank wall. LEWIS *is blind.*

Where are you?

LEWIS works along the wall. In a state. ELAINE *comes up to him.*

ELAINE. You are making a spectacle.

LEWIS. I can't find the door.

ELAINE. This is what your father wants you to be like.

LEWIS. MOTHERFUCKER!

ELAINE *pulls him gently away.*

ELAINE. Well now, you never said a truer word. And I'm sure your mom is truly grateful. 'Cause if he gets all fired up like that in his pulpit then what does he get in his bed. (*Beat*). Least you don't get to see their faces.

LEWIS. I don't need their faces. I heard the tuts.

ELAINE. 'Swellin' with your devil's child'. Uh huh!

LEWIS. All those Christian women and their audible disapprobation. You know the sound of righteous disapproval?

ELAINE. No thank you.

LEWIS. Two hundred sateen asses squirming on wooden bench. Big, big sighs. And tuts spittin' like rifle fire.

ELAINE *chases . . . and fails to hail another taxi.*

ELAINE. Ain't there no black cabbies work these streets?

LEWIS. Some of you remember a boy . . .

ELAINE *watches quietly.*

. . . up here in white beside me singing the Lord's praises. That fine mind, that perfect ear for beauty, those hands that shaped the sweet sounds of his innocence, took up and offered in the ceremonies of the nameless one.

ELAINE. Shit.

LEWIS. Just look at him now where he sits – the hundred dollar coat, the arrogance, the pride that mocks our simple piety. Look at the street woman swelling with his devil's child. That man amongst you was my son. I say was because . . . I repudiate him. I reject him. I cast him out. Brothers and sisters here before you in the Lord's sight . . . I take back his name!

Silence.

ELAINE. Such a perfect memory for pain and you never played a note of it.

LEWIS (*quietly*). I know.

LEWIS takes off his coat.

BERNIE appears in the darkness. Sees LEWIS. Almost comes forward and then falls back to watch in the shadows.

LEWIS. I'm hot now.

ELAINE. Put your coat on.

LEWIS. I don't feel so good.

ELAINE. You'll catch a fever.

LEWIS. I don't feel so good.

ELAINE. You got to start listening to me.

LEWIS. I wanted . . .

ELAINE. He ain't going to give you nothin'. Listen to *me* now. I want things too.

LEWIS. I'm still hot.

ELAINE. Listen to me Lewis, 'cause I mean it.

LEWIS. What?

ELAINE. Just the regular things, some of the regular things, that's all.

LEWIS slowly begins to spin.

Oh Christ! Cab!

ELAINE steps forward for a cab.

BERNIE steps out of the darkness with his record in his hand.

BERNIE. I can't talk –

LEWIS (*shocked*). What?

BERNIE. Not in person, like.

In front, ELAINE *has found a cab.*

ELAINE. At last.

BERNIE. Here. It's on here. Play this.

BERNIE pushes the record into LEWIS's hand and goes.

LEWIS. What? (*Terrified.*) Elaine?

ELAINE. Yes?

LEWIS. What was that?

ELAINE. On the street?

LEWIS. Yeah.

ELAINE. Nothing.

Terrified, LEWIS *turns the record in his hand.*

ELAINE *bends to pick up his coat. He knows she is doing this.*

LEWIS. Leave it.

ELAINE. A hundred dollar coat?

LEWIS. Leave it!

ELAINE. Now I'm warning you, don't you go crazy on me, because I won't stand for it. Git in that cab.

They go off to the cab. LEWIS *clutching the record as if it were poison.*

(*To the* CABBIE.) Sugar Hill . . .

BERNIE *comes out of the darkness. picks up the coat. Puts it on . . .*

Lights change.

Scene Five

JENNIFER *singing 'That Lovely Weekend'.* ACCOMPANIST *accompanies. At end of song –*

ACCOMPANIST. One from the heart.

JENNIFER. Hmm.

ACCOMPANIST. I was in the war.

JENNIFER. What as, a target?

ACCOMPANIST. ENSA. How the British got their kamikaze units. Men'd face certain death sooner'n our concert party twice in a month. Honestly duck, you'd a been Betty Grable. (*Beat.*) Time the great healer eh. (*Looks out over the audience.*) Nobody's going to tell me she's alive.

They laugh.

What was he? Did you give yerself to him in the long grass on the last night of his leave? Here's a bit to remember me by love.

JENNIFER. You'll get over me, pianist.

ACCOMPANIST. Is that a promise? (*Beat.*) It must have been messy to bring you, a person like you, down to this.

JENNIFER. The Queen Mary?

ACCOMPANIST. Morgue on The Queen Mary. And a kitchen steward for company – who is really a bricklayer incognito. I can see the ending now – personalised pointing trowels.

She laughs.

His and her bibs and braces hanging up in the hall. (*Beat.*) Who are you trying to remember? Tell us yer tragedy Jen, I'd tell you mine if I had one. Flyboy? Guards Officer?

JENNIFER. Know what you are, pianist?

ACCOMPANIST *settles back.*

ACCOMPANIST. Should be good this.

JENNIFER. A species of insect. A shiny, hardbacked –

ACCOMPANIST. Very hardbacked.

JENNIFER. – glittering iridescent beetle. But if you take this thing in your hands.

ACCOMPANIST. I'm interested.

JENNIFER. And crack its back, the grey slime oozes out – the real, the essential you – Norman. When you make your suggestions, your clammy, moist, insinuating offers. It sounds just like you want to feed off me.

ACCOMPANIST. (*Beat*). So it's Mr and Mrs Brick after all.

JENNIFER. For the foreseeable future.

ACCOMPANIST. How long is that?

JENNIFER. Minute to minute.

ACCOMPANIST. Where you come from . . . ?

JENNIFER. Shropshire.

ACCOMPANIST. I bet you think it's the heart of England. Meself
I come from back streets. Outside toilets. The midden man and
his cart on Friday to empty them with his shovel. That's the
heart of England, duck. The pile of shite we iridescent insects
learned to live on. And that's where you have to learn to live
too. Isn't it? (*Beat.*) Had to be a flyboy.

JENNIFER. Local infantry. Solicitor's son. Second Lieutenant. A
real let down for the folks. Okay?

ACCOMPANIST. Where'd he cop it?

JENNIFER. Norway.

ACCOMPANIST. A right cock up that.

JENNIFER. I was glad it was a defeat. I couldn't have borne a
glorious victory.

ACCOMPANIST. The long grass?

JENNIFER. Mind your own shitty business.

ACCOMPANIST. I thought so.

JENNIFER. Married actually. Gretna Green actually. Oh God the
folks were furious. (*Beat.*) Even worse when I didn't want the
baby, not posthumously. People are so morbid.

ACCOMPANIST. You was all broke up then, kid?

JENNIFER. Don't get soft on me. I wouldn't believe it for a
second.

ACCOMPANIST. Just me natural oiliness, nothing to worry
about. How much of all this does Mr Brick know?

JENNIFER *shrugs*.

Guessed? Noticed?

JENNIFER. The pity is . . . you can't go back home, not after
you've been away for so long. Here I am. Condemned to
wander the oceans in perpetuity. Like the Flying Dutchman.
Only with a much smaller orchestra.

Offers glass for drink. He takes it.

ACCOMPANIST. I'd tek you back.

JENNIFER. You?

ACCOMPANIST. I'm ready for Blighty. Open up a nightclub.

England Expects. Wouldn't let you sing though. (*Beat.*) I'll even let you get him out of yer system. And then . . . I'll leave you to it. On yer own. (*Beat.*) It's one of them clammy offers.

JENNIFER. I've been alone for a long time.

ACCOMPANIST. And how was it?

He walks off. She does too, the other way.

Lights down.

Scene Six

Music – 'Ornithology', Charlie Parker 1945.
Lights change to LEWIS's *bare apartment in the late afternoon.*
Door to hall. Door to bedroom and bathroom. Somewhere a piano.
Somewhere else a pile of records next to a record player. Chair. Coffee
makings. No other furniture.
LEWIS *sits on the floor by the record player.*
In the hall the door clicks open. LEWIS *reacts. Produces a gun.*

LEWIS. Hey you with the door . . .

The door shuts.

Come and get it.

ELAINE *peeps round the door.*

ELAINE. You gonna kill me?

LEWIS (*puts up the gun*). It's just something I say when the neighbours drop by.

ELAINE. On Sugar Hill?

LEWIS. This neighbourhood is on the move.

ELAINE. They took the furniture with them?

LEWIS. Well . . . You haven't been here in a long time.

ELAINE. A month. And it flew right past.

LEWIS. You gettin' big?

ELAINE. Not to speak of.

Walks round. Wipes dirt.

LEWIS. They miss me on the street?

ELAINE. I don't ask.

LEWIS. They miss me.

She checks out the bedroom.

ELAINE. You keeping livestock in that bedroom these days?
    Worse to worser.

LEWIS. Worser than worse is unallowed. So . . . how's tricks?

ELAINE. Oh, you don't sluff me that easy – my baby is your
    baby. Except I'm the one gets to drag ass round town, get sick
    with it twice a day. Fact I just come by case I luck out and get
    to mess your Persian rug – which you don't seem to have no
    more.

LEWIS. Coffee?

ELAINE. Coffee?

LEWIS (*proud*). I can make coffee.

ELAINE. Don't talk, do – I wanna see.

He stands and goes to the coffee maker.

LEWIS. You don't understand.

ELAINE. You got it.

LEWIS. Well, I don't understand it either. Leastways I can't put
    it into words yet.

ELAINE. That's okay. (*Beat.*) Fuck your life, my life, the baby's
    goddam life and if you are not ready to put whatever you are
    doing into words then I am relaxed. (*Beat.*) No fuckin' problem
    for me at all.

He drops the coffee percolator.

LEWIS. I'll do it!

ELAINE. I ain't moving.

Gets on hands and knees, looking for the coffee.

LEWIS. Leavin' was all your own idea.

ELAINE. That's because you went crazy, honey.

LEWIS. You call this crazy?

ELAINE. I call it crazy.

LEWIS. Well I call it a journey of self-discovery.

ELAINE. Man, your behaviour –

LEWIS. What's wrong with my behaviour?

He finds the coffee on the floor, begins scraping it into the pot.

Okay my behaviour is a little peculiar – but I know I have to do this.

ELAINE. Do what?

LEWIS. Go back, inside myself.

ELAINE. Man. You ain' never been outside yourself, that's your problem. (*Suddenly angry.*) MY BABY! (*Quiet.*) Is growin'. One day soon now I'm gonna feel it inside me. That is infinitely more real than jerkin' off with the self-discovery bullshit.

LEWIS. This is serious.

ELAINE. Oh yes.

LEWIS. It's a cultural matter.

ELAINE (*beat*). Honey . . .

LEWIS. Yeah?

ELAINE. I don't want coffee no more.

LEWIS. Why say, then?

ELAINE. Because I hadn't seen where it gets to.

He dumps the coffee. She walks wiping more dirt.

Swear this apartment ain't been cleaned in a month. What's that woman do for her money?

LEWIS. I let her go.

ELAINE. With the furniture.

LEWIS. Some. Some acquired by persons unknown.

ELAINE. And I guess by now you're broke?

LEWIS. You know what I'm like with money.

ELAINE. Duke Ellington next door and the man is broke. Where's the saxophone?

LEWIS. Hocked it.

ELAINE. Jesus, never would have believed that.

LEWIS sits by the wall.

LEWIS. The Duke. (*Beat.*) I lived here oh . . . eighteen months and never heard him the once. Goddam shame. Dutch wouldn't have built so damn thick if they knew niggers was going to live here.

ELAINE. Music is what you do. It's all you do. (*Loses her patience.*) You go to work.

LEWIS. We been through this.

ELAINE. Play or you are nothin'.

LEWIS. Listen – the more I blow, the emptier it sounds, the less it means.

ELAINE. Get you ass back to work, Lewis.

LEWIS. Woman, do you think I can't hear what is in your voice – *money*! And I am struggling –

ELAINE. My baby –

LEWIS. – with great things.

ELAINE. Little things are more important. Little things are necessary.

Hits him.

I hate you, musician, artist, selfish full of shit dreamer. Care about something real. Care about us.

LEWIS. I didn't choose –

ELAINE. You did.

LEWIS. It happened –

ELAINE. You like it. Because it is one more thing to make you important.

She goes to the bedroom so he can't hear her cry.

LEWIS. Elaine? . . . E-la-ine??

ELAINE (*off*). (*Pause.*) I know you hear every breath I breathe.

LEWIS. Whose asking on the street?

She comes on.

ELAINE. Nobody.

LEWIS. Somebody's askin'!

ELAINE. Folks forgettin' so fast you dead already.

ELAINE *puts her coat on.*

It don't end here, Lewis. I'm gonna straighten you out.

ELAINE *goes.*

LEWIS *sits by the record player, drops the stylus on the record. The swish of static. Another of* BERNIE's *records.*

Lights up on BERNIE *in the recording booth.*

BERNIE. Mad trying to talk t' you like this, but I cannat think of any other way. I'm the one give you the record outside that church.

LEWIS. What the –

Lights down on LEWIS. *Stay up in booth tight on* BERNIE.

BERNIE. And I've got your coat an' all. I'm lookin' after it for ya. The time comes when you've got to tek your life in yer hands and do what really matters. There's summat I want to ask ya. In person. I've decided to come and see you meself.

BERNIE *opens the door.*
Continuous with . . .

Scene Seven

BERNIE *walks tentatively out. Snap lights up on* LEWIS's *apartment.* LEWIS *appears with a gun.*

LEWIS. Hands.

BERNIE (*hands up*). Jesus.

LEWIS. Kneel.

BERNIE. For Christ sakes.

LEWIS. KNEEL!

BERNIE *falls to his knees.*

BERNIE. I'm kneeling, right?

LEWIS (*pause*). Right.

BERNIE. Don't shoot . . . I'm kneelin' . . . All the time I'm talkin' I'm on me knees . . .

LEWIS. With your hands in the air?

BERNIE. Gorra be some mistake here.

LEWIS. You bet your ass. (*Cocks the pistol.*)

BERNIE. Some kinda mistake man, honest.

LEWIS. The voice.

BERNIE. Look . . .

A standoff. LEWIS *points the gun in the very general direction of* BERNIE, *still kneeling.*

BERNIE. Me arms.

LEWIS. Yeah?

BERNIE. Can I put them –

LEWIS. Higher!

Tentatively BERNIE *puts his hands down anyway.*

LEWIS. Don't think I don't know what you did then. (*Beat.*) Who are you? And why are you here?

BERNIE. I came to see you.

LEWIS *finds the chair, sits – with the gun still cocked on his knee.*

LEWIS. Don't consider moving.

BERNIE. No. (*Beat.*) Door was open. So I came in. I'm sorry, I . . . shoulda knocked. But the door was wide open.

LEWIS. Wide open?

BERNIE. Mebbe not wide, burrit was open.

LEWIS. That voice.

BERNIE. I thought mebbe something was up.

LEWIS (*pause*). Okay – relax. For the moment.

BERNIE. So I came in. I didn't want to disturb yer.

LEWIS. These days folks take my apartment for Grand Central Station, walk through whenever they've a mind. Month ago this apartment was fully furnished. Nice things.

BERNIE. What happened?

LEWIS. Too soft. I needed hard edges. Basics. So I let them go. Also the criminal fraternity visited. Man, vulnerability is an undesirable attribute.

BERNIE. Aye.

LEWIS. Only thing left is the piano on account of it came in through the window, however the landlord seems prepared to try the stairs – in lieu of rent. That and the phonograph which I may yet dispense with on account of this weird voice speaking in the records.

BERNIE. A weird voice?

LEWIS. I'm a little worried about my state of mind. I wanted . . . retreat, reorientation. Things have got to have meanings. If I can't play . . .

BERNIE (*shocked*). You can't play?

LEWIS. Then I guess I'm crazy anyway. Are you actually there?

LEWIS *waves the gun in* BERNIE's *direction.*

Speak!

BERNIE (*slumps*). This is ridiculous. You can't see.

LEWIS. But I can shoot your ass off, inside twenty feet.

BERNIE. Mebbe.

LEWIS (*puts up gun*). I'm tired now. And I don't understand.

BERNIE. I wanted – want you to teach me.

LEWIS. The voice on the record. Are you really there?

BERNIE. Yes. Teach me.

LEWIS (*beat*). Absolutely not.

BERNIE. Not the basics of the instrument.

LEWIS. Absolu –

BERNIE. No, no, no. I've had lessons since I was fifteen from this guy who used to be in the army – army band. I want you to teach me to play jazz.

LEWIS. There is no –

BERNIE. Like *you*.

LEWIS. Man, do you listen?

BERNIE. A little bit like you anyway. I sent the records.

LEWIS. The record.

BERNIE. The first I made in Newcastle, England, I actually come from Whitley Bay just up the road on the coast – it's awful. That one I made before me first trip. The second I made in Southampton in the turnaround because I didn't know whether you'd heard the first one or not. Department stores, they've got these booths. (*Beat.*) Don't put me on. I'm not a fan. I'm a musician burra I cannat play, not the way I hear in me head anyway, like you tharris, burr I know it's in me too.

LEWIS (*beat*). I thought they spoke English in England.

BERNIE. I'm working the boats, tried to get in the band, bastards wouldn't have us, so I sent the records – second through the post, first in your hand. I've come three thousand miles, twice.

LEWIS. I didn't ask.

BERNIE. Listened to *your* records and I had to come, and you've gorra listen to me. At home, right –

LEWIS. I don't know if I'm crazy and you ain't there but if you are there then you got to be crazy to think –

BERNIE. That's what they say at home. Daft Bernie. Tek the piss all the time, but what they cannat bear is somebody not bein' like them, settlin' for shite like them, well I'm not gonna, I refuse.

LEWIS. Man!

BERNIE. I play in this dance-band.

LEWIS *laughs*.

Aye, why, you'd laugh even louder if you heard them. One of the lads come back from Germany on leave.

LEWIS. This can't possibly be imagination –

BERNIE. Charlie Parker, Dizzy, Monk, Lester, you.

LEWIS. Weird ofay flattery.

BERNIE. Honest admiration.

LEWIS. You are really there?

BERNIE. Touch me.

   LEWIS *throws himself back. Drops the gun.*

LEWIS. NO! – I want to stop now.

   BERNIE *grabs* LEWIS's *hand.*

BERNIE. Here. Feel.

LEWIS. They're hard.

BERNIE. Callouses.

LEWIS. A musician?

BERNIE. A musician who also works, with his hands. I'm a
   brickie. Was. The skin gets hard from the tools and the bricks.
   Dirt gets grimed in, all teks a long time to wear off. (*Beat.*)
   You're mad, you know that?

LEWIS. One of us sure is, one of us is way off planet.

BERNIE. Teach me.

LEWIS. How is it I can touch you like this and it all mean so little
   to me? What do you want?

BERNIE. To be clever.

LEWIS. Like me. Jazz. You know what the word means?

BERNIE. No.

LEWIS. Fuckin'. Dirty. Low down.

BERNIE. That's not how you play.

LEWIS. Played!

BERNIE. You play clear and cold.

LEWIS. Played!

   BERNIE *picks up his sax case.*

LEWIS. That your sax?

BERNIE. Tenor sax.

LEWIS. Okay. (*Pause.*) 'Ornithology'?

BERNIE. Charlie Parker.

LEWIS. You know it?

BERNIE. Off by heart.

LEWIS. Bird's solo? . . . Sing it.

> BERNIE *tries to sing it. Gets it wrong.* LEWIS *sings the solo perfectly.*

> Real music comes from the human voice, I'm just good with the dots – like words without meaning. Ten dollar lesson, fella.

BERNIE. I'll give it the landlord and you can keep the piano. For next time.

> BERNIE *goes.* LEWIS *gets the gun, goes to the piano.*

LEWIS (*shouts after him*). Next time I might just blow your ass right off. (*Suddenly sings.*) Precious Lord / Take my hand / lead me on
. . .

The ACCOMPANIST *comes in.* LEWIS *makes way for him at the piano . . . and* LEWIS *goes off. The* ACCOMPANIST *plays.*

Lights change . . .

Scene Eight

Lights change . . .
The lounge of the Queen Mary. JENNIFER *joins* ACCOMPANIST *by the piano.* BERNIE *comes in. They look at each other.* JENNIFER *sings 'I'll Be Seeing You'. During the chorus the* ACCOMPANIST *talks over her singing.*

ACCOMPANIST. Heard them all, I have: good, bad . . . and this is pure shite. I mean, some poor bugger spent a birra actual effort writin' that tune down, least she could do is try and sing it.

The ACCOMPANIST *takes an elaborately unimaginative solo.*

To be fair, singing as such int the main thing. (*Grins.*) Strictly class though – we're all Cunarders here – (*Interpolates 'Rule*

Britannia' into his solo.) – upper crust. I like just being among
them. They're truly different. Show you worra mean. Try this,
try and imagine Princess Elizabeth and Princess Margaret on
the toilet; go on, close your eyes and have a go. (*Pause.*) I
admire that, mass hypnosis like that made Britain great. – And
our Jenny's part of it all. – Oh yes, there's a story there and no
mistake.

JENNIFER *sings back chorus.*

On the other hand, not exactly Anne Shelton is she?

Song over. They pack up.

JENNIFER. Oicky.

BERNIE. Jen.

JENNIFER. I missed you.

ACCOMPANIST. Like the tune. But you know I respect you, in
me 'eart of 'earts.

JENNIFER. Your heart, my dear, is part of your digestive system.
The end of it.

ACCOMPANIST. Mother always said I should keep me bowels
regular.

Silence. They stare.

Hope he fucks berrer than he plays, Jen.

JENNIFER (*leans close*). He does.

Still a tense moment. Then he laughs.

ACCOMPANIST (*to* BERNIE). Tell us, duck, d'ya runs go straight
or d'you stick the bricks in special places?

ACCOMPANIST *off with his music.*

BERNIE. That's what they call being a pro?

JENNIFER. Where did you get to?

BERNIE. The kitchens. Nearest I've ever been to slavery.

JENNIFER. And how was Fifty-Second Street? What an
imaginative naming system.

BERNIE. I don't know. I took the A train up to Harlem. Tracked
down me man. He lives in this big house on Sugar Hill next

door to Duke Ellington. Billy Eckstein and Sarah Vaughan just up the street. Burr he's gone mad.

JENNIFER. Perfect. In all the time I've sloshed around this great big ocean you are by far the most exotic creature I have encountered.

BERNIE. Me?

JENNIFER. You.

BERNIE. I don't get it.

JENNIFER. An orchid blooming on a dung heap. What on earth do they make of you at home?

BERNIE. They think I'm mad. You know what they call us?

JENNIFER. Daft Bernie?

BERNIE. How d'you know that? When I went to pick up me cards, told them I was goin' to New York and all that, the boss says I'm the daftest bugger he's ever had workin' his walls.

JENNIFER. Is there Daft Bernie's Girl?

BERNIE. There was when I left, burra doubt there is now.

JENNIFER. What did she say about New York?

BERNIE. She told me about you. Aye. Burra didn't think I'd get lucky this quick.

JENNIFER. You are crazy to be doing this.

BERNIE. Aye, but you don't understand the alternative: bricks.

JENNIFER. Well, no.

BERNIE. You might, if you tried.

JENNIFER. Bricks?

BERNIE. Why not? I'll show ya.

JENNIFER. You mean actually . . .

BERNIE. Yeah.

JENNIFER. How?

BERNIE *mimes laying bricks as he talks through this next part.*

BERNIE. It's not bricks first, first it's founds –

JENNIFER. You're serious.

Pounds the floor.

BERNIE. Why aye! Foundations. Rubble from houses that's been knocked down and that. It's pounded in. Compacted. Deep. That's the past.

JENNIFER. You know I'll laugh.

BERNIE. You might.

JENNIFER. I will.

BERNIE. Then again you might not. (*Mimes.*) Get the founds absolutely flat. Set the line for your run. Then it's mortar, trowel, brick. Worr happened to you Jennifer?

JENNIFER. Well, darling –

BERNIE. No, I mean really? Birrof an orchid on shite yourself.

JENNIFER. That'll teach me. (*Pause.*) A boy. The war.

BERNIE listens as he mimes.

Hereford teashops. You know the expression 'a broken heart'? Well it's true. I felt it happen. When he died, when I got the telegram, I actually felt it snap and stop working. People don't know these things like they should.

BERNIE. Shush . . . man at work. Mortar, trowel, brick.

JENNIFER. God, you're taking me seriously. (*Pause.*) No one's taken me seriously for years.

BERNIE. I know how you feel.

JENNIFIER. That's clever, Oiky. Oh my. Something stirs. (*Laughs.*) Strange bedfellows, you and I.

BERNIE. I remember it as a lifeboat.

JENNIFER. (*Beat.*) I also remember where it is.

BERNIE. Just as well, I can't tell starboard from port.

JENNIFER. Leave all that to me.

JENNIFER and BERNIE off.

Scene Nine

The apartment. ELAINE *comes in with* LEWIS. *They have just made love. She kisses him.*

ELAINE. Well then?

She is out of cigarettes.

I need a cigarette (*Stops.*) Oh, man . . . I'm gettin cravins, I'm getting them cravins people talk about. Coal. (*Thinks.*) I don't want coal, I want . . . Hershey bar.

LEWIS. No.

ELAINE. Peanut butter, grape jelly and . . . anchovies.

She goes to the kitchen. Comes out disappointed.

You live on air. (*Beat.*) Lewis, go down to the deli.

LEWIS. The deli? Man, it'll take me all day.

He goes to the piano, plays around with a few notes.

ELAINE. I thought you didn't play no more.

Instantly, he stops playing.

LEWIS. Not connected. Not the same thing as the horn.

She goes to the piano.

ELAINE. Who's this? (*Sings.*) 'My fingers itchy, got to get out and jam. Take me somewhere.'

LEWIS. That was before.

ELAINE. Not connected, my ass.

LEWIS. You are wasting your time, Elaine. You won't get nowhere. The devil been here already.

ELAINE. No shit.

LEWIS. No shit. I been tempted.

ELAINE. No shit.

LEWIS. But my ear is perspicacious. This . . . guy, he pretended to some kind of kinship, but I know he was seducing me.

ELAINE. Seducing you? The serpent been here? (*She moves up on him, raunchy, singing Bessie Smith –*) Nineteen men livin' in my neighbourhood . . .

LEWIS (*prim*). I said guy. The serpent is a feminine aspect.

ELAINE (*close*). . . . eighteen of them are fools, and the one – he ain't no doggone good. Well, in my experience, the serpent is definitely in the trousers.

She plunges her hand into his trousers. He breaks away.

LEWIS. Come on now!

She goes to the window. Looks out. LEWIS begins to pick out a tune.

ELAINE. Fresh snow. (*Pause.*) Ain't you cold?

LEWIS. No.

He plays sad, minor chords . . . a hint of dissonance . . . continues . . .

ELAINE. That piano is out of tune.

LEWIS. You'd know, huh?

ELAINE. Nobody knows like you, honey.

LEWIS. Nope. (*Sighs.*)

Pause. She touches the glass. He plays.

ELAINE (*to herself*). Oh, love . . . is ice. Snow . . . falling in all the empty, grey spaces. (*Beat. Turns sharply from the window.*) There's frost on your glass, Lewis.

LEWIS. It's that time of year.

LEWIS *is slipping into Debussy. 'Des Pas Sur la Neige.'*

ELAINE. That sounds so . . .

She hums to it.

What is it?

LEWIS. French. Des pas sur la neige. Love – know the word?

ELAINE. I've heard it used from time to time.

LEWIS. What's it mean to you?

ELAINE. Oh . . .

LEWIS. A word is a sound, right?

ELAINE. This what the devil tell you?

LEWIS. A tissue of sound and means a thing too. So I figure you take a word like love which means something.

ELAINE. Don't count on it.

LEWIS. And say it over: Love, love, love, love, love, love, love, love, love, love –

ELAINE. You are gonna get sick this way.

LEWIS. Love, love, love, love, love, love, love . . .

ELAINE. Real sick.

LEWIS. Love, love, love, love, love, love . . .

ELAINE. And I will not be around.

LEWIS. Love, love, love, love, love, love, love – maybe a hundred times, love, love, over and over.

ELAINE. Not this time.

LEWIS. And all there is – is noise. Obeying all the rules of meaning. Nevertheless, meaningless.

ELAINE. Things have moved on for me.

LEWIS. That's what happened.

ELAINE. FOR ME! A man can't be a child all his goddam life. Time comes when he has to make way, take responsibility for himself. Not the universe, just himself.

Stops playing.

LEWIS. You know what a gnostic believes? God and the devil swapped over and nobody noticed.

ELAINE (*beat*). So Dorothy and her little dog Toto are in the land of The Soul, where wearing a coat don't make no difference.

LEWIS. I don't want a coat.

ELAINE. Cold, food, kid – don't matter shit.

LEWIS. I DON'T WANT A COAT!

ELAINE. You want to be cold?

LEWIS. And clear.

ELAINE. Time you were somethin' else. (*Beat.*) I want – me me me me me – *I want!* . . . a house, a square of deep green grass. An apartment with its own front door. A serious situation. (*Beat.*) You were a nice guy once. For a musician you were even a slightly regular person, but you had to go back to the tabernacle when you *knew* how he would be?

LEWIS. I still had to . . .

ELAINE. Yeah. Well look what it done to you honey – what you done to yourself.

LEWIS. My father had me figured for the massed choirs.

ELAINE. You told me.

LEWIS. Singin' up so loud and sweet God *had* to hear it.

ELAINE. But Lewis wanted to play the devil's music.

LEWIS. Clever, fast, pure, cool. I got the theory good as those cats at Juilliard can teach. And all the clumsy street people, let them flounder in their ignorance.

ELAINE. That how you see us?

LEWIS. I don't see you, I hear you.

ELAINE. And you so good.

LEWIS. Comp-lic-ated. I get cleverer and cleverer, and all the ignorant cats get righter and righter, love, love, love, love . . . you sing and it means something.

ELAINE. I can hardly read the dots.

LEWIS. I know, and it burns my ass because you sound like I feel – here – but can't play shit. (*Beat.*) Can't touch the horn, not even touch it. Can't bear the feel of the metal on my fingers. Know why?

ELAINE. At last.

LEWIS. Because of that.

Plays a note on the piano.

When Lester play it, it's Lester. When I play, it's Adolphe Sax, the instrument, just the instrument. Know that?

ELAINE. Sure.

LEWIS. But where do I start?

ELAINE (*beat*). In that church, you cried.

LEWIS. Not for my father.

ELAINE. For Precious Lord.

LEWIS. So did you.

ELAINE. You can tell?

LEWIS. These days you cry all the time. All the time.

> LEWIS *sighs. Stands. Walks away. Stumbles into a slow spin.*

ELAINE. Honey . . .

LEWIS. Maybe I should try – Monk spins.

ELAINE. I hate to see you like this.

LEWIS. It works for Theolonius, maybe it'll work for me.

ELAINE. You ain't gonna find centre by fallin' all the way around it. What are you, a planet?

LEWIS. What you know about planets?

ELAINE. I listen to the radio.

LEWIS. The radio, not the voice on the –

ELAINE. Stop!

> *He stops. Sits on the piano stool.*

I remember – first time you played with Monk, him spinnin' one side, you the other, absolutely still. You don't need that.

> *She takes his hand.*

LEWIS. The ofay has the hands of a workin' man.

ELAINE. A horny handed devil.

LEWIS. Callouses – here, and here. I can't figure this guy.

ELAINE. Then you got to pretend, because keepin' yourself outa Bellevue is becoming a big priority. Look, the ofay was just a fan.

LEWIS. He paid my rent.

ELAINE. The hell you say.

LEWIS. To keep the piano. Offers me undiluted adulation. I

think. Because I can't hardly make out a goddam thing he says.
But I know I have to listen. Maybe . . .

ELAINE. Honey?

LEWIS. Yeah?

ELAINE. Honey . . . all I want is the regular things.

Long pause.

LEWIS. Maybe later.

Angrily, she spins him in the piano stool. Walks off into the bedroom.

LEWIS. Elaine?

He plays the last chord of the Debussy. BERNIE *comes on.*

BERNIE. What you got me to sing on me last trip. I decided it
was some sort of riddle.

LEWIS. Yeah?

BERNIE. I looked it up – Ornithology is the study of birds, yeah?

LEWIS. Hence –

BERNIE. Bird's title. So. That's what you set me to do. Kinda like
. . . homework.

LEWIS. *Homework?*

BERNIE. A test. And I've been practisin'. I've driven them mad
in the kitchen. Daft to think lessons like these'd be anything
else other than – extraordinary. So . . .

LEWIS. So?

BERNIE. Riff first.

BERNIE *sings 'Ornithology' riff. From now on, everything in strict time.*

Okay, the entire record from the top. Drum intro. Followed by
alto, trumpet, tenor unison. Piano break. Then the solos.

BERNIE *sings the first chorus . . . and when the time comes,* LEWIS
*can't help sketching in the piano break. Shakes his head. The dedication
gradually impresses him.* BERNIE *sings the repeat and keeping time . . .*

Two bar breaks, then Bird's solo –

Sings Charlie Parker's solo – perfectly. LEWIS *likes it.*

Trumpet . . .

Still in time, **BERNIE** *picks up the Howard McGhee trumpet solo.*

LEWIS. Well.

BERNIE. Tenor . . .

> **BERNIE** *picks up the Wardell Gray tenor solo but abruptly . . .*
> **LEWIS** (*singing*) *takes over powerfully and silences* **BERNIE** *. . . one*
> *chorus of Wardell Gray then, a new chorus from* **LEWIS** *– his own.*
> *. . .* **ELAINE** *drawn on . . .*
> *The piano break – a few chords from* **LEWIS**.
> *Then they sing the two riffs again in unison.*
> *Silence.*

BERNIE. The second chorus was you.

LEWIS (*self-contempt*). All me. Every last God damn note.

ELAINE. Uh-huh!

BERNIE. I paid your landlord.

LEWIS. I know. How much?

BERNIE. Twenty-seven dollars and fifty cents.

LEWIS. Ten dollar premium. So. Is twenty-seven dollars and fifty cents real money?

BERNIE. Oh aye.

LEWIS (*pause*). Listen, Tristano teaches jazz school in the Bronx. He's got all the credentials except colour, which don't signify for you: Bird friend, *great* musician, romantically blind. Leave me be.

BERNIE. No, I want you. You spoke to me in your records.

LEWIS. Which is how you get to speak to me in yours. And tell me about myself. Tell how great I am.

> **BERNIE** *takes his sax out of its case.*

BERNIE. I've got to tell you about me first.

LEWIS. Is that your sax?

BERNIE. Music. There are rules.

LEWIS. Sure are. I know them all.

BERNIE. They're in the books. But there's also a feelin', a *freedom*. I don't know how the books and the feeling go together –

LEWIS. Neither do I.

BERNIE. I haven't got the education. But I'm trying to understand.

LEWIS. This is college for you, huh?

BERNIE. Never went to college anywhere else.

LEWIS. Well I did and what I learned there was how to be you, white man.

BERNIE. Not me.

ELAINE. Just because you don't pick it up don't mean it ain't yours.

BERNIE. Not mine. I'm like a slave too.

LEWIS. You sonofabitch.

BERNIE. It's the same. It's all power.

LEWIS. Power.

BERNIE. It's true. On the boat. Back home: gerrup, go to work, clock on, head down, worrever you do never think about none of it, nothin', head down, work, head down and never ever think because if you do – then you begin to desire, *desire* . . . something . . . expression . . . freedom . . .

LEWIS. It's a matter of cultural tradition.

BERNIE. What's that to me, I'm a bricklayer. I build walls for a livin' and every day they get higher.

LEWIS. What does he look like, Elaine?

ELAINE. Short, stocky.

LEWIS. Is he a man of colour, to any extent?

ELAINE. What about them perspicacious ears of yours. Can't they even pick out that?

BERNIE. I don't expect you to do it all for nothin'. I'm payin' me way.

LEWIS. If I can't do it for myself how can I do it for you?

BERNIE. Do it with me.

LEWIS (*pause*). Oh shit. (*Sighs.*) You and me buddy are gettin' all tangled up with each other, and we gotta get straightened out.

Okay. Sing the Blues, Elaine. You like the way I play? Now this is the difference. -- Elaine? The man pays his way, he gets his lesson. (*Beat.*) For me?

ELAINE. For you.

ELAINE *sings 'It Hurts Me Too', first two verses. Unaccompanied. Very powerfully. She sings it for* LEWIS.

ACT TWO

Scene Ten

JENNIFER *and the* ACCOMPANIST. *At the piano, fiddling with their music in a quiet moment.*

JENNIFER. New York. Again. There's a song about this.

ACCOMPANIST. Several. But after a while you only notice the dirt.

JENNIFER. Well yes.

ACCOMPANIST. Not that I mind.

JENNIFER. No (*Wistful.*) But every time we come in there's just a little . . . hmm . . . a little –

ACCOMPANIST. Bit more oil on the water, rubbish on the piers.

JENNIFER. Quite.

ACCOMPANIST. Here's your mate. He's a romantic too. Just try not to go down with him, eh.

JENNIFER. No.

BERNIE *comes on with a trowel.*

BERNIE. I bought this in Southampton. To show him.

JENNIFER. Some form of tool.

BERNIE. Pointing trowel.

ACCOMPANIST. Monogrammed?

ACCOMPANIST *goes off.*

JENNIFER. Couldn't you think of something more conventional, a sack of cement perhaps?

BERNIE. The wall.

JENNIFER. No, Bernie.

BERNIE. I'm going to show him the wall.

Throughout the following speeches, BERNIE *mimes building the wall.*

BERNIE. Tie your line –

JENNIFER. Oh!

BERNIE. Take your time.

JENNIFER *walks off.* BERNIE *continues miming the wall.*

Where you goin'?

JENNIFER. I've seen the act.

BERNIE (*mimes*). Okay. Handlin' the trowel's the key: Saw off the mortar, load the trowel and lay the sausage . . . in the frogs . . . smooth your joint. Then it's brick – butter – trim – lay. Snug. And so on.

Looks up and ELAINE *walks on from one side.* LEWIS *from the other. Lights change. They are in* LEWIS's *apartment.*

LEWIS. Go on.

BERNIE. Check your level: straight, rake, rake. That's how it goes – all day and every day, course after course. There's skill. But after a while it's just mortar, trowel, brick, level, straight –

ELAINE. Rake, rake?

BERNIE. First's gettin' it right, second's gerrin it fast, and then it's – when's tea? when's dinner? when's home? hope there's overtime, hope there isn't. And after then, one of two things happens – either you stop thinkin', or you start.

ELAINE. And you?

BERNIE. I started. You get the picture?

LEWIS. Work is mindless, boring shit?

BERNIE. It robs you.

LEWIS. Of what?

BERNIE. I don't know. That's why I'm a socialist.

LEWIS. They don't have walls in socialist countries?

BERNIE (*wriggling*). Not worra mean.

LEWIS. Walls are bad? (*Beat.*) Well I'm with the man there, all I do is walk into the goddam things. But what worries me is how do we hold up the roof? We go for pillars, huh? We go for sticks or something like that?

ELAINE. Lewis, what is all this crazy stuff?

LEWIS. I started it because of you. (*Ironic.*) And that blue feel.

ELAINE. You wanna do something for me? Get your horn outa hock and go make money.

LEWIS. I'll go when I'm ready. (*Beat.*) People talk about me down there? They ask about me?

ELAINE. Truth is, you such an arrogant sonofabitch, they just glad to see you gone.

LEWIS. I don't believe it.

LEWIS *drinks from the bottle of scotch.*

Okay. The Blues.

BERNIE *opens up his sax case, puts his trowel in and takes out the sax. Sets it up.*

ELAINE. I don't get this Lewis.

LEWIS *demonstrates to* BERNIE *on the piano.*

LEWIS. Twelve bar.

ELAINE. Lotsa blues.

LEWIS. We are doing the twelve.

ELAINE. Why?

LEWIS. Because the guy is paying for the lessons *I* am giving. (*To* BERNIE.) To understand we go back to basic structure. (*To* ELAINE.) Ethnomusicology.

ELAINE. Missin' the point, professor.

LEWIS (*to* BERNIE). I call it, you play.

ELAINE (*to* BERNIE). Ain't what's written, honey, ain't the bones, it's the wind blows through.

LEWIS (*to* BERNIE). And listen up good. To me. Blues in F. You are a tone up.

BERNIE. I know.

LEWIS *plays the piano.* BERNIE *plays the sax.*

LEWIS. -F- -Bb -F- -F- Listen - oh yes, hear the harmonium in this -Bb- -Bb- -F- -F- . . . sure hear where this . . . -C- . . . come from . . . -C- cadence -C- to -F-.

They stop.

BERNIE *(making it).* I did it.

LEWIS. The devil went to church. And harmonised. Simple chords. Lots of possibility in between to be himself.

ELAINE. Better.

BERNIE *plays.*

LEWIS *(to BERNIE).* Let's use some of that possibility. First variation on the simple twelve. Elaine?

ELAINE. Maestro?

LEWIS *(plays).* -F9- -Bb9- -F9- (*To* ELAINE.) Go down the corner and --- -C-, -Gminor7-, -F7- --- and get some barbeque, huh?

ELAINE. I'll git you a heart attack first.

LEWIS *(to BERNIE).* Listen. -B diminished- -F9- . . . Hear it? -C- -F- -C- . . . that harmonium again -F9- . . . except . . . -Gminor7, C7, the end.

And BERNIE *lost.*

ELAINE *(to BERNIE).* If I wasn't an intelligent person I might think you'd put a spell on this guy.

ELAINE *picks up the scotch.*

LEWIS. I've taken up with alcohol again.

ELAINE. Yeah? Well I've taken up with the bottle.

She tucks the bottle under her arm.

LEWIS. A little chicken sandwich from the deli? I ain't eaten in days.

ELAINE. Explain all this to me!

LEWIS *(to BERNIE).* Still lots of inbetween here. Blow.

Plays first variation blues, quite straight.

ELAINE *takes* BERNIE's *chair, walks out.*

ELAINE (*going*). The man has had a conversion to socialism and now he teaches nightschool for ofays in the building trade – I can't stand it!

LEWIS. Improvise.

BERNIE *shudders to a stop.*

BERNIE. On what?

LEWIS. The chords.

BERNIE. But there's no tune.

LEWIS. Make one up.

BERNIE. I can't, not without the words.

LEWIS. Just fool around.

BERNIE. Which notes?

LEWIS. The ones in your mind, tonic, subdominant, dominant – mortar, trowel, brick – you wanna do – do.

BERNIE *falters as he tries to play fast, fails, they stop.*

BERNIE. This is hard.

LEWIS. This is masterclass, whiteass – BLOW!

BERNIE. I'm nervous.

LEWIS. TRY!

BERNIE. Give us a minute.

LEWIS. Okay, just . . . forget I'm here.

BERNIE. How can I when you're shouting arrus all the time. (*Beat.*) Come on then.

BERNIE *tries to play.*

LEWIS (*Immediate*). No man . . . no! Not like that. You don't understand what you got.

Irritated, grabs the sax before he realises what he is doing. He is shocked by the touch. But handles it confidently.

You have a column of air – diaphragm to roof (*Mouth.*) – laid alongside your heart. The aim is to connect the air to the horn and make one whole thing of inside your body and out. Diaphragm to bell. (*Of sax.*) Use this (*Head.*) and the throat tightens, the connection breaks and that puny little sound comes out.

BERNIE *starts to play.* LEWIS *is instantly dissatisfied.*

NO! Think.

BERNIE. But you said –

LEWIS. With your fingers; connect your fingers to the air inside your body. (*To himself.*) Body moulds the sound. Air wets it with blood. (*To* BERNIE.) The blues is a moan.

BERNIE. That's norr how you sound.

LEWIS. A physical thing.

BERNIE. You nowt like that.

LEWIS. Not disconnected.

BERNIE. Not that kinda gutsy tenor at all. You're more . . .

LEWIS. Cerebral. Shit, I know.

LEWIS *points to the piano. They work (silently) on stage.*

Lights change . . .

Scene Eleven

Lights change . . .
Continuous . . .
The landing outside LEWIS's *apartment.*
JENNIFER *walks on – as part of walking up and down, obviously waiting.* ELAINE *comes out of the doors.*

ELAINE. Sonofabitch.

Puts the chair down and sits in it, her back to the door.

Something of a situation.

JENNIFER. Excuse me?

ELAINE. I said . . . (*Looks her over.*) Forget it.

JENNIFER (*Beat*). I beg your pardon?

ELAINE Another Limey.

JENNIFER. I'm afraid –

ELAINE. Ofays!

JENNIFER. There's no need to be –

ELAINE. Crawl up your accent lady.

JENNIFER (*Beat*). I think perhaps you may not have understood who I am. The impression I must be giving. Standing out here. Like this. As I am. I think perhaps –

ELAINE. I think you are spectacular. And Lady Creamass you may sound, but I think you still look dumb enough to be in the hall waitin' for your even dumber friend in the apartment. Which makes two of us. I don't know how he done it but he sure inveigled his way into Lewis's mind, which is one helluva bizarre operation these days. (*Beat.*) You do bricks too huh?

JENNIFER. Actually I'm a singer.

ELAINE. Like the machine? You sew?

JENNIFER (*freezing*). I sing. On the Queen Mary.

ELAINE *imitates Queen Mary whistle.*

JENNIFER *taking up the challenge, imitates Queen Mary whistle – not as well.*

ELAINE. Uh huh. I win. You sing even worse than he plays.

JENNIFER. You can't tell from that.

ELAINE. I can tell. The Queen Mary is just under straight A and you were some way over it. I know about these things. But don't tell the guy in there, he thinks I am some kinda child of Nature.

JENNIFER. How do I get into these situations?

ELAINE. You askin' me?

JENNIFER. It's been like this for years.

ELAINE. Yeah, years and years.

JENNIFER. These situations.

ELAINE. Hanging round.

JENNIFER. Waiting for men.

ELAINE. You know what's goin' on in there?

JENNIFER. Well, actually, I don't know.

ELAINE. Actually I don't know neither. And the guys in there 'runnin' things', they don't know – *nobody* knows. Crazy.

JENNIFER. It's true. I can't sing. But I don't see why people have to point it out all the time.

ELAINE. No offence, honey.

JENNIFER. I make a living.

ELAINE. Tell me.

JENNIFER. You see, where I sing – ish – no one ever listens.

ELAINE. Oh sure.

JENNIFER. I mean literally. I'm just an after-dinner confection. A piano and something sweet with the coffee in the lounge.

ELAINE. Like Petits Fours?

JENNIFER. Exactly like Petits Fours. For the dinosaurs who find Geraldo just a little bit too . . . umpfy.

ELAINE. Geraldo?

JENNIFER. The orchestra. I'm just something for the old ladies to look at while they fall asleep.

ELAINE (*impressed*). You sing for old ladies?

JENNIFER. Yes. Old ladies. Very rich, very old ladies.

ELAINE. That is *class*. I sing for pimps and elevator operators. No offence, but the old ladies don't hear much huh?

JENNIFER. They don't really need the voice at all, it's the scene they like, the Palm Court ambience.

ELAINE. Just keep on talkin'.

JENNIFER. Why?

ELAINE. I'm gettin' to like it.

JENNIFER. Well . . . (*Beat.*) I haven't the slightest idea what to say.

ELAINE. Say . . . am-bi-ence.

JENNIFER. Ambience.

ELAINE. You talk more interesting than you sing.

JENNIFER. Would you mind if we changed the subject?

ELAINE. No offence. Cigarette?

JENNIFER. Oh . . . yes . . . ah . . . hmm . . . err . . . are they . . .?

ELAINE. Just Luckies.

JENNIFER (*disappointed*). Oh. Thank you.

ELAINE. Drink?

She offers the bottle.

JENNIFER. No, really . . . I promised myself.

ELAINE. Oh sure we all promised ourselves.

JENNIFER. Thank you. (*Taking the bottle. Drinks.*)

ELAINE. You're right, I shouldn't be doin' none of this since I'm very much with child at the moment. (*Moves over on the chair.*) Rest your feet, honey. Half a chair is the best you gonna get.

JENNIFER *sits beside her on the same chair. They continue to drink.*

You been pregnant?

JENNIFER. Once.

ELAINE. I hate men, don't you? How was it?

JENNIFER. Brief.

ELAINE. Uh huh! I know what you mean. But time to move on from one stage in life to another else you get trapped – in the perpetual girl situation.

JENNIFER. Are you . . . err? (*Nods to room.*)

ELAINE. No way. (*Beat.*) And you? (*Nods to room.*)

JENNIFER (*shrugs*). Hmmm – ish.

ELAINE. Even I, knowing England for a piece of shit can tell you and him opposite types.

JENNIFER. Lady Creamarse.

ELAINE. 'Arse'. Jesus, I'm a sucker for bullshit.

They laugh.

JENNIFER. Totally opposite.

ELAINE. But opposites attract, goddam it. Which just means arguments all the time. You really goin' with him?

JENNIFER. Well, sort of. I mean, only just.

ELAINE. Oh honey ain't it always *sort of*, and only just, and in-spite-of, and if-it-wasn't-for uh! -maybe-it'd-be-worthwhile.

JENNIFER. Always.

ELAINE. Every time. (*Beat.*) The bricks? Are the bricks on the level?

   JENNIFER *stands.*

JENNIFER (*mimicking*). 'Absolutely FLAT.' (*Hits floor.*)

ELAINE. That's him.

JENNIFER. 'The founds have gorra be deep'. 'Compact'.

ELAINE. You got him.

   JENNIFER *stamps around like* BERNIE.

You've had it too?

JENNIFER. Up to here.

ELAINE. Hell, I can't figure that man. I mean I hear that shit he says but I can't figure if he believes it.

JENNIFER. Art.

ELAINE. Oh, art.

JENNIFER. And soul.

ELAINE. Art and soul. (*Beat.*) I'm gettin' to like you. The funny guy in there, forget it – but you I like. (*Beat.*) What we doin' out here in the hall, instead of sittin' in there . . . on the floor . . . because this is the last of his chairs. And carpets. He got rid of it all in the interests of somethin' ridiculous. You understand that?

JENNIFER. You mean there's nothing in there?

ELAINE. Listen . . .

On the other part of the stage, there is a fragment of music from the piano, BERNIE *copies it.*

One chair, one piano – the guy's nuts. The guy had it made.
And then – I was there – stopped dead in his tracks in the
middle of a chorus. Packed up his horn and left. I said honey,
all these people, what's wrong? He said – 'uh!'. Three days of
questions later and finally he says 'it's a cultural matter', and
three days after that he went back to his daddy's church to be
humiliated. Been in communication with himself ever since.

JENNIFER (*beat*). My father was in the church too. A bishop.

ELAINE. You know what my man does with the money your man
gives him?

JENNIFER. Not exactly my man –

ELAINE. Burns it.

JENNIFER. Money?

ELAINE. Burns it.

JENNIFER. But *why*?

ELAINE. Because it's a cultural matter. And a matter of power.
He must be empowered in this undertaking with the ofay,
whatever it is – beggin' your pardon. Money unempowers. You
know what he makes on Fifty-Second Street? You know where it
all is now, I don't. I say let it unempower *me*, but no, it is
something he got to do, he got a helluva lotta things he *gotta do*,
his whole goddam life is fulla things he *gotta do* which is why I
gotta do so many goddam things too. Or did. Because I am *out*!
(*Beat.*) Except I been sayin' it for a month which maybe makes
me think I am in up to my neck. Shit. (*To her womb.*) You
listenin' to all this down there? Little mother. Took me over
when I wasn't looking.

ELAINE *stands, walks.*

End to the girl situation. And tell the truth I wasn't ready. You
been – I asked you that, forget it, forget I said it. Ain't had a
drink in a month and this one has kicked me like a mule in the
head. You know, we are degrading ourselves drinkin' out the
bottle like hobo women, people like us oughta have glasses.

JENNIFER. You are right. We deserve them.

ELAINE. Sonsabitches.

JENNIFER. If we are appendages then we need the little
attentions of appendage.

ELAINE. Right! Right! You know what you're doin' here?

JENNIFER. Tell you the truth, I have absolutely no idea at all.

ELAINE. Now you're sayin' it. Me neither. No idea at all.

JENNIFER. I could be in the Waldorf Astoria.

ELAINE. The Waldorf Astoria!

JENNIFER. With a rich old man.

ELAINE. I like you.

JENNIFER. Or the Astor.

ELAINE. Yeah. Keep talkin'.

JENNIFER. Or the Saint Regis.

ELAINE. Yeah, yeah. Dream, dream.

JENNIFER. Or . . . or The Plaza. Or . . .

ELAINE. And here you are drinkin' hooch on the step in Sugar
    Hill. (*Beat.*) *Why?*

JENNIFER. I have no . . . absolutely no idea – shall we get

    glasses?

ELAINE. You want to go in?

JENNIFER. And listen to that music?

ELAINE. The way your man plays it?

JENNIFER. Not exactly my *man*.

ELAINE. I'll get em. I'll go get glasses.

    ELAINE *gets up and goes off.* JENNIFER *sits and waits. Lights
    change . . .*

Scene Twelve

Lights change . . .
. . . continuous.
BERNIE *and* LEWIS *are at the piano.*

LEWIS (*getting frustrated*). Just pay attention –

LEWIS *plays a more elaborate version of the blues form in staccato chords, shouting out the changes to* BERNIE *who tries vainly to keep up. Fast.*

Bar 3 . . . Cminor7 – F7 – then Dflat minor, Fsharp minor – Bb13 – –Bb– –Dbmajor7– . . . more modern – A minor7 form of F major7, chromatic Aflatminor 7 – Ebminor7 – then Gminor 7 to C8 – then –F–, and – Fsharp minor 7 to Fsharp 7.

Silence. BERNIE *totally confused.*

BERNIE. Give me time. Take it slower . . .

ELAINE *emerges from the same door.*

ELAINE *(interrupting).* The appendages in the hall want glasses.

LEWIS. Saywhat?

ELAINE. I said –

BERNIE. I'll get them.

LEWIS. You stay where you are and work.

LEWIS *points to the music.*

ELAINE. Excuse me for interrupting these cultural matters, but I SAID . . . You got glasses or you lick it off the floor around here these days? My friend and I – I got a new friend – my new friend and I are partying and we gettin' ugly.

LEWIS. Saywhat?

ELAINE. In the hall.

ELAINE *gets on his knee – ironically.*

LEWIS. Elaine, I'm trying to get with something serious here. My creativity –

ELAINE. Your creativity? Lewis . . . you been walkin' round with your creativity hanging outa your pants for a month and more. Lewis . . . you have been insane for weeks and weeks and weeks and now IT IS MY TURN! I am out here talking things I care about.

LEWIS. The glasses are like always, man. *(To* BERNIE.) Come on, blow.

ELAINE *walks off into the kitchen.*

BERNIE *plays hesitantly.* LEWIS *pushes him with the chords.*

Listen . . . Listen . . . Pick your way.

ELAINE *comes on, with some glasses.*

ELAINE. Obliged. (*Stops by the piano.*) I SAID –

LEWIS *stops playing.*

LEWIS. You're welcome, ma'am. You reconsidered that chicken sandwich?

ELAINE. Choke!

LEWIS. No, huh?
Okay, now, this is *jazz*, the idea is – play off, not on. Rhythm goes that way (*Horizontal.*) and harmony that (*Vertical.*), Jazz is makin' the one kinda jog the other.

ELAINE *bursts into raucous laughter.*
They watch her as she goes into the hall.
Lights change . . .

Scene Thirteen

Continuous . . .
Lights change . . .
JENNIFER *shares a look with* ELAINE. *Walking and sitting down.*

ELAINE. Scotch is acceptable but best is gin, English gin.

ELAINE *offers glasses.* JENNIFER *pours.*

Tastes green, like a forest. Smell the pine. I like all kindsa clean smells. But best of all I like them country smells because they're clean even when they're dirty. Lady Creamarse.

JENNIFER (*in* ELAINE's *accent*). 'Uh huh?'

ELAINE. Where you hail from, they got grass? I mean extensively?

JENNIFER. Meadows and fields and hillsides. Miles and miles and miles. Grass in profusion.

ELAINE. Sheep and cows and stuff?

JENNIFER. Yes.

ELAINE. Brown cows?

JENNIFER. Yes.

ELAINE. Like in 'Gone With The Wind'?

JENNIFER. Brown cows.

ELAINE. Oh shit. Where you come from, what's it called?

JENNIFER. Shropshire.

ELAINE. The name – oh, conjures up a cow right out of your mind. Nice house huh?

JENNIFER. Yup.

ELAINE. Stone?

JENNIFER. Yup.

ELAINE. Like in 'Wuthering Heights' with moss and ivy and all that stuff?

JENNIFER. Better. Old wisteria thick as a man's wrist. But it's called 'The Elms'. Because there are also elms.

ELAINE. How can you bear to leave it?

JENNIFER. Because elms and wisteria is all it has got. No . . . champagne, silk, or nylons, or steak au poivre, or stuffed olives or the Foxtrot, or any of the things that make life really worthwhile.

ELAINE. Yeah. But grass that ain't dirty . . .

JENNIFER. Quite nice, yes, but the carpets in the Waldorf Astoria . . . infinitely better than grass.

ELAINE. No shit.

JENNIFER. No shit. First of all they're dry. Grass, grass is often wet. Second they're very very soft, that deep! And third they are valeted.

ELAINE. Valeted. Like soft, deep, valeted grass?

JENNIFER. Yup.

ELAINE *stands. Takes* JENNIFER *by the hand*.

ELAINE. C'mon, honey, this I got to see. (*Pause.*) They let sepia in?

JENNIFER. The front door.

They share a look, and roar off growling with determination.
Lights down.

Scene Fourteen

LEWIS *explains harmony as* BERNIE *plays*.

LEWIS. So take the chromatic addition and stretch it to the very furthest point of tonality. (*Beat.*) And then come back to where you started. Or maybe not. Either way real fast.

BERNIE. Why?

LEWIS. Because that's how it is.

BERNIE. But why d'ya have to come back?

LEWIS. The Laws of Harmony. Ignorance.

BERNIE. The whole point is I don't know any of the technical stuff and you know all of it. That's what we started with. But none a that's talent.

LEWIS. You heard the expression: making bricks without straw?

BERNIE. Aye but I never understood it because they don't use straw.

LEWIS (*beat*). Man this is hard work. Okay.

LEWIS *pushes the ashtray towards* BERNIE.

Now.

BERNIE. This is ridiculous.

LEWIS. Pay your way.

BERNIE. It's puttin' me on.

LEWIS. I thought you were big on political understanding.

BERNIE. Big on expense more like.

LEWIS. Listen – obviously, your *ear* tells you to come back.

BERNIE. But is it true for everybody, I mean are everybody's ears built the same way?

LEWIS. It's a sense of completeness.

> LEWIS *waits.* BERNIE *unfolds a big white five pound note.*

(*Listening.*) Is that a bedsheet?

BERNIE. Five pound.

LEWIS. English money?

BERNIE. I didn't have time to change it.

LEWIS. I'm going to have to consider this.

BERNIE. Ask me, you're mad. Don't even eat properly and you burn money. Look, why don't I bring you a steak from the ship.

LEWIS. Entrecote?

BERNIE. If you want?

LEWIS. Bring it for next door. Duke Ellington's dog eats entrecote. So what is five pounds in hard currency?

BERNIE. Twenty dollars.

LEWIS. Let's go.

> LEWIS *leans back and* BERNIE *rolls up the note, lights it.*

BERNIE. Why don't you keep it?

LEWIS. Money I get lotsa ways. This way I get power.

BERNIE. Over me?

LEWIS (*smiles. Sings* –). Somewhere there's moonlight / somewhere there's song – The lesson continues with: The Popular Song.

BERNIE. All right. Me question – is it the way your ears are made? Is there only one . . .

LEWIS. Tonality. Sonofabitch.

BERNIE. Worrave I said this time?

LEWIS. How High The Moon. Chorus.

> BERNIE *plays the chorus.* LEWIS *speaks over it.*

Listen . . . Listen all the time . . . Stretch your ear . . .
Bricklayer, we gonna build a new wall, with new bricks . . .
crazy elastic bricks that still fit. Because there's more than one

kind of wall – huh? And you know how we gonna do it? (*Changes abruptly into 'Georgia'*). Keep playing.

BERNIE (*stopping*). Aw man!

LEWIS (*Southern accent*). We goin' back down South . . .

BERNIE. Is it gonna make sense?

LEWIS (*sings*). Georgia . . . Georgia . . .

BERNIE. Is this some kinda answer?

LEWIS (*talks*). My daddy was a Georgia boy. Elevated hisself up North. Satin swish on the polished floor. The light laughter of high-spirited young womanhood.

BERNIE (*walks away*). I'm lost.

LEWIS (*stops abruptly*). You want me to go on?

BERNIE. It's all meant as humiliation.

LEWIS. Education. You guys, the ones shipped us over, you oughta hear how it all turned out.

BERNIE. Not people like me – the higher ups.

LEWIS. Oh, the big guys said put 'em on the ships and the little guys like you went right ahead and did it. – Yes boss! *Git* your black ass!

BERNIE. Hundreds of years –

LEWIS. You forget, we remember. The door is there. And this is the *only* way I go on.

BERNIE. Go on.

LEWIS (*plays, picks up the theme exactly where he left off*). . . . . the orchestra whispers . . . virtue to the young folks lingerin' amongst the magnolias of temptation. But out there in the night . . . deep in the shadow . . . darkies!

BERNIE. Christ.

LEWIS. Amazed! By the simplicity of the music, the monotony of the rhythm. Sugar songs touch nothing, get nowhere near the ache. This . . . this is nearer the ache.

He rips the melody apart rhythmically.

Much better. Much closer to that not forgotten, but hid, Africa. And you know what?

Boogie Woogie . . .

The white folks dig them jungle rhythms too. Oh . . . magnolias. Oh . . . temptation. O . . . Lordy! Let the niggers tell them how it is to let go. So steal it.

Hits a dischord, stopping abruptly.

When you oppress a people you lose a part of yourself in that people and the only way to get it back is steal.

But too late, we done made it different. We had an idea. (*Plays swing à la Count Basie.*) So steal that too.

But BERNIE *shakes his head, drifts away and watches.*

Change, steal, change and steal, steal the voice out of the black mouth, no song no rebellion. Not history but now. Okay *this time* it's gonna be so fast so impenetrable, chords and counterpoint so clever they can't even work it out. Atonal? Hindemith suck your ass. (*Beat.*) And you *still* left with the ache.

BERNIE. I don't understand any of this.

Silence.

LEWIS. Our writers write like yours, our painters paint like yours, there's only music – I thought I was playin' the devil's music, but I was just real good at cleaning up the act. You so goddam right you sonofabitch. Ignorance led you straight there.

BERNIE. Are we still talkin' about music?

LEWIS. We are talking about everything. Four hundred years the black fights a little way out of oppression and what does he find – everything done, everything planned – what do you build when all the bricks are white, fella, but white houses and white streets. And YES there has to be another way. But I can't feel it in me. My mind gets in the way. My clever white mind.

BERNIE. Know the trouble with you?

LEWIS. Please . . . tell me the trouble with me.

BERNIE. Too flash by half.

LEWIS. A regular smartass.

BERNIE. I cannat talk like this. I haven't been trained. I can't put the way I feel into words.

LEWIS. And I can't get rid of the words. A word needs meaning to get it out of your mind.

BERNIE. All self. Listen! While I try and say summat for once.

LEWIS. Your solo.

BERNIE. Takin' the piss again. People have always taken the piss outa me. It's easy cos what puts me in the way of it is not acceptin' what they say.

LEWIS. They?

BERNIE. Yes they.

LEWIS. Who is they?

BERNIE. I don't know who they are, but I know the buggers are out there all right. And they say what marrers. I don't know how, burra know they do. And what marrers about a workman . . . is what he can make . . . in how much time . . . because that decides how much money he can make in the same time and all that means it doesn't matter buggery what he is *personally*. Who cares what a machine thinks? What the cogs say to each other? It doesn't marrer shite, man.

LEWIS. Back to walls huh? I'm beginnin' to find the wall a limited concept.

BERNIE. So how do ya think I feel about it? Do you know what you sound like when you play this (*Sax.*) I can't say the word, I daren't because I'm waitin' for the whole World to tek the piss. (*Pause.*) The word is beautiful. Doesn't that sound strange in my accent, eh? Beauty. Clarity. Intelligence. All the embarrassin' things I can think of, all the things machines aren't supposed to know. That's what you are capable of. And summat else an' all, summat that lifts it all – up, puts it all together, summat's that's only in Jazz.

LEWIS. Rebellion.

BERNIE. Aye, that's right! What's the word . . . ?

LEWIS. Incitement. But not your rebellion, mine. Against you.

BERNIE. Not me. They. The others, the ones that say what goes.

LEWIS. You.

BERNIE. No. I keep on sayin' –

LEWIS. But you are who I can get to, little guy.

BERNIE. Not me. They. Burn their money, they gorra lot more
of it. Insult them. And teach me to play, to rebel. Against them
with you. I wanna . . . the word, the word?

LEWIS. Strike?

BERNIE. No.

LEWIS. Attack.

BERNIE. No . . .

LEWIS. Assert.

BERNIE. Say I'm free . . .

LEWIS. Express.

BERNIE. Oh yes, fight back. If I stop tryin' to do that, I die,
mentally, I die and become that machine. Help me.

LEWIS. This is something you can't make, you can only imitate.

BERNIE. Why not?

On the piano . . .

LEWIS. The scale right. The diatonic . . . *(Plays it.)* Musical reality?
European reality. Missy on the harmonium. One way. Give me
your hands.

BERNIE. What?

LEWIS. Your hands. Doh – Ray – Me – Far – So – Lar – Tee –
Doh.

*Takes BERNIE's hands and fuses them onto the piano keyboard, pulls
them off as the diatonic scale. Spread.*

But there's another. Niggers in the darkness remembered this
. . . Doh – Ray – Me – So – Lar. African reality. The pentatonic
scale.

Plays the pentatonic scale and spreads five fingers of his own hand.

And Jazz. Is this –

Jams his hands into BERNIE's and crashes the tangle onto the keyboard.

Harmonium in the parlour. Hymns in the church. Niggers in the fields. Work shouts, ring songs . . . Nearer my God to thee . . .

Pulls BERNIE *round.*

And puttin' it all together somehow. Africa and Europe. Five into eight, one reality crushed into another making – a bloody, confused mess of music and history. Which belongs to me. Only way to be a nigger in a field is *be* a nigger in a field. (*Calms.*) Slave holds, pens and plantation and chain-gang. The devil's music is full of ghosts.

BERNIE. Ghosts?

LEWIS. In between the notes, blowing through the bones, the ghosts of my people. (*Beat.*) Let go of my hand, man.

BERNIE. No.

LEWIS *tries to drag himself free.*

LEWIS. Let go of my hand!

BERNIE. It belongs to me too. Five into eight, eight into five.

LEWIS. You want a rebellion? Make your own.

BERNIE. It isn't just black people.

LEWIS. You can tell who is speakin' here.

BERNIE. It's more than you.

LEWIS. Yep, there it is – more. The only really original musical thing made in the new world is black and the white man says mine, more . . . you got everything else, so why MORE? Let go of my hand!

BERNIE. No. It's your gift. You cannat keep music for yourself. Once you set it off you cannat stop it goin' out and influencing people, nor if it's alive.

LEWIS. It gets owned, our humanity gets taken away, and used. (*Beat.*) Let go of my hand.

ELAINE *and* JENNIFER *come on.*

JENNIFER. You boys really have a good time when the girls ain't around.

ELAINE *puts a wrapped packet on their joined hands.*

ELAINE. Chicken. On wheat.

JENNIFER. What are they doing?

ELAINE. Secret things – between men.

ELAINE *and* JENNIFER *go off*.

(*Going*). Looks like a cultural matter to me.

LEWIS. Let go of my hand.

BERNIE *lets go*. LEWIS *is left with the sandwich on his hand*.

(*Pause.*) Chicken sandwich? (*Offers it to* BERNIE.) This is my gift.

BERNIE *gives up the hand*.

BERNIE (*pause*). I want to go on with the lesson now. I've paid. In humiliation.

LEWIS. Know what impresses me about you?

BERNIE. You owe me goin' on.

LEWIS. Your total disregard for the rules of possibility, for what can be.

BERNIE. Bugger that.

LEWIS. Talent, education, knowledge –

BERNIE. We've all got the talent but we just can't . . . shape it.

LEWIS. It's magnificent. Rebellion. But the wrong kind. You in trouble.

BERNIE. I've got to go on.

LEWIS. Yes?

BERNIE. I can't afford not to.

LEWIS. No.

BERNIE. We're norral like you, livin' in a hole complainin' about how disappointin' genius is.

LEWIS. Man. An ear for the streets is what you got. Listen then: that's all you got. I can't teach you nothing.

BERNIE. Please.

LEWIS (*beat*). You don't have the talent.

BERNIE. Please.

LEWIS. Okay. (*Pause.*) Take me to church.

BERNIE. What?

LEWIS. Take me to the cathedral. I hardly seen the outside in a month. Coat, man – Coat, man.

BERNIE gets the coat he rescued from the snow outside the Baptist church, gives it to him.

BERNIE. I kept it for ya.

LEWIS. And now I want to walk.

They stand, walk . . .
Lighting change . . .

Scene Fifteen

Lighting change . . .
To a cathedral. High light. Choral Mass.

LEWIS. I can hear the air go clear up to wherever. Listen to that mathematical perfection. It runs in the air like water, a whole lake of air trembling.

Stands and listens.

What's the root of all music?

BERNIE. The human voice.

LEWIS. Inside the body and out, a bridge between realities. So what do you feel?

BERNIE. Angry.

LEWIS. Me too. In a different way. I listen to this and I hear light. Is there light?

BERNIE. From the windows high up.

LEWIS (*holds his hands up to it*). Cold light?

BERNIE. Very.

LEWIS. Describe it for me.

BERNIE. Aw!

LEWIS. No really. No put on. Do it.

BERNIE. At the best of times –

LEWIS. Try.

BERNIE. White up high and lower down, stained, with colours.

LEWIS. Colours . . .

BERNIE. From the stained glass. Red. Blue.

LEWIS. Like sound, tone and variation.

BERNIE. No, sound is air vibrating, you can feel it. Light is not a thing, but what shows you things.

LEWIS. Illuminates.

BERNIE. As usual, the right word.

LEWIS. All I know is the word. This isn't my culture, it's a foreign language, though I speak it exceedingly well.

Stands out.

Do I have a shadow, here, now?

BERNIE. Yeah.

LEWIS. Listen to all that purity. Do you hear it?

BERNIE. Yes.

LEWIS. Do you like it?

BERNIE. It's not my . . . style.

LEWIS. But do you *like* it?

BERNIE. I've never really –

LEWIS. Old, pure beauty. But it casts a shadow. (*Beat.*) Black man is the tabernacle of white man's imperfections. God and devil. Neither whole without the other. And how the white man needs his shadow to steal from. And what an unhappy thief he is, brutalised by beauty.

BERNIE. You hate us?

LEWIS. Yup. All those notes were hate. Not . . .

BERNIE. Asserting.

LEWIS. I never asked your name?

BERNIE. Bernie.

LEWIS. Well, Bernie . . . all of Lewis's young life he listened to God, in the Gospel choir, and then one day the devil spoke. Tenor saxophone. It was ravishing. But, god and the devil gotta start gettin' on in the man's mind. (*Beat.*) There is a little act of assertion I have chosen to perform here. It may cause you some embarrassment –

LEWIS *walks away from* BERNIE, *who is stunned.*

(*Sings.*) Precious Lord / Take my hand / Lead me on / Let me stand /

. . . *the chant fades.*

I am tired / I'm so weak / I am worn . . .

THE VERGER (*American*) *comes on quickly, speaks to the stunned* BERNIE.

VERGER. Friend, friend – let me explain: This is strictly a Catholic establishment we have here, we don't go in for that kind of thing, not here.

LEWIS *stops.*

A word please.

VERGER *goes off.*

LEWIS (*sings*). Through the storm / Through the night /

VERGER *comes on.*

VERGER. Now – look!

LEWIS. Lead me on / To the light /

VERGER. Don't misunderstand I'm not saying we're strangers to inspiration, only we prefer it kept to ourselves. Private. Silent.

LEWIS. Take my hand – take my hand /

VERGER. What would happen if they all took to it. We get quite a few in here you know.

LEWIS. Precious Lord /

VERGER. Off the street and so forth.

LEWIS. Lead me – on . . .

VERGER. Things could get out of hand.

LEWIS. . . . Oh yeah.

Silence.

VERGER. Have I asked politely?

ELAINE *(off)*. *(Sings.)* When my way / draweth near

VERGER. Jesus.

ELAINE *comes on.* JENNIFER *is with her.*

VERGER. It's the cops then, okay. Okay – if that's how you want it – *okay*! *(To audience.)* Sorry about this folks, if you could all just get back on your knees, the normal service will be resumed as soon as possible.

ELAINE. Precious Lord / linger near / When my life / is almost gone / And my pride / And my song / Hold my hand Jesus / Precious Lord / Take me home.

ELAINE *walks up to* LEWIS.

VERGER. Fantasists.

ELAINE *(talks)*. You through with this foolishness?

LEWIS. Bernie?

BERNIE *stares straight ahead.*

LEWIS *(shrugs)*. I'm through.

ELAINE *and* LEWIS *go off. Leaving* JENNIFER *with* BERNIE.

JENNIFER. Bernie . . .

JENNIFER *reaches out her hand, drops it, goes.*

BERNIE *in his own world.*

Lighting change . . .

There is a sudden storm of noise from the Count Basie Band. LEWIS *comes on and gives him his sax.*

BERNIE. I never thought this would happen. Not in me wildest dreams. You taught me so much.

LEWIS. Forget it, man.

BERNIE. Gave me the chance to show worr I could do.

LEWIS. Forget it, man. If Geraldo won't take you. Then Count Basie will. Solo.

BERNIE. Solo.

LEWIS. Take it. Man.

> BERNIE *stands and takes the solo with a confident booty tenor style. As he plays his silhouette is projected on to a screen behind. At the end. The sound sheers to silence. Bring up the noise of traffic.*
>
> *Lights change . . .*

Scene Sixteen

New York. Fifty-Second Street. BERNIE *still on with sax.* JENNIFER *slightly behind.*

BERNIE. The bastards won't let me play on the boat –

JENNIFER. Bernie –

BERNIE. Because I'm not one of the lads.

JENNIFER. It's not the end of the world.

BERNIE. Because me face doesn't fit.

JENNIFER. What did he say to you?

BERNIE. Because I'm not a member of their club.

JENNIFER. What did he say?

BERNIE. Right then, right – talent depends on opportunity. Doesn't it?

JENNIFER. To a certain extent.

BERNIE. All I need's the chance. I'll prove him wrong. If I can cut it in one of these clubs. Sittin' in here, these clubs – white, black, all you have to be is good right?

JENNIFER. That's a lot.

BERNIE. They don't look at the colour of your skin, they listen to what you play, right?

JENNIFER. This is a tough test.

BERNIE. Burr I'll pass it. And we'll see if I can cut it or not.

JENNIFER. Here?

BERNIE. Here. Fifty-Second Street.

Fade up voices. From the club doorways people are touting for business.

JENNIFER. This is the biggest hustle in the World.

BERNIE. I'm not listenin'.

VOICE. Ben Webster goin' on.

JENNIFER. Fifty-Second Street.

VOICE. Just goin' on, Ben Webster.

BERNIE. Ben Webster, *himself*.

VOICE. Lady Day.

JENNIFER. Not here, Bernie.

VOICE. Bird here tonight.

BERNIE. Jesus.

VOICE. Dizzy Gillespie Quartet.

JENNIFER. You can't walk on to a stand here and now.

VOICE. No minimum for Dizzy.

BERNIE. It's after the shows I'm thinkin' of, later on.

VOICE. Lady Day right now!

BERNIE. There's a club the musicians gather in after the shows and jam. They have these competitions against each other to see who can play the longest, the best, the most choruses for hour after hour.

VOICE. Charlie Bird Parker is here and going on right now.

BERNIE. Late into the morning.

VOICE. The President.

BERNIE. Play all night.

JENNIFER. Oh.

BERNIE. I want to play all night, Jennie.

VOICE. Adolphe Sax gave it a shape.

JENNIFER. We did once or twice.

BERNIE. I mean . . . create.

JENNIFER. No, we never got round to that.

VOICE. Listen to the man who gave it a sound.

BERNIE. Lester . . .

VOICE. Lester Young . . .

BERNIE. I'm gonna do it, Jennie, I'm gonna jam with them. This is freedom, Jennie. All this.

JENNIFER. It's a mistake.

BERNIE. I have to.

JENNIFER. Why?

BERNIE. Because there's nowt else worth havin'.

JENNIFER. Not worth having?

BERNIE. I've got to go.

JENNIFER. Well, if you must, then you must. (*Turning to go.*) But afterwards – keep to your kitchen.

BERNIE. This can be heard everywhere. This is the capital of the World. This is the sound of all the people of the Earth who want to be free. Now. And here.

BERNIE *goes.*

Snap lights into next scene . . .

JENNIFER. No!

Scene Seventeen

Lights change to the Queen Mary. JENNIFER *crosses stage and sits at piano where the* ACCOMPANIST *waits.*

ACCOMPANIST. Ah!

JENNIFER. Yes – ah!

ACCOMPANIST. Where are we exactly?

JENNIFER. Well, we're back down to earth.

ACCOMPANIST. With a bump?

JENNIFER. Yes, bit of a bump.

ACCOMPANIST. Burris he out of the system yet?

JENNIFER. Not quite yet. But soon. Innocence, romance, hope – my last fling I think.

ACCOMPANIST. Oh good, because there's a lot to be gerring on with.

JENNIFER. These innocents are such cruel bastards.

ACCOMPANIST. No, there's norra lot of choice when you come down to it is there, me duck?

JENNIFER. I'd love to say yes.

ACCOMPANIST. And?

JENNIFER. No. (*Beat.*) A nightclub wasn't that it?

ACCOMPANIST. Oh yes. The way I see it is a piano in the hollow of a kidney-shaped shiny black floor. Not shite like this one – a grand. White. With silver trim to catch the dazzle. Watered drinks. Girls with big tits. And a very intelligent roulette wheel in the corner. We'll make a fucking fortune. Up on the wall, right – in black crotchets –

JENNIFER. England Expects?

ACCOMPANIST. Or – The Nelson Touch. All this boating about has really got to me. It'll be real classy.

JENNIFER. And where does the money for all this come from?

ACCOMPANIST. From you. I told you, I'll tek you back to your folks.

JENNIFER. I see.

ACCOMPANIST. They've got the capital, I've got the plans, you haven't have you?

JENNIFER. And this is what I settle for.

ACCOMPANIST. Reason I never lost me way, Jen, is because I never tried to go anywhere in the first place. I'm one of Nature's conservatives. Blue, in tooth and claw.

JENNIFER. I quite see that.

ACCOMPANIST. And I'm about to become a thriving species. Never did understand what an experienced realist like you saw in a dreamer like him. All he ever had for brains were hopes. Come on, let's get back home and gerron with it.

JENNIFER. You're so banal.

ACCOMPANIST. So what. – Home time, Jen.

JENNIFER. Shropshire? 'The Elms'.

ACCOMPANIST. How long have you been away?

JENNIFER. Ten years.

ACCOMPANIST. Ever since Norway?

JENNIFER. More or less.

ACCOMPANIST. Time you were getting back then.

JENNIFER. They won't take me back, not after all this time.

ACCOMPANIST. Oh yes they will. You *and* me. We're all there is. Right?

JENNIFER (*long pause. She decides*). Right.

They go off.

Lights change.

Scene Eighteen

ELAINE *now heavily pregnant comes back in with a Persian rug and throws it on the floor.*

ELAINE. Hmmm . . . just here.

She sets the rug.

LEWIS. How's it look?

ELAINE. Exotic.

LEWIS. That landlord is one helluva guy. I can't get round his apartment without falling over my things.

ELAINE. Lewis.

LEWIS. Yeah?

ELAINE. You always liked this rug.

She sits on the rug.

So I am gonna make one helluva mess on this rug. Me and my baby.

LEWIS. What?

ELAINE. I'm gonna give birth right here.

LEWIS. Forget it.

ELAINE. Right here. From now on my big ambition in life is gettin' in your way. I'm gonna break you Lewis Page, I'm gonna bend you to my will. You are gonna be my thing.

LEWIS. What did I say?

ELAINE. I intend me and my child will rule the Earth from this rug. You are on notice. So watch out. I am gonna crack your balls like walnuts. I got somethin' for you out back.

ELAINE *goes out, comes back with a sax.*

ELAINE. I stole the pawn ticket from your wallet.

Puts the sax down on the piano.

Go to work.

LEWIS. Suddenly I'm frightened.

ELAINE. Man! Rise above it.

LEWIS. It would be like startin' over. What I did before was contrived.

ELAINE. I kinda liked it, in a way.

LEWIS. Little pieces of theory laid end to end.

ELAINE. So make it better.

LEWIS. And people said who is *that*? But now . . .

ELAINE. Let me hear the pain.

LEWIS. And give up all my advantage?

ELAINE. Man. If you don't say what you feel, then why live? You hear the way I feel all the time.

She picks up a record. Walks to the record player.

Your friend –

LEWIS. Bernie.

ELAINE. – sent you this. A record. Entitled 'Ofay Blues'. You think he got a sense of humour at last?

ELAINE puts it on.

Lights change . . .

Scene Nineteen

Lights up in the recording booth. Swish of static. BERNIE makes a recording.

BERNIE. It's me. The last time. Thought I'd let you know worr happened. I went into this club. These guys were playin'. After a bit I went on the stand and started playin'. (*Beat.*) It was like one a them dreams where you haven't got no trousers on. And then wakin' up from the dream to find you haven't got no trousers on. Never played another note. And I gorra new sound for ya.

Lifts two bricks together and clicks them.

Me old firm took me back on and now I'm buildin' a council estate. Home safe. The lads are still tekin' the piss but they'll gerrover it. When it comes to the sax . . . I'm useless. Sorry for the embarrassment and all that but I hope I was some use to you. Oh aye, and there is summat else. If I had been talented then mebbe you would have been wrong. As it is . . .

He clicks the bricks again.
Lights change.

Scene Twenty

ELAINE. Listen to what the guy is telling you. Musicians play music. Go to work, man.

LEWIS walks to the sax. Picks it up. Puts it to his mouth.
Lights down.
A howl of pain from the sax.

BOLD GIRLS ■ RONA MUNRO

RONA MUNRO was born in Aberdeen in 1959. After studying history at Edinburgh University she worked as a cleaner and later as a receptionist before getting her first professional commission for *Fugue* at the Traverse Theatre, Edinburgh, in 1982. Since then she has written for stage, radio, television and several community theatres. Her work includes *Watching Waiters* and *The Dirt Under the Carpet* for BBC radio, *Hardware* and *Biting the Hands* for television and *Piper's Cave* and *The Way to Go Home* which was commissioned and performed by Paines Plough Theatre Company. She travels as much as she can, including trips to Nicaragua, Turkey and South America. She also appears with Fiona Knowles in a feminist double act called the Msfits, who perform their show in Aberdonian and have toured all over Britain. Her short play *Saturday at the Commodore* was performed by 7:84 Scottish People's Theatre as part of *Long Story Short: Voices of Today's Scotland* in 1989, and in 1990 the company commissioned and toured *Bold Girls*, which was joint winner of the Susan Smith Blackburn Award for the best play by a woman in the English speaking world, 1991. Her current commission *Your Turn to Sweep the Stair* is scheduled for performance in autumn 1992 at the Traverse Theatre, Edinburgh.

For Pat

Bold Girls was commissioned by 7:84 Scottish People's Theatre and first performed at Cumbernauld Theatre, Strathclyde on 27 September 1990 with the following cast:

DEIRDRE	Andrea Irvine
MARIE	Paula Hamilton
NORA	Joyce McBrinn
CASSIE	Julia Dearden

Directed by Lynne Parker
Designed by Geoff Rose
Lighting by Stephen McManus
Music by Debra Salem

This production subsequently toured during October and November 1990 to Glasgow, Stirling, Lochgelly, Greenock, Musselburgh, Blairgowrie, Dundee, Govan, Dumbarton, Kirkintilloch, Ayr, Edinburgh, Paisley, Belfast, Kilmarnock and Selkirk.

Scene One

MARIE*'s house.*

It is irons and ironing boards and piles of clothes waiting to be smoothed, socks and pegs and damp sheets waiting for a break in the Belfast drizzle for the line; it's toys in pieces and toys that are just cardboard boxes and toys that are new and gleaming and flashing with lights and have swallowed up the year's savings. It's pots and pans and steam and the kettle always hot for tea; it's furniture that's bald with age and a hearth in front of the coal fire that's gleaming clean. At the moment it's empty, an unnatural, expectant emptiness that suggests this room is never deserted; it's too stuffed with human bits and pieces, all the clutter of housework and life. There is a small picture of the Virgin on one wall, a large grainy blow-up photo of a smiling young man on the other, he has a seventies' haircut and moustache. DEIRDRE *is not in this room, she's crouching on all fours on her own talking out of darkness in which only her face is visible.*

DEIRDRE *moves from all-fours.*

DEIRDRE. The sun is going down behind the hills, the sky is grey. There's hills at the back there, green. I can't hardly see them because the stones between here and there are grey, the street is grey. Somewhere a bird is singing and falling in the sky. I hear the ice cream van and the traffic and the helicopter overhead.

Lights off on DEIRDRE.

MARIE *bursts into the room with her arms laden with four packets of crisps, two of Silk Cut and a packet of chocolate biscuits. Drops one of the crisps, tuts in exasperation, looks at it, shouts back out the door.*

MARIE. Mickey! Mickey were you wanting smoky bacon? . . . Well this is salt and vinegar . . . well, why did you not say? Away you and swap this . . . Catch now. (*Hurls the bag.*) No you cannot . . . No . . . because you'll not eat your tea if you do. Mickey pick up those crisps and don't be so bold.

MARIE *comes back into the room and starts two jobs simultaneously. First she puts the crisps etc., away then she fills a pan with water and throws it on the stove; she starts sorting her dry washing into what needs ironing and what doesn't; she sorts a few items then starts peeling potatoes; all her movements have a frenetic efficiency.*

NORA *comes in with a pile of damp sheets.*

NORA. Is that the last of them, Marie?

MARIE. Just the towels . . . Oh Nora, you didn't need to carry that over, wee Michael was coming to get them.

NORA. Och you're alright. These towels is it?

MARIE. That's them.

NORA. This'll need to be the last, I've a load of my own to get in.

MARIE. Oh here Nora, leave them then!

NORA. No, no, we're best all getting our wash done while it's dry. We'll wait long enough to see the sun again.

CASSIE *sticks her head round the door.*

CASSIE. Can I ask you a personal question, Marie?

NORA. Have you left that machine on, Cassie?

CASSIE. Do you have a pair of red knickers?

MARIE. I think I do, yes.

CASSIE. With wee black cats, with wee balloons coming out their mouths saying 'Hug me, I'm cuddly'?

MARIE *(stops peeling potatoes briefly, gives* CASSIE *a severe look).* They were in a pack of three for 99p.

NORA. You see if you leave it, it just boils over, you know that Cassie.

CASSIE. And did you put those knickers in the wash you just gave my mother?

NORA. It's because that powder isn't really biological, it's something else altogether.

MARIE. What's happened to them?

NORA. I think it's for dishwashers. But it was in bulk, cheap you know? I got a load of it at the club last month, awful nice young man, do you know that Dooley boy?

CASSIE. And did my Mummy just drop those bright red knickers with their wee cats, right in the middle of the road, right by the ice cream van as she was coming across from our house to yours?

NORA. Did I what?

MARIE. Oh *no*! (*Increases the pace of her peeling.*)

NORA. Cassie, will you get back over the road and see to that machine before the foam's coming down the step to greet us.

MARIE. Where are they?

CASSIE. At the top of the lamp-post, I didn't know wee Colm could climb like that, he's only nine.

NORA. Och I'll do it myself. (*Moves to exit with a heap of towels.*)

MARIE. Hold on Nora, I'm coming too.

CASSIE. I wouldn't. After what's been said about those knickers I'd just leave them alone, pretend you never saw them in your life.

NORA. All my lino's curled after the last time. I'll never find a colour like that again.

NORA *exits.*

CASSIE. And did you know your wee Michael's just swapped a packet of salt and vinegar crisps for a wee plastic cup full of raspberry ice cream syrup?

MARIE (*erupting towards the door*). MICKEY!

CASSIE. I'll get him. (*Calling off.*) Mickey, come here . . . 'Cause I want you.

MARIE *finishes the potatoes, dives into the ironing again.*

MARIE. He doesn't just drink it, he wears the stuff.

CASSIE (*talking off*). Give me that cup now.

MARIE. In his hair and everything.

CASSIE (*off*). Because it's poison.

MARIE. Then he won't eat his tea and what he does eat comes straight back up again.

CASSIE (*off*). I am an expert on poison, a world expert, and I'm telling you that stuff will kill you. I do know. I took a G.C.S.E. in identifying poisons.

MARIE. Threw his hamburger clear across the room last time. Frightened the life out of his Aunty Brenda.

CASSIE (*off*). It gets your intestines and eats them away till they just shrivel up like worms. Its worse than whisky.

MARIE. I wouldn't mind but he doesn't even like the taste, he just likes being sick.

CASSIE (*off*). I'll tell you what happens to all those men that drink whisky and all those wee boys that drink raspberry ice cream syrup; their intestines get eaten away and their stomachs get eaten away and all the other bits inside just shrivel up and die. Then they've no insides left at all and all they can do is sit in front of the television all day and cough and shout for cups and cups and cups of tea because that's the only thing that can fill up their awful, empty, shrivelled insides . . . Yes just like him . . . and him as well, so will you give me that cup? That's a good boy.

CASSIE *comes back into the room with a plastic cup of red syrup.*

MARIE. Your tea's on the table in half an hour, Michael.

CASSIE (*to* MICHAEL). What? (*To* MARIE.) Can he still have his crisps.

MARIE (*wavers*). Och . . .

CASSIE. No. Best let the poison drip its way through your intestines as fast as possible. Crisps would just clog it up.

She moves into the room, takes a swig of the syrup.

CASSIE. Put some vodka in that and it would make a great cocktail.

MARIE. Do you want a beer? I've cans in.

CASSIE. No, I'll wait a while. Are you still on for the club tonight?

MARIE. Oh . . . well . . .

CASSIE. Marie!

MARIE. I've no one to watch the kids.

CASSIE. I thought Brenda was coming in?

MARIE. She said she'd try but I think her John's out tonight.

CASSIE. When is he not? Well we'll take Mickey and Brendan down to hers before we go.

MARIE. Och . . .

CASSIE. What?

MARIE. I've nothing to wear.

CASSIE. What about your red dress?

MARIE. I've nothing to go with it.

CASSIE. What about your cuddly kitten knickers? Look, when did you last have a night out?

MARIE. I was over at yours watching that video just the night before last.

CASSIE. Oh, it'll take you a while to get over the excitement of that, I can see.

MARIE. Well it cost me a bit of sleep Cassie, that film.

NORA *comes back in.*

NORA. Marie I need your mop. What did I tell you, Cassie?

CASSIE. Sure it was only a film. Nothing real to it at all was there, Mummy?

MARIE *fetches the mop.*

NORA. Foam right up the walls.

CASSIE. You know that video we saw with Marie, *The Accused*, remember? Her winning the court case and all, who could believe that?

NORA. I came in the kitchen and all the stuff out the bin was floating around on top of it, a packet of fags bobbing out the door . . .

CASSIE. Oh not my *fags.* (*Grabs the mops and exits.*)

NORA *settles herself down.*

NORA. She was no good, that girl, if you ask me.

MARIE. Who?

NORA. Jodie Foster or whatever you call her. I'm not saying she deserved it, mind, but she should've known better, she should've known what'd be coming to her.

MARIE. But was that not the thing of it Nora, that no woman deserves . . .

NORA (*interrupts*). Och she should've learnt better at her age. What do you think of that?

NORA *hands* MARIE *a fabric sample.*

NORA. The colour of it, what do you reckon to the colour? It's unusual isn't it? Unusual. Different. I don't think I've ever seen the like of that.

MARIE. It's lovely.

NORA. So it is, and it's a good heavy fabric you see, you could do your curtains in that and your loose covers.

MARIE. You could.

NORA. Well I'm getting the end of a roll of that; fifteen yards of remnant and that'll be my front room just a wee dream again.

MARIE. That'll be some price will it not?

NORA. Oh I've a deal worked out with your man at the club, it won't be shop prices he'll be charging. Anyway, they won't cut off the electric or the gas this month and we must be due some summer by next month and who knows if I'll live longer than that, so I'll be alright for a while, and I'll have my room the way I want it.

MARIE. It is a nice bit of cloth. (*Handing it back.*)

NORA (*stroking it*). Just feels rich doesn't it? So are you coming out with us tonight, Marie?

CASSIE *sweeps back in, brandishing the mop.*

CASSIE. A wee bit of foam just dripping over the top! I thought I'd need my aqualung the way you were talking.

NORA. I hope you didn't let it drip on my good lino!

CASSIE. And what I'd like to know is, if everything in the kitchen was bone dry, how was it my fags were sopping wet on top of the machine?

NORA. Sure it wasn't me that put them there.

CASSIE. Sure it wasn't you puffed that packet down to two and them too damp to light at all now.

NORA. Och you're killing yourself with those.

CASSIE. And what are *you* doing? 'Bit of interior decor?' Tar-filled lungs: what the best dressed bodies are wearing.

NORA. To say nothing of the money you're burning up.

CASSIE. Oh they're a terrible price, you're right there, just as well you've mine to puff on. Here Marie, put these under the grill for me will you?

Hands MARIE *soggy cigarettes.* MARIE *takes them and then offers both* CASSIE *and* NORA *out of her own pack.*

NORA. Thanks Marie. (*To* CASSIE.) Our Martin never grudged me a cigarette.

CASSIE. That's because our Martin smoked mine as well.

NORA. You! You'd grudge a dry hand to a drowning man.

MARIE. Maybe I will come out tonight.

CASSIE. There's no maybe about it.

NORA. Are you not coming out with us, Marie?

CASSIE. Yes she is.

MARIE. I just don't know if I can get a sitter.

NORA. Sure, put Brendan and wee Michael over with our two. Our Danny's watching all of them.

CASSIE. Well our Danny's watching *Nightmare on Elm Street 365,* but I daresay that'll keep him awake long enough to notice if they try and run away from home.

MARIE. Well . . .

NORA. I know how you feel love, but you can't mourn forever.

CASSIE. Who's mourning?

NORA. Cassie!

CASSIE. Michael's been dead three and a half years Mummy. I should think she could try a wee smile on for size now and then don't you? Sure he was hardly here when he was alive.

NORA. God forgive you, Cassie.

CASSIE. And who was that came out with us last month drank a pint and a half of vodka and tried to climb into the taxi driver's lap on the way home to show him how to change gear?

MARIE (*laughing*). Well he was in second, the eegit, the whole way.

CASSIE. Was that Michael Donnelly's mourning wee widow carrying on like that or was I hallucinating?

NORA. God forgive me for bringing a child into this world with a heart of flint and a tongue to match.

NORA *exits.*

CASSIE. Heart like a Brillo pad, that's me. That was B.T.'s taxi, by the way; it was broke.

MARIE. Was it? Why did he not say?

CASSIE. I think he tried but you were too busy trying to remember all the words of *Life in the Fast Lane*. Then he couldn't breathe too well by then either, not with you squashing him into the steering wheel like that.

MARIE. Cassie! You should've stopped me!

CASSIE. There was no stopping you, Marie. B.T.'s never been able to get it past first since.

MARIE. I don't remember any of it, you know.

CASSIE. Just as well. So why won't you come out?

MARIE. Have you fallen out with your Mummy?

CASSIE. I fell out with my Mummy on the delivery room floor. Why won't you come out Marie?

MARIE. Och, I've things to do here.

CASSIE (*looks round*). Looks great to me. Want me to help you dust the lightbulbs?

MARIE. I just need a bit of quiet, time on my own.

CASSIE. Well you're in the wrong house for that.

MARIE. No, sometimes I get a sit to myself, by the fire, when the kids are in bed.

CASSIE. And what do you do?

MARIE. I just wait.

CASSIE. Wait for what?

MARIE (*hesitates*). Cassie . . . Do you believe in ghosts?

> CASSIE *stares at her for a minute, then casts a quick nervous glance at the photograph on the wall.*

CASSIE. Has he been back? Have you seen him?

MARIE. No, not Michael. It's a wee girl, all in white.

CASSIE. A wee girl?

> MARIE *nods.*

CASSIE. Well, who is it?

MARIE. I don't know.

CASSIE. Well, who does it look like?

MARIE. She looks like Michael.

CASSIE. Sacred Heart!

MARIE. You know how me and Michael always wanted a wee girl.

CASSIE. I remember.

MARIE. Then other times . . . she looks like me.

CASSIE. But . . . you're not dead.

MARIE. Well, you remember that dress I was married in, that wee white mini-dress?

> CASSIE *nods.*

MARIE. Then when Michael brought me here . . . I'd never seen it. Even on my wedding day I still thought we were moving into his parents' back room . . . then he brought me here, asked me how I liked our wee home . . . and I just stood at the end of the path there and stared . . .

> MARIE *stops.*

CASSIE. Yes?

MARIE. That's where she stands. And stares.

CASSIE. Oh Marie!

MARIE (*laughs*). So am I cracking up at last, Cassie?

CASSIE. I think you should get out of this house and get a good stiff drink or twelve down you.

MARIE (*laughs again*). I think you're maybe right.

There is the sound of a distant explosion. Both stop for a moment. They don't appear unduly alarmed.

CASSIE. What side was that from?

MARIE. Sounded like it was down the front somewhere.

CASSIE. Sounded like it was a good way from here.

MARIE. Och, it's time I was getting the kids in anyway.

She wipes her hands and exits. We hear her calling off.

MARIE. Mickey! Brendan! That's your tea ready.

CASSIE *gets up slowly, looking after* MARIE. *She hesitates a second, then moving fast she goes to the photograph of Michael senior on the wall, she scrabbles down her front and pulls out a wad of money; she conceals it behind the picture. She straightens the picture again, steps back, then turns. She freezes in shock, staring out the window.*

NORA *enters. She now has a towel round her head.*

NORA. There's buses burning all the way up the Falls.

CASSIE (*distracted*). What?

NORA *looking to the window.*

NORA. What is it?

MARIE *enters.*

MARIE. That's the Brits coming up the road. Close that blind, will you Nora?

NORA *moves to do so.* MARIE *is talking to her kids off.*

MARIE. Alright, you can have it in your room, but don't you be dropping chips on those clean downie covers.

NORA (*peering round the edge of the blind as she closes it*). Ahh! Will you look at what those great boots are doing to my nasturtiums!

MARIE (*to* CASSIE). Brendan got one of those computer games for his birthday, can hardly drag the pair of them out of there now (*Putting food on plates.*)

NORA. I've only got two feet of garden, you'd think they could walk round it.

MARIE. He had it in here but I couldn't take the noise, so then he shifted it through; he'll sit through there in front of it even when he can see his breath and he's got to wear gloves to punch the wee buttons. Did you hear that Brenda's put a heater in every room in her house there? I says Brenda, if you switch them all on they'll be bringing you the bill by parcel post. Just steams the damp out anyway; it's like a Turkish Baths in her front room. Are you O.K. Cassie?

NORA (*turns*). The only flowers in the whole road and they have to go and jump on them . . . Are you O.K., Cassie?

CASSIE. Sure, why wouldn't I be O.K.? So what's happening?

NORA. There's buses burning all along the Falls.

MARIE *exits with two plates of food.*

CASSIE. What?

NORA. There's one just outside the supermarket there and there's a great lot of smoke further back as you look along the road.

CASSIE. Well, what's that for?

NORA. Sure it doesn't have to be for anything does it?

CASSIE. Well, what's the date?

NORA. No there's no anniversaries or nothing. I was just asking your wee woman there, we couldn't think of anything.

MARIE *re-enters.*

MARIE. They're saying there's shooting on the main road.

CASSIE. Who's shooting?

NORA. No one seems to have a clue, but there's a road block going up the top of the road there.

CASSIE. Well, we thought we heard something going up down the front there didn't we Marie?

MARIE. Put the radio on. There'll maybe be something in a minute.

Lighting change.

DEIRDRE *speaks again from her own space.*

DEIRDRE. It's raining. The sky is grey.
There's a helicopter up there, in the sky, I can hear it. It watching.
It's raining on the shops. On the smoke, on the kids. It'll come in round the windows, it'll beat in the doors, can't keep it out.
I'm wet, I'm cold. I want to get inside.
There's burning, making the sky black. The sky's full of rain and the sound of the helicopter.
I want to get inside, Can't keep me out.

MARIE. It was a terrible wet day when I got married.
A wet grey day in 1974 and I couldn't get to the church for the road blocks. I was standing out on my step there with my Mummy screaming at me to come before I got my good white dress dirty from the rain . . . only I was wetter from crying than the clouds could make me, because Michael Donnelly was the only boy I'd ever wanted for myself and me just seventeen. He was the only boy I'd wanted at all and it was still a miracle to me he wanted me back . . . but then since I've always had to work hardest at believing miracles and anyway I knew they only fell in the laps of the pure in heart, now it seemed certain to me that a pile of Brits and a road block would lose me Michael altogether . . . for why would he wait an hour or more at the church, when he'd that smile on him that made you feel wicked and glad about it and that look to him that caught your eye when he was walking down the street. Just with the way he put his feet down, bold and happy together, and those hands that were so warm and gentle you hardly worried where he was putting them and why would a man like that wait two hours in a cold church for a wee girl in a damp wedding dress?

And my Mummy's trying to pull my Daddy in 'cause he's shouting at the Brits saying this was the greatest day of his daughter's life and hadn't they just spoiled it altogether? Then this big Saracen's pulled up and they've all jumped out and my Mummy's just going to scream when do they not offer us an escort through the road block? So that was my bridal car to the wedding, a big Saracen full of Brits all grinning and offering us fags and pleased as punch with themselves for the favour they were doing us. I hardly dared look at them. I was certain the big hulk sitting next to me was one of them that had lifted Michael just the year before but oh they were nice as anything.

There was wanted men at the wedding and everything. Sure I'd grey hairs before I was ever married.

And then I was married and Michael brought me here and the rain stopped; it even looked like the sun had come out and I stared and stared, just standing at the top of the path in my wee white dress that was still half soaked. It felt like we'd won through everything, the weather and the road blocks and the Brits and there were never going to be bad times again . . . because I was never going to be without him again.

Well . . . I was just seventeen after all.

Lighting change.

NORA. 'Reports of disturbances in the west of the city'? As if we hadn't noticed. Can I borrow your hair-dryer Marie?

MARIE. Sure help yourself, it's just by my bed there.

NORA *moves to leave.*

NORA. Well, it looks like none of us will be getting out tonight.

CASSIE. Why not?

NORA. You'll not get a taxi down this street tonight, Cassie.

CASSIE. They'll be gone before you've your face on Mummy, with the time you take.

NORA. Well I hope you're right. Our Danny won't get home from his work.

NORA *exits.*

MARIE. Our Brenda's probably stuck in town as well.

CASSIE. Well what's it all for; that's what I want to know?

MARIE. Someone'll know. Here, I'll get you some dinner, Cassie.

CASSIE. No, no, you're alright.

MARIE. Come on, I've it all ready here.

CASSIE. No, no, we've a meal ready for us across the street; we were just waiting on Danny. I gave my crowd theirs before I came out.

MARIE. Will they be alright?

CASSIE. Eileen's over there, her telly's been lifted.

MARIE. They never came to her house?!

CASSIE. They did, half the street out watching them stagger out the door with it, took her video as well. She said she didn't mind the publicity but she was half way through watching *Home and Away* and they wouldn't even wait till she saw if they caught those two in bed or not . . . No but I'm on a diet.

MARIE. A diet! What for?

CASSIE. To lose weight!

MARIE. That's what I mean. What for?

CASSIE. Have you ever seen me in a bikini, Marie?

MARIE. I have not and I shouldn't think anyone else will either unless you were planning on sunbathing on that wee tuft of grass your Mummy calls a lawn, or unless you've got some toy-boy hidden away just waiting to sweep you off to Spain.

CASSIE. Well when I meet him, Marie, I want to have the figure for it. Anyway I've got this calorie chart, so all I can have today is half a grapefruit.

MARIE. Half a grapefruit!? What kind of diet is that?

CASSIE. You have to weigh it up, a little of this or a lot of that. Do you know how many calories there are in a gin and lime? And I'm only allowed 1300 a day so if I'm wanting a drink tonight that's all I get to eat.

MARIE. That can't be healthy, Cassie.

CASSIE. Sure it is, you balance it out over the week. Fruit juice and yoghurt all day tomorrow.

MARIE. And ten gin and limes and half a grapefruit today?

CASSIE. *Six* gin and limes, I worked it out . . . mind you, I could always give the grapefruit a miss couldn't I?

MARIE. Cassie, that can't be healthy at all . . .

Her words are cut off by a few gunshots; they sound close at hand. Both freeze for a second.

MARIE. That was at the back of us, wasn't it?

CASSIE *nods.* MARIE *goes to peek out past the edge of the blind.*

CASSIE. Must be something big.

MARIE *is looking carefully up and down the street.*

CASSIE. Anything?

MARIE *(shakes her head, still looking out).* . . . So why don't you try that B.B.C. diet? Brenda lost ten pounds with that.

CASSIE. I want something quick. You wait, Marie, I'll have a completely new body by the end of the month.

MARIE. Whose will you have?

There is a sudden thunderous knocking at the door. Both CASSIE *and* MARIE *stare at each other, terrified.*

CASSIE. Sacred Heart!

MARIE *runs to the door to the hall and shouts out.*

MARIE. Mickey, Brendan, you stay in that room!

She waits there, just looking back at CASSIE. *More knocking.* NORA *catapults into the room, her hair half dried.*

NORA *(frightened).* That's someone at your door Marie.

MARIE *moves over to peer round the blind again.*

MARIE. I can't see the step from here.

CASSIE. Just leave it Marie.

MARIE. Sure if it was anybody to worry about they'd've had the door in by now anyway. *(She hesitates looking towards the hall.)*

CASSIE. Just *leave* it, Marie.

MARIE. Maybe it's someone needing to go through to the back.

CASSIE. And they wouldn't be knocking either, it'd be excuse me Mrs and straight through your kitchen with the Brits on their heels.

MARIE *starts to move towards the door.*

MARIE. I'll keep the chain on the door.

CASSIE. *Marie!*

MARIE. You stay here.

MARIE *exits.*

NORA *(crosses herself).* Mother of God, did you hear those shots?

CASSIE *nods.*

They wait, watching the door.

DEIRDRE *comes into the room. She looks about fifteen but could be younger or older, she's wearing a white mini-dress, damp and grubby, battered white trainers on her feet. Her legs are bare and scratched, there are more scratches on her arms. She has heavy black make-up on, smudged slightly around her eyes as if she's been crying. She stands uncertain in the centre of the room.* MARIE *enters behind her; all the three older women just stare at* DEIRDRE.

DEIRDRE. Can I stay here till I'm dry, Mrs? They won't let me up the road.

There is a pause then MARIE *finally stirs.*

MARIE. You better sit down by the fire.

DEIRDRE *does so. The others slowly sit as well, watching her.*

NORA. I don't know your face.

DEIRDRE *says nothing. She doesn't look up from the fire.*

NORA. Well where are you from?

DEIRDRE *jerks her head without turning.*

NORA. Where?

DEIRDRE (*sullen, quiet*). Back of the school there.

NORA. What's that?

DEIRDRE (*loud*). Back of the school there.

NORA. Those houses next the off-licence?

DEIRDRE *nods.*

NORA. I know where you are. So what happened to you then?

DEIRDRE *shrugs. She looks up and catches* CASSIE's *eye.* CASSIE *turns quickly to look at the television.*

MARIE. Will you take a cup of tea, love?

DEIRDRE *nods.*

MARIE *goes to make it.* NORA *stares at* DEIRDRE *a while longer, then turns to* CASSIE.

NORA. So Cassie, looks like that wee brother of yours will miss his tea altogether.

CASSIE (*eyes on telly*). Looks like he might.

NORA. I hope he's the sense to stay in town.

CASSIE. Sure he'll phone next door, let us know what's happening.

NORA. Aye he's a good boy.

A pause while everyone watches the telly in uncomfortable silence.
MARIE brings DEIRDRE the tea and some biscuits. DEIRDRE takes it without saying anything, starts to eat and drink furtively and ravenously. CASSIE and MARIE exchange glances over her head.

MARIE. Turn the sound up on that will you Nora?

NORA moves to do so.

CASSIE. Is that *Blind Date?*

NORA. You should know, you've been sitting here staring at it.

CASSIE. Will you look at what that woman's wearing!

NORA. What's wrong with it?

CASSIE. She looks like she's ready to go in the oven for Christmas dinner.

NORA. I like Cilla Black, she'd a great singing voice.

CASSIE. Pity she hasn't the dress sense to match.

Another pause. All of them, including DEIRDRE, keep their eyes fixed on the screen.

MARIE (*turns to DEIRDRE*). Have I not seen you around here before?

DEIRDRE shakes her head.

MARIE (*certain*). I thought I had.

CASSIE (*pointed*). Me too, Marie. I'm sure I've seen her.

DEIRDRE. No.

MARIE. Just outside the house there.

DEIRDRE. Wasn't me.

MARIE. So you got caught in the rain?

No response.

MARIE. You shouldn't be out without a coat in this weather; you'll catch your death.

DEIRDRE *shrugs.*

MARIE. Will your mother be worrying about you?

DEIRDRE *shakes her head.*

NORA. The woman next door's got a phone love; you could pop in there and give her a ring, sure she'll be worrying about you with everything going on.

DEIRDRE. She's out.

NORA (*distracted by the T.V.*). Oh look at that one, oh he's the kind that'll sing, I love it when they do that.

Another pause.

MARIE. I'll need to get my dinner if we are going out tonight. You'll take something Cassie?

CASSIE. No, no, I told you.

MARIE. Nora?

NORA (*eyes on screen*). No you're alright pet, we've a fry to eat when Danny gets in . . . (*At telly.*) Oh here he goes, look Cassie! (*Sings along.*) 'You are the sunshine of my life . . .' Oh do you see him Cassie!?

CASSIE. I hate when they do that, it's just embarrassing.

MARIE *has fetched herself a plate of food. She divides half its contents onto another plate which she gives to* DEIRDRE. DEIRDRE *again takes it without comment.*
There is another shot, more distant.

MARIE, CASSIE *and* NORA *look at each other.* DEIRDRE *keeps her eyes on the screen.*

MARIE. Turn the sound up on that will you, Nora?

NORA *moves to do so, speaking to* DEIRDRE.

NORA. Did you see what's going on out there?

DEIRDRE *shakes her head.*

NORA. You didn't see nothing?

DEIRDRE (*mouth full, eyes on screen*). Buses burning and Brits everywhere.

NORA (*to others*). Wonder what it's all about?

CASSIE *shakes her head.* MARIE *looks at her watch.*

NORA. When's the next news, Marie?

MARIE. 6.30.

NORA (*turning back to the telly*). Oh look! Oh will you look!

MARIE. What?

NORA. They've got a weekend in the Caribbean! Oh look, Cassie!

CASSIE. I see it.

NORA. Oh wouldn't that be great! She looks pleased, doesn't she?

CASSIE. I suppose she's got a weekend to find something better than the singing spring onion she picked for herself there.

NORA. Oh I think he's lovely. What do you think, Marie?

MARIE (*not listening*). Hmmm?

CASSIE *turns back to* DEIRDRE.

CASSIE. That's quite a walk from the school down to here.

No response from DEIRDRE.

CASSIE. You've got friends down here then?

Still nothing.

Maybe that's where I've seen you, visiting your friends round here.

DEIRDRE (*to* MARIE). Can I get another cup of tea, please?

MARIE (*surprised*). Yes, of course.

CASSIE. Yes it's the best café in the road here.

MARIE *throws* CASSIE *a look.*

NORA. Have you nothing warmer to wear pet, sure you'll be catching a chill there.

DEIRDRE (*quiet*). I'm O.K.

NORA. What's that?

DEIRDRE. I'm O.K!

NORA. I think I'm going deaf, Cassie.

CASSIE. No I don't think you are, Mummy. (*To* DEIRDRE.) No, I just thought I saw you outside there, just about a quarter of an hour ago, at the end of the path.

MARIE (*struck*). Did you see her?

CASSIE. I'd swear I did.

DEIRDRE (*mutter*). No.

CASSIE. What?

DEIRDRE. It wasn't me.

CASSIE. Must've been some other wee girl in a white dress then.

NORA *is flapping a hand at* CASSIE *trying to get her attention. She mouths the word 'glue'.*

CASSIE. What, Mummy?

NORA (*flustered*). Nothing, I was just looking at these three girls here . . . oh it's the adverts . . . (*Mouths again 'Glue'.*)

DEIRDRE *is apparently watching the screen, oblivious.*

CASSIE. What?

NORA (*piercing whisper*). Glue!

DEIRDRE *does not react.* CASSIE *looks at her speculatively.*

CASSIE. Hmmm . . . maybe.

MARIE *hands* DEIRDRE *another cup of tea; exchanges another look with* CASSIE.

DEIRDRE. I've seen you though.

NORA. Who pet?

DEIRDRE (*looks at* CASSIE). Her.

CASSIE. Have you though? Where was that?

DEIRDRE. It was a long time ago, years ago.

NORA. You couldn't miss her anyway.

CASSIE (*to* DEIRDRE). What are you talking about?

No response.

CASSIE. Well where, then?

DEIRDRE *shrugs.*

CASSIE. It's the Night of the Living Dead here, Marie . . . So you know who I am? You know my name?

Nothing.

CASSIE. I'm Cassie Ryan and this is my mother Nora and this is Marie Donnelly.

DEIRDRE *gives a brief nod.*

CASSIE. So what's your name?

DEIRDRE *(mutters).* Deirdre.

CASSIE. What?

DEIRDRE. Deirdre.

CASSIE. Deirdre what?

Nothing.

CASSIE. Deirdre what?

DEIRDRE *(to MARIE).* Can I use your bathroom, please?

MARIE. Sure you can love; it's first left in the hall there.

DEIRDRE *exits.* NORA *has become absorbed in the telly again,* CASSIE *and* MARIE *look at each other.*

CASSIE *(quiet).* Is that her?

MARIE. It is.

CASSIE. I saw her as well.

MARIE. Did you?

CASSIE. End of the path there. Staring.

NORA *(eyes on screen).* What did she say her second name was?

CASSIE *(louder).* She didn't, Mummy.

NORA. Deirdre . . . There was a Deirdre McMahon used to live up there . . . sure but she'd be twenty-five now at least . . .

CASSIE. Is it time for the news yet?

MARIE. Oh here, put it on.

CASSIE *moves to the radio. Lighting change.*

DEIRDRE. I need a knife. A wee blade of my own. It's quieter than a gun. You can hold it quiet in your hand. Maybe I'd like that.

I see a lot of things. This time I saw a man holding another man outside the circle of light the street lamp made on the road. He kept him pinned on the wall in the dark with a wee blade. It was the neatest thing you ever saw, wee and thin, like he had a metal finger he could point where he liked and he was saying, 'Is that the truth then? Is that the truth?' but the other man never says anything back at all and I thought to myself that maybe it wasn't a question, maybe it was the knife he was talking about. It was the truth. I thought I'd like that. A wee bit of hard truth you could hold in your hand and point where you liked.

Lighting change.

NORA. Well, if that wasn't a pack of lies what was it?

CASSIE. You'd think if they didn't know what was going on they'd just tell you 'stead of making it up for themselves.

MARIE. I hate it when that's all they give you, 'reports of casualties' and you're left wondering who or how many.

CASSIE. Sounds like they've got someone though, doesn't it?

MARIE *moves over to put the telly back on.*

NORA. Have you got your pass through for tomorrow?

MARIE. I did, but they've put the wrong date on it.

NORA. Sure they'll not bother about it, they're nice as anything at the Kesh these days.

MARIE. It's some change isn't it?

NORA. Something to be grateful for Marie, we've a lot to weigh us down, the two of us; one man dead and the other in a prison cell. A lot to weep over.

CASSIE. And here's me never stopped dancing since they took mine away.

NORA. Cassie!

CASSIE. Sure they did me a favour when they lifted him.

MARIE (*laughing*). You'll be telling me next you made the phone call.

NORA. Marie!

CASSIE. I did not, a useless bastard he may be, but he doesn't deserve what he's had in there, no one does.

NORA. Oh do you remember the night they took Jo? You should've seen me, Marie.

CASSIE. She was something that night, Andytown's own Incredible Hulk, 'Don't get me angry'!

NORA. Well Marie, there was wee Cassie . . .

CASSIE. Wee? I'm wee again am I?

NORA. . . . just a week out the hospital with the stitches still in from the section that gave us Teresa, and I open my door and here she is running up the road . . .

CASSIE. . . . That was when we had our own house, you know, at the end there . . .

NORA. Squealing 'Mummy! Mummy!' . . .

CASSIE. . . . One hand clutching my stomach 'cause I'm sure the whole lot's going to fall out.

NORA. . . . 'Mummy! Mummy! They're taking Jo!' Well I just felt my blood rise . . .

CASSIE. She was a lioness. She was.

NORA. I marched back up the road and here they were, dragging the poor man out of his own house without even a pair of shoes on his feet . . .

CASSIE . . . He'd been snoring away in front of the football, toasting his toes, with a pie in one hand and a can in the other.

NORA. Sure he'd not been ready for any trouble; why would he be?

CASSIE. . . . And the rest of them are throwing everything every which way and all over the house and the baby's screaming and the child's calling for her Daddy . . .

NORA. . . . And he keeps his hand tight round this pie the whole time they were dragging him away. And I goes up to this big R.U.C. man and I says . . .

CASSIE. . . . She picked the biggest.

NORA. I says, 'What's the charges? Where's your warrants?'

CASSIE. And he's peering down at her like he's a mountain and she's a beetle at the bottom of it.

NORA. And he says 'And who are you?' And I says, 'I'm that boy's mother-in-law, and before you take him you'll have to answer to me!'

CASSIE. Can you beat it, Marie?

NORA. And he says, 'You get out of our way Mrs or it'll be the worse for you.'

CASSIE. He didn't say it as nice as that Mummy, there was a few fucking old . . .

NORA. *We* do not need to use language like that Cassie! 'Out the way or it'll be the worse for you,' he says. Oh he was a big bastard Marie. 'Oh,' I says, 'Oh would you strike a woman that could be your own mother? Would you now?' (*Starts to laugh.*)

MARIE. What happened?

CASSIE. Wallop! Knocked her straight through the hedge.

NORA (*still laughing*). Would you hit a mother? Sure I got my answer on the end of his fist.

CASSIE. Nearly choked on her false teeth.

NORA. I did.

CASSIE. I didn't know which of them to go to first, Jo, or Mummy in the hedge with her little legs waving in the air.

NORA (*wiping her eyes, still laughing*). Oh . . . oh but that was a terrible night. (*Getting serious.*) Sure, when they took our Martin there was no one for me to battle with. He just never came home, his dinner drying up and waiting and waiting till you knew something had happened . . . then waiting some more.

MARIE. It was the same with our Davey.

NORA. And him only a child. The pain of that just killed your Mummy, didn't it Marie? . . . Just finished her off.

Pause.

NORA. I wish our Danny would get safe home.

CASSIE. Well I'm telling you Marie. It's Mummy here had the temper in our house. We were all terrified to leave our shoelaces undone.

NORA. Your Daddy had a temper.

CASSIE. Daddy! I'll tell you how much he could stand up for himself. He hated eggs.

MARIE. So?

CASSIE. So a big yellow-eyed egg he got in the middle of his fry every Saturday and never said a word about it.

NORA *(getting sharp)*. He had a temper when he had a drink in him.

CASSIE *(sharp back)*. If he was pushed.

NORA. He had a temper.

CASSIE. My Daddy never had a word to say for himself.

MARIE. I wonder what that wee girl's doing in the bathroom all this time?

All look towards the door. MARIE *gets up; listens.*

MARIE. She's taking a shower.

NORA. She's not!

MARIE. I can hear her.

CASSIE. Well do you like the cheek of that?

MARIE. I better put the hot water on, she'll have the tank emptied.

CASSIE. Marie!

NORA. She looked like she could do with a wash.

CASSIE *(getting up)*. I'm going to bang on that door.

MARIE. Oh leave her, Cassie.

CASSIE. Leave her!?

NORA. That child needs help from someone.

CASSIE. She needs something Mummy, or she's after something. I wonder you can have her in the house, Marie.

MARIE. Well . . . maybe we'll find out what's been going on.

CASSIE. You'd be better asking questions of a can of beans than that one.

MARIE. Is the road block still there?

CASSIE *crosses to the window to look.*

CASSIE. There's still a crowd of them up the top there.

MARIE. I was wanting out with my crumbs.

NORA. Crumbs?

MARIE. For the birds.

NORA. What do you want to do that for?

MARIE. I just like to.

NORA. I'd've thought birds were one thing that could look out for themselves in this town.

MARIE. It's only crusts; I just like to feed them.

CASSIE. You remember when Marie was a child Mummy and they'd been burnt out, had to spend a few months in those big flats.

MARIE. That's when I got started, I'd throw crusts out the window and see if the birds could get them before they hit the ground. And they did you know, they never let a scrap go to waste.

CASSIE (*sarcastic*). Amazing isn't it Mummy?

MARIE. I like the birds.

DEIRDRE *comes back into the room, hair wet, wrapped in a towel. All turn and gape at her.*

DEIRDRE. Do you have a hair-dryer?

Pause.

MARIE. It's in the bedroom.

DEIRDRE *turns to exit.*

CASSIE (*calling after her*). Just make yourself at home!

NORA. She'd nothing on at all!

CASSIE. We saw.

NORA. That wee girl is trouble, Marie.

CASSIE. You tell her, Mummy.

MARIE. Well you wouldn't have me turn her out on the street in a towel would you?

Pause. CASSIE *looks out the window again.*

CASSIE. Oh I think they're moving off. They'll be around the place for the rest of the night, but.

MARIE. Still, maybe we'll get out to the club after all.

NORA. Oh you're coming, Marie? Oh that's great.

MARIE. Sure I've nothing to keep me in now, have I?

CASSIE (*meaningfully*). Not as long as you get her clear of the house before you go.

MARIE (*moving to the door*). I'll see if I can get Brendan to go down now.

CASSIE. Is he sleeping better?

MARIE. Well he goes down alright; then he's up in the night.

CASSIE (*to* NORA). Bad dreams.

MARIE. He thinks he sees his Daddy.

NORA. Sure, but he was only a baby.

MARIE. One of the wee boys at the school has been tormenting him, saying his Daddy had his head blown off.

NORA. Oh that's cruel! That's cruel!

MARIE. So he's dreaming about it.

NORA. Wee boys are terrible cruel.

CASSIE. Tell her what you say to him, Marie.

MARIE. I just bring him into the fire and I hold him and I rock him and I say . . . (*Getting dreamy.*) Your Daddy was a good man and a brave man and he did the best he could and he's in heaven watching out for you and when you're good he's happy, he's smiling at you and that's what keeps us all together, keeps me going, keeps me strong because I know your Daddy can see us . . .

Pause.

NORA (*choked*). Marie . . . That's lovely. (*Gulps.*) I'll away and get Danny's fry on, Cassie.

NORA *exits hurriedly.* MARIE *looks at* CASSIE.

MARIE. I know Cassie, but he's a child; it's good for him to hear it like that. (CASSIE *doesn't respond.*) I know, I know he was no saint . . . but I miss him.

CASSIE. I know you do.

Pause.

(*Sudden vehemence*). Oh Marie, I wish I was out of this place!

MARIE. Cassie?

CASSIE. I'll see you later, better go and find what the kids have left of my sacred wee brother's dinner.

CASSIE *leaves the room.*

Lighting change.

CASSIE. Oh my Daddy was a lovely man. Gentle. He'd hold you in his lap like you had fur and he didn't want to ruffle it. He held me like that anyway. There's been men that've told me I'm pretty and men that've told me I'm clever and men that've sworn I'm some kind of angel come down to pull them out of a sea of whisky and give them the kiss of life.

Lying hounds every one of them.

My Daddy said I was the best girl that ever stirred her Daddy's tea for him. The best girl that ever sat on his lap or combed his hair or did any of the wee things he wasn't fit to do for himself. My Daddy said I was special.

My Daddy never lied to me.
So it must've been me that lied to him.

MARIE *is slowly tidying up and shredding bread for the birds.*

MARIE. I like the pigeons. I saw a pigeon fly across the sky and when it crossed the clouds it was black but when it flew past the roofs it was white. It could fly as far as it liked but it never went further than Turf Lodge from what I could see.

I used to watch for that bird, the only white bird that wasn't a seagull.

He wasn't even the man they wanted, but they shot him; that made him the man they wanted.

You have to imagine the four of them. All men you'd look at twice one way or another. Michael, my husband, because he had that strong feel to him. You felt it in the back of your neck when he came in a room. People turned to look without knowing why. Davey, my brother now, you'd look again but you'd say, what's that wee boy doing in his Daddy's jacket. Nineteen and he looks more like nine, though they've put age in his eyes for him now. He's got old eyes now. Martin, Cassie's brother, you'd look and you'd cross the street in case he caught your eye and decided he didn't like the look of *you*, he's got the kind of eyebrows that chop short conversations, slamming a glower on his face like two fists hitting a table . . . and Joe, Cassie's husband. You'd look at him to see what the joke was, Joe's always laughing, Joe's always where the crack is.

Davey's in the Kesh. Martin's in the Kesh. Joe's in the Kesh . . . and Michael is dead.

They didn't really go round together, the four of them, just every odd Saturday they'd be in here playing cards till they were three of them broke and Joe stuffed with beer and winnings. Singing till they were too drunk to remember the words then waking and eating and drinking some more till they were drunk enough to make up their own. Sure it was a party they had. And Davey felt like a man and Martin smiled and Joe sang almost in tune and Michael would tell me he loved me over and over till he'd made a song out of that.

Sometimes he said he loved me when he'd no drink in him at all. Sometimes he even did that.

MARIE *finishes tidying, exits.*

DEIRDRE *comes into the empty room. She has her hair swept back, her face made up. She is wearing tight white jeans and a shiny white top. She has jewelry on. She looks stunning. She also looks about 21. She stands for a moment, admiring herself then wanders over to look at the portrait of Michael. She studies it, then almost leisurely reaches behind it and removes the money* CASSIE *has hidden there.*

DEIRDRE *exits.*

Scene Two

The Club.
This could be a community hall or an ancient warehouse but it has been
jazzed up with glitterballs and spots. The chairs and tables are cheap and
battered. There are double doors at the back of the room. MARIE, NORA
and CASSIE *have got themselves a table overlooking the small dance floor.*
There is a small stand like a lectern on one side of it. The place is crowded,
bright with the colours of the women's dresses and great misty clouds of
cigarette smoke whorling in the fans. CASSIE's *dress is quite revealing*
though not extravagantly so. It is silent. The three women are standing by
their chairs, heads bowed as if by a grave-side. No one moves. they speak in
whispers.

MARIE. I didn't know him.

CASSIE. There's that cramp again, in my leg, I'll wobble.

NORA. That's his aunty there, is it not? She shouldn't be here
   drinking sure she shouldn't.

MARIE. Can't put a face to him at all.

CASSIE. My *shoes*, a size too small and I've swelled with the heat.
   Oh God, don't let me fall off them.

NORA. His mother's sister-in-law's sister; it's close enough. She
   should be with that poor woman.

MARIE. Was he young?

CASSIE. Just a boy too.

NORA. Is that not a minute over?

MARIE. Is that not a minute now?

CASSIE. Can I get off my feet?

   There is a sudden burst of music and a loud buzz of talk. The women
   shout over this as they claim their seats with jackets and handbags.

MARIE. Did you get my ticket for the competition, Cassie?

CASSIE. I got us all ten.

NORA. Ten?

MARIE. Money to burn.

CASSIE. I'm feeling lucky.

MARIE. So it's a gin and lime and a black Russian for you, Nora?

NORA. No, I'll get these.

CASSIE. Sure I'll get them.

MARIE. No you're alright, I've my money in my hand. (*Waving a fiver at the waitress.*)

CASSIE. Let's have a kitty then, fiver in and start us with doubles, Marie.

MARIE. I can't catch her eye.

NORA. Did you know him then, the poor wee boy?

CASSIE. It was him with the dog.

NORA. At the chemist's?

CASSIE. His brother.

MARIE. Always seems such a long minute.

NORA. I was just in that chemist's today.

MARIE. I hate it. Never know what to fill my head with.

NORA. They still hadn't got my prescription in.

MARIE. I didn't know him. What can you fill your head with if you can't picture his face?

CASSIE. You'd know him if you saw him. Just nineteen, trying to grow a moustache like dust on a ledge.

NORA. His mother's youngest. The last one at home.

MARIE (*shivers*). I still can't see him. I just think of coffins.

NORA. She's all on her own now. All on her own.

CASSIE. Marie, will you hurry up getting that drink, it's the only nourishment I've got coming to me today. This is going to be the wildest of wild nights. I'm telling you Mummy, all the times I've been coming here, the best ones have always been when we've come on our own, just the three of us.

MARIE *is waving her money for the waitress again.*

She exits.

NORA. Remember the first we knew of what had happened to Michael was when they asked us to stand for him?

CASSIE. Marie had never been out of her house, never told a soul till we came in to her.

NORA. Oh, but he was well respected.

CASSIE. Just sitting by the fire and the fire dead for hours and the baby crying and crying . . .

NORA. They sang for him as well, do you remember?

CASSIE. Her just sitting there.

NORA. He's still missed; there's some men you don't forget.

CASSIE. He was popular, I'll say that for him.

NORA. He was.

MARIE *returns with two glasses for each of them balanced on a tray.*

NORA. Oh Marie, do you remember when my Sean took all that money off your Michael?

MARIE (*smiles*). Betting on a dog that never was.

NORA *turns to relate the story to* CASSIE *who doesn't display much interest, she's heard it.*

NORA. He had some terrible tall stories, your Daddy.

MARIE. He says, 'I know a dog can run up the side of a wall.' If he'd left it at a ten pound bet we'd've been alright . . .

NORA. Oh Sean could be bold.

MARIE. I can hear him yet. 'Now Michael,' he says, 'I wouldn't want to take your money.'

NORA. Egging him on . . .

MARIE. Did I tell you the plotting and planning that was spent on that idea? Grown men, sitting in our front room with cans and sandwiches and paper and pens and rulers, little scale drawings of walls, talk of alsatians and dobermans and greyhounds and wind speed and how if Sean was talking about a terrier then he was a liar for sure. They took it so seriously.

NORA. Well it was a two hundred pound bet by then. It was serious.

MARIE. The drinking was serious. There'd been some serious drinking when they all went out the back of the club and saw a little terrier dog jump a ten foot wall.

NORA (*shaking her head*). Two hundred pounds.

MARIE. It was worse Nora. That car we gave you was worth at least five hundred with its wheels on.

NORA. I don't know where they found that cat.

MARIE. I don't know who cut the tail off it but they should be ashamed of themselves.

NORA. And dressing it in my good mohair jumper. I never saw that jumper again.

MARIE. Well you wouldn't, the jumper and the cat were half way to Galway before anyone had even a quarter sobered up and looking no more like a terrier than they ever could unless you were looking through the bottom of a whisky glass. And when Michael found out he just laughed. That man's sense of humour nearly ruined us. Laughed himself black in the face and started plotting how to get that car back off your Sean.

NORA. We'd sold it by then.

MARIE. He had all these schemes . . . (*Quieter.*) never got to try them though.

NORA (*matching her tone*). And Sean dead himself just three months after . . .

Pause.

CASSIE. Are we going to drink to that, then?

MARIE. What?

CASSIE. The dear departed?

NORA. Cassie!

CASSIE. Well, are we going to drink to something?

MARIE (*laughs*). Come on then. (*Clinks her glass off* CASSIE's.)

CASSIE *raises hers.*

CASSIE. To the bold girls.

NORA. And who are they?

CASSIE. That's us.

NORA. There's only one bold girl here, Cassie Ryan, and she's broadcasting it to the world.

CASSIE. What do you mean?

NORA. What do you think I mean?

CASSIE. Well I don't know, Mummy, that's why I'm asking.

NORA. And you with your man inside.

CASSIE. And what about him?

NORA. What about you?

MARIE. Oh look do you see B.T. and that other boy looking over here? What's on their mind do you think?

NORA. Oh we're great entertainment tonight, Marie.

CASSIE. Mummy if there's something on your mind, would you just out and say it please?

MARIE (*looking out past the dance floor*). Oh here's Jimmy going to call out the numbers. Have you got your tickets, girls?

CASSIE *is still confronting a stony-faced* NORA.

CASSIE. Come on!

MARIE. Cassie, you've got them all in your bag there.

CASSIE. All what?

MARIE. Come on down, he's calling out the numbers.

CASSIE. Oh . . . right. (*She rummages in her bag.*)

MARIE. Come on, he's called one already.

NORA. What was that one Marie? I didn't hear him right.

MARIE. Ninety-six.

NORA. Have we got a ninety-six Cassie?

CASSIE (*spreading the tickets to look, sullen*). No.

MARIE. And . . . seventy-two.

NORA. Seventy-two Cassie?

CASSIE. No.

MARIE. Eh . . . wait a minute . . . Oh he's dropped the cards Nora!

NORA. Jimmy Dooley was on the whisky before he was weaned.

MARIE. Here we are . . . one hundred and three.

CASSIE (*picking out card*). One hundred and three, that's your ticket Marie.

MARIE. What!?

CASSIE. One hundred and three. Look.

MARIE. . . . That's not mine!

CASSIE. It is so, I got you the first ten.

NORA. Go on Marie, they're waiting on you!

MARIE. Oh no Nora, you take it!

CASSIE. Go *on*, Marie!

MARIE. Oh I hate standing out in front of everyone. (*Moves to cross to the dance floor, looks back.*) You'll shout the prices out to me?

CASSIE. Yes! Go *on*!

MARIE *goes to stand behind a little plinth on the dance floor, smiling round her nervously.* CASSIE *and* NORA *take a long swig of their drinks. They don't look at each other.*

NORA. Oh she's shaking. Look, we'll need to keep her right, Cassie.

CASSIE. So is it because I've no bra on, is that what's eating you?

NORA (*shock*). You've no bra on!

CASSIE. Well, where did you think I would fit it under this?

NORA. Cassie Ryan you're sitting here, bare-breasted in front of the whole town!

CASSIE. Well, you didn't notice did you?

NORA. I noticed that dress!

CASSIE. Good.

NORA. There's nothing good about it.

CASSIE. What's that? (*Peering.*) A Black and Decker drill? Ninety-five pounds, what do you say?

NORA. No . . . Fifty-nine pounds, ninety-nine.

CASSIE. Could be right.

CASSIE *shouts across to* MARIE *who is looking up at them anxiously.*

CASSIE. Fifty-nine, ninety-nine.

NORA *shows five, and three nines with her fingers.* MARIE *nods and starts writing on a big sheet of paper in front of her.*

CASSIE. Joe always liked this dress.

NORA. Joe isn't here, is he?

CASSIE. Oh so I should just get back in my box and wear bin liners till he's out should I?

NORA. You know there's been talk.

CASSIE. No I don't know, what talk?

NORA. Did she get it?

CASSIE *looks over at* MARIE. *She has displayed her price. Now crumples it.*

CASSIE. No . . . What talk?

MARIE *prepares a fresh sheet of paper.*

NORA. What's this coming now? (*Peering.*)

CASSIE. A tea set. What talk, Mummy?

NORA. Danny said one of the boys had words with him.

CASSIE *says nothing. She takes a long drink.*

NORA. That'd be thirty pounds or so, what do you think?

CASSIE *still says nothing.* NORA *mimes thirty at* MARIE. MARIE *nods and writes.*

NORA. So Danny says to me, 'Mummy, I know our Cassie isn't doing a line and so do you, but there's plenty will think she is.'

CASSIE. And what business is it of Danny's?

NORA. He's just looking out for you, Cassie.

CASSIE. And what business is it of the boys?

NORA. I should think they're thinking of Joe.

CASSIE. They might've thought of him before they let him take the rap for a job he wouldn't have had the brains to understand if they'd tattooed it on his wrist.

NORA. You're just determined to let the world think the worst of you, are you?

CASSIE. I don't care what the world thinks. (*Peers.*) Computer games. Eighteen pounds, ninety-five.

NORA. Twenty-five pounds.

CASSIE. Eighteen ninety-five, I've seen them in a catalogue. (*Shouts.*) Eighteen ninety-five. (*Mimes the numbers.*)

MARIE *writes.*

NORA. You're bringing shame on this family, Cassie.

CASSIE. Well I won't be the first.

NORA. What do you mean?

CASSIE. Our Martin was never too good at keeping his belt buckle fastened, was he?

NORA. Your brother was a good boy, the best boy a mother ever . . . !

CASSIE (*interrupts*). Well, you tell that to the wee girl in Turf Lodge.

MARIE *crumples another sheet of paper.*

CASSIE. Oh she just missed it!

NORA. That was not Martin's child.

CASSIE. Oh it just borrowed that nose and that red hair off another friend of the family did it? (*Peers.*) A magi-mix, oh it'd be great if she got that.

NORA. I asked her to her face, I said, if you can look me in the eye and swear by the Virgin that this is my grandchild I'll not see you short, just look me in the eye and tell me.

CASSIE. Forty-five pounds! Marie! (*Mimes.*) Forty-five pounds!

NORA. And all she said was, I'm not wanting your money, Mrs Ryan.

CASSIE. Do you know you never put a plate of food in front of me before he had his.

NORA. She was nothing but a wee hoor.

MARIE *holds up her sheet.*

CASSIE. Oh she's put eighty-nine ninety-nine. Oh Marie!

NORA. What has food got to do with it?

CASSIE. The only time you gave me food before him was when I was to serve him. I never *once* got my dinner before he'd his in his mouth. Not *once*.

NORA. What are you talking about Cassie?

MARIE. I've got it!

MARIE *waves at them excitedly.*

CASSIE. Oh Mummy! She's won the magi-mix!

MARIE *stands with her hands up in triumph then stares as* DEIRDRE *walks over the dance floor to her carrying her prize. There is ragged applause.* DEIRDRE *hands the big box over with a model's grin.*

MARIE. Thanks.

DEIRDRE *turns and smiles at the applause.*

MARIE *wanders to the side of the dance floor where* NORA *and* CASSIE *are waiting for her.*

CASSIE. Was that your white top, Marie?

MARIE. It looked like it. It looked like my earrings as well.

NORA. Did you not used to have a pair of white trousers like that, Marie?

MARIE. I did. They were exactly like that.

NORA. That wee girl is trouble.

CASSIE (*moving towards her*). And I'm going to find out what kind.

MARIE. Cassie, wait. (*Catching* CASSIE'*s arm*). She's not going anywhere.

CASSIE. Marie, when will you stand up for yourself? You're a mug! That girl's making a fool of you!

MARIE. And when I get the chance I'll hear what she has to say but it won't be here with half the town hearing it as well Cassie!

CASSIE *hesitates.*

NORA. Well I'm dry, I think we should get ourselves another drink.

MARIE. That's a great idea, Nora. What'll you have?

NORA. No, no, we'll use the kitty, like before.

CASSIE. I'll get them.

MARIE. No, I'll do it, Cassie.

CASSIE. *I'll get them.*

MARIE *and* NORA *sit down.*

Lighting change.

CASSIE. My Mummy taught me how to raise my family. How to love them, how to spoil them. Spoil the wee girls with housework and reproaches, the length of their skirts and the colour of their lips: how they sit, how they slouch, how they don't give their fathers peace, how they talk, how they talk back, how they'll come to no good if they carry on like that. They're bold and bad and broken at fourteen but you love them as you love yourself . . . that's why you hurt them so much.

Ruin the boys, tell them they're noisy and big and bold and their boots are too muddy, ('Clear that mess up for me Cassie.') Tell them to leave their fathers in peace and come to their Mummy for a cuddle, tell them they'll always be your own wee man, always your own bold wee man and you love them better than you love their Daddy, you love them best of all . . . that's why they hurt you so much.

Lighting change. There is dance music playing behind the talk. CASSIE *picks up a tray with another double round on it and moves back to the table.* NORA *is in the middle of a story.*

NORA. That's your woman up the street came to me crying and sobbing: her man lifted, her kids running wild, the phone and the electric off and on again as often as she could drag herself up the town to argue with them. 'Oh Nora,' she says, 'Nora I don't know what to do.' I says 'Well Sheila, for a start you could wash those front windows of yours and when you've done that you better do the curtains as well for the whole street will be able to see the colour of them then.' 'Oh Nora,' she says, 'I'm living in hell, I'm just living in hell.' 'Well,' I says, 'if this is hell it could do with a lick of paint and I've a couple of tins left over from my bedroom I could lend you.'

Oh but she never stirred herself to get it done. Her kids are just wild wee hoods, took that paint and painted her lawn roseblush white, took the magnolia and went out painting F . . . (*Nods 'you know the word I mean'.*) the I.R.A. on all the walls, but you could hardly read it. That's the beauty of that magnolia, it'll blend in with just anything. (*Takes a drink.*)

MARIE (*drinking*). Thanks, Cassie. You did a lovely job in your bedroom with that magnolia, Nora.

NORA. It was nice, it was, while it lasted.

CASSIE. That was the damp brought it all down.

MARIE. No!

CASSIE. Oh, the paper's hanging off the wall in there.

NORA. Still I'll get my front room nice again.

MARIE. It'll look great with that material you showed me, sure it will.

NORA. Oh but I'll never have my bamboo suite again. Do you remember my bamboo suite, Marie?

MARIE. It was lovely.

CASSIE. Are you coming up dancing Marie?

MARIE. Oh but there's no one else up yet.

CASSIE. So?

NORA. And I had those big potted ferns, remember, just like I saw it in the magazine.

CASSIE. Mummy, come dancing with me.

NORA. I'm not dancing, Cassie what do you think this is, a wedding? Oh Marie, it just sickened the heart out of me when that suite got broke.

CASSIE. Oh your man's still watching us. I think he's got his eye on you Mummy.

CASSIE *starts dancing in her chair to the music.*

NORA. Sit at peace, Cassie. Now your wee boy, he went round it didn't he? Comes in my door like he's Ireland's best chance at the Olympics, right through the room and he says 'Sorry Mrs,' he does, nice soft wee voice and him running for his life. But he runs *round* my lovely bamboo suite and jumps out the window.

CASSIE *starts to sing along with the music.*

NORA. And then the Brits are through and do they not run over it? Boots like anvils, they were wearing my suite before I'd time to open my mouth. And then kicking and swearing and trying to pull their feet out of it . . .

CASSIE. Marie knows, Mummy, you told her half an hour after it happened and you've never stopped telling her.

NORA. Cassie stop wriggling about.

CASSIE. I'm just giving your man there something to look at.

NORA. 'Course I tried to stop them . . .

MARIE. Oh your poor ribs.

NORA. Well I thought this one looked like he'd a bit of sense, Marie.

CASSIE *snorts.*

NORA. Well he was older than the rest, you know, they're just young animals but he looked like Michael Aspel.

CASSIE. Do you not love this song Marie?

NORA. So I says, 'You'll not wreck my house son,' 'course he keeps coming so I says . . .

CASSIE *joins in mimicking her tone.*

BOTH. 'Oh but you'll not hit a woman.'

MARIE. That was an awful dig he gave you.

NORA. I'd those ribs taped for months. Oh but my bamboo suite, Marie. Two hundred pound and I'd only had it a week. I'd saved, ten months it took me, sliding a note out of Sean's pocket every time he was too puddled to know how many fivers he'd poured down his throat.

CASSIE. Poor Daddy.

NORA. Easy to see you didn't have the carpet to mop up after him.

CASSIE. Well I'm up for a dance myself.

CASSIE *gets up and crosses to the dance floor, starts to dance.* MARIE *and* NORA *gape at her.*

NORA. Holy mother of God, what is she doing!?

MARIE. I don't know, Nora.

NORA. Oh Marie get up with her!

MARIE. What!

NORA. We can't leave her on her own there, performing for the whole town!

CASSIE*'s dancing becomes more extravagant.*

NORA. Marie!

MARIE (*getting up*). Oh Nora I don't even like dancing.

MARIE *crosses over and joins* CASSIE *who beams, applauding her.* MARIE *starts shuffling cautiously from foot to foot.*

CASSIE. I'm telling you this is a great diet Marie, you really feel the benefit of the gin.

MARIE. Well maybe you should go easy now, Cassie.

CASSIE. Oh I'm a long way from lockjawed.

NORA *is beckoning at them frantically.*

MARIE. Your Mummy's asking us to come and sit down.

CASSIE. The song's just started.

MARIE *glances round nervously.*

CASSIE. What? Are they all watching us?

MARIE. They are.

CASSIE. Let them.

MARIE (*shaky laugh*). Feel a bit like the last meat pie in the shop out here, Cassie.

CASSIE. Well let them stay hungry. They can just look and think what they like.

MARIE. Cassie, what's wrong?

CASSIE. Oh I'm just bad Marie, didn't you know?

MARIE. No. I never knew that.

CASSIE. You remember that wee girl in Turf Lodge, the one Martin couldn't get enough of? She was a decent wee girl. She's bad now. Ask my Mummy.

MARIE. Have you had words?

CASSIE. He's out in less than a year, Marie.

MARIE. *Martin!?*

CASSIE. Joe.

MARIE. I know. It'll be alright Cassie.

They stop dancing, they look at each other.

It'll be alright, Cassie.

CASSIE. I tell you Marie I can't stand the smell of him. The greasy, grinning, beer bellied *smell* of him. And he's winking away about all he's been dreaming of, wriggling his fat fingers over me like I'm a poke of chips . . . I don't want him in the house in my *bed, Marie.*

MARIE. You'll cope.

CASSIE. Oh I'm just bad. I am.

MARIE. Don't. Don't say that about yourself.

CASSIE. I'll go crazy.

MARIE. I won't let you. You won't get a chance Cassie, I'll just be across the road, I won't let you go crazy. You just see what you'll get if you try it.

Slowly CASSIE *smiles at her.* MARIE *puts a hand on her arm.*

MARIE. Now will you come and sit down?

The doors at the back bang open, hard white light floods everything.

Oh Jesus it's a raid!

All the women freeze, legs apart, arms raised as if they're being searched. The same hard light stays on them.

DEIRDRE. Brick in your hand, hard in your hand, hit skin and it'll burst open and bleed, hit bones and they'll break, you can hear them break, hear the snap.

MARIE. Why are you asking my name, you know my name.

DEIRDRE. Smell the petrol, lungs full of the smell of it. Blow it out again and you'll be breathing fire. Throw fire in a bottle and it runs everywhere like it's water.

MARIE. Everyone know where I live.

DEIRDRE. Get a car, fast car, drive it till its wheels burn, leave it smoking, burning, exploding.

MARIE. Everyone knows all about me, don't they? So what do you want to know? What do you want?

DEIRDRE. The whole town's a prison, smash chunks off the walls 'cause we're all in a prison.

Lighting change.

CASSIE *running up to the table.*

CASSIE. Mummy are you alright?

NORA. I'm fine, I was just thinking about getting another drink here.

CASSIE. I was sure you would hit someone again.

NORA. I won't say I didn't think about it. They searched me Cassie!

CASSIE. I saw. I thought you'd give her a swipe in the gub.

NORA. Terrible cold hands she had.

CASSIE. Here where's my drink?

NORA. I gave it to that big peeler there.

CASSIE. What? What did you do that for?

NORA. Well he was leaning on that table over just there shouting in Bobby's face and I'm looking down and here's his socks.

MARIE. Where?

NORA. On his feet, in his boots. Pale blue socks, you could see the whole back of his heel there, I don't think his boots were fitting too well. So your drink was just on the edge here Cassie, (*Demonstrates with empty glass.*) so I just gave it a wee nudge. (*Knocks it over.*) Poured in as neat as you please. Oh he was desperate angry. I just stared him down.

CASSIE *starts to laugh.*

CASSIE. Oh you're doing your bit for the struggle alright Mummy.

MARIE. Give them all wet socks!

NORA. Here I'll get you another one Cassie.

NORA *waves for a waitress.*

CASSIE. Should've known they'd be in tonight.

MARIE. They're saying it was a break-out from the Crumlin Road.

CASSIE. Is that what was happening?

MARIE. That's what I heard up at the bar there. Maybe three of them got away.

CASSIE. Oh it'll be road blocks the rest of the night then.

NORA *(calls)*. Can we get a drink here?

DEIRDRE *comes up to their table with a tray. They stare at her.*

DEIRDRE. What're you having?

Pause.

MARIE. Well the jeans don't fit anymore so they're yours and welcome and I never was desperate fond of that top so you can have it, but those earrings were a present from my husband so I'll be having them back.

DEIRDRE *fingers the earrings for a minute then unfastens them and hands them over.*

MARIE. Thank you. Now it's a Black Russian a gin and lime and a pernod and blackcurrant.

DEIRDRE *nods, turns on her heel.*

CASSIE. Well! Marie!

MARIE. What?

CASSIE. I see Oxfam's come to Andersonstown. Any time we want a new outfit we'll know where to come!

MARIE. Would you've had her strip where she stood?

CASSIE. I'd've had an explanation out of her!

MARIE. She was probably wanting new clothes.

CASSIE. And wasn't she lucky that Mother Teresa here was ready to hand them over!

NORA. You should've said something to her Marie.

MARIE *just shakes her head.*

CASSIE. You're not letting her away with it altogether?

MARIE. She's a look about her.

NORA *and* CASSIE *look at each other.*

NORA. What do you mean?

MARIE. I don't know. I don't know what it's got me thinking of but she's a look about her.

CASSIE. She's not a ghost Marie.

NORA. She's a thieving wee hood.

MARIE. It's like she's looking for something.

CASSIE. Trouble.

MARIE *just shakes her head again.*

NORA. I don't know, Marie. (*Lighting up a fag.*) Cassie's right, she's making a mug out of you. Oh, will you look at that.

NORA *shows them her hand which is trembling violently.*

CASSIE. It's the D.T.'s.

NORA. It's the R.U.C.

CASSIE. Oh don't let it get to you.

NORA. So let's see your hand!

CASSIE *holds hers out, it is also shaking. They both laugh.*

CASSIE. It's our life style Mummy, we'll have to change our life style.

NORA. Is that right?

CASSIE. We're living too fast so we are, it's the same problem the film stars have, we'll burn ourselves out with all the excitement.

NORA. Me and Joan Collins both.

CASSIE. You can write articles for the women's magazines, 'Stop and Search, would your manicure stand up to the *closest* inspection?'

NORA. Let's see Marie's hand there.

MARIE *is lost in her own thoughts.* CASSIE *pulls her hand out. They study it.*

CASSIE. Steady as a rock.

NORA. Ah she's got a clear conscience.

CASSIE. Either that or she's in a coma, are you with us Marie?

MARIE. Hmmm?

NORA. Wired up but not plugged in.

MARIE. Are you reading my palm?

CASSIE. I will if you like.

DEIRDRE *is approaching their table with a tray of drinks.* CASSIE *glances up at her, then bends theatrically over* MARIE's *hand.*

CASSIE. Oh, you're going to meet a dark stranger Marie, all in white but with a black wee heart. You better watch out for she'll thieve the clothes off your back but you'll not have peace till you nail the wee snake down and ask her what she's up to.

DEIRDRE (*handing out the drinks correctly*). Black Russian . . . gin and lime . . . pernod and blackcurrant.

CASSIE. So what about you Deirdre, if it is Deirdre?

DEIRDRE. It is.

MARIE. Cassie . . .

CASSIE. I hope you've not taken a fancy to anything else that's caught your eye, like my handbag.

DEIRDRE *stares at her for a minute.*

DEIRDRE. It was in a car. A blue car.

CASSIE. What?

DEIRDRE. That I saw you before.

CASSIE. You're a lying hoor, you never saw anything.

DEIRDRE. With a man. With him. With . . .

CASSIE *lunges at her before she can get another word out.*

CASSIE. You bastarding wee hoor! Come here till I get the skin off you!

CASSIE *attacks* DEIRDRE *as* NORA *and* MARIE *try to pull her off.*

NORA. Cassie!

MARIE. Cassie *leave* it!

CASSIE. I'll finish her! I will!

DEIRDRE *shields her head and face but makes no move to defend herself.* NORA *and* MARIE *manage to pull* CASSIE *back.*

CASSIE. I'll have the tongue out of you! Then we'll see what tales you can tell!

NORA. Marie, get you outside with her, I'll see to a taxi.

MARIE (*trying to pull* CASSIE *away*). Come *on* Cassie.

CASSIE. I'll finish her! I will!

MARIE *drags her off.* NORA *watches* DEIRDRE *as she straightens up.*

NORA. Well your Mummy didn't do much of a job with you, did she? (*Calls.*) B.T., we're needing a taxi, son.

DEIRDRE *exits.*

Lighting change. NORA *stands for a moment.*

NORA. Oh I could say plenty I could. I've poems in my head as good as anyone. I could talk so it'd burn the wee hairs out your nose. I could. But will you tell me what the use is in talking? . . . I've a man to see about fifteen yards of pale peach polyester mix. That's what I'm doing.

Lights down.

Scene Three

Outside the club. Bare wasteground. Moonlight. MARIE *and* CASSIE *are sitting on the ground, watching the sky.*

MARIE. This is ruining my good dress, Cassie.

CASSIE. It is not.

MARIE. It is so; I can feel the damp through the back of it.

CASSIE. That is not ruining your best dress.

MARIE. So you know what my bum's feeling better than I do?

CASSIE. You are ruining *my* best dress that you've had on loan since last Easter.

MARIE. Oh . . . well I shouldn't think you'll want it back now.

CASSIE. Will you look at that. (*To the sky.*)

MARIE. Nearly all gone now.

CASSIE. Do you know what that is?

MARIE. Well of course I do. It's an eclipse.

CASSIE. It's the shadow of the earth. That's our very own shadow swallowing up all the light of the moon.

MARIE. So where's the sun?

CASSIE. Australia.

MARIE. They won't be getting an eclipse then?

CASSIE. No, they'll be getting a suntan.

MARIE. Why did you go for that wee girl like that, Cassie?

CASSIE. Belfast gets an extra dark night and they get a suntan. Do you ever think there's no justice in the world at all?

MARIE. What did she say to you?

CASSIE. Well they'll all get skin cancer so we'll have the last laugh. Wet and wrinkly as feet in a bath but at least we've *got* skin.

MARIE. *Cassie.*

CASSIE. You heard what she said.

MARIE. I didn't hear any harm in it.

CASSIE. Bastarding wee hoor's been spying on me.

MARIE. Have you been seeing someone Cassie?

CASSIE *doesn't answer for a minute; she looks at* MARIE, *hesitating, then she drops her eyes.*

CASSIE. No.

MARIE. Well I'm just saying I wouldn't blame you if you had Cassie, I wouldn't blame you at all.

CASSIE. What about the sacred bonds of marriage? What about my martyred wee Joe, pining for me in his prison cell?

MARIE. I'm not saying you wouldn't be doing wrong, but it's wrong that's been done to you often enough. Sure there's worse things you could be doing.

CASSIE. Marie Donnelly I'm surprised at you.

MARIE. Oh I'm just the wee prude amn't I? Cleaner than a prayer book me.

CASSIE. You're drunk.

MARIE. I am not. Just . . . well if you are Cassie, you need to be more careful.

CASSIE. If I was, Marie, you'd all know for sure. You can't keep a secret in this place. It's like trying to keep a snake in a matchbox. Oh they'll have me tarred and feathered before the week's out.

MARIE. Don't joke about it, Cassie.

CASSIE. Who's joking?

MARIE. I don't know how you coped with all Joe's carry on. I don't. You were the martyr there, Cassie.

CASSIE. It gave me peace.

MARIE. No but I couldn't have stood that, just the lying to you, the *lying* to you. I used to say to Michael, 'If you go with someone else it'll tear the heart out of me but tell me, just tell me the truth 'cause I'd want to know, I couldn't bear not to know.' He never did though. So I never worried.

CASSIE. No.

MARIE. Do you know he was like my best friend. Well sure you're my best friend but if a man can be that kind of friend to you he was to me, could tell each other anything. That's what I miss most. The crack. The *sharing*.

CASSIE. Marie . . . (*Stops.*)

MARIE. What?

CASSIE. Aw Jesus I hate this place!

CASSIE *gets up, kicking the ground.*

MARIE. We'll get a weekend in Donegal again soon, the three of us and the kids. Sure we could all do with a break.

CASSIE. I'm leaving.

MARIE. What?

CASSIE *says nothing.*

MARIE. What do you mean, you're leaving?

CASSIE. Do you know she gives me a tenner before every visit to go up town and buy fruit for them, 'poor Martin' and 'poor Joe'. That's all she's allowed to give them, all she can spoil them with, fruit, so she wants them to have grapes and melons and things you've never heard of and shapes you wouldn't know how to bite into. I'll bring her home something that looks and smells like the Botanic Gardens and she'll sniff it and stroke it like it was her favourite son himself, 'stead of his dinner . . . And I'll have three four pounds safe in my pocket, saved, sure she doesn't have a clue of the price of kiwi fruit.

I've two hundred pounds saved. I'm going, Marie.

MARIE. Going where?

CASSIE. It's desperate, isn't it? Thirty-five years old and she's stealing from her Mummy's purse. Well I thought about asking the broo for a relocation grant or something you know, but it seems to me all they can offer you is the straight swap of one hell hole for another.

MARIE. You talking about a holiday?

CASSIE. I'm talking about getting out of here.

MARIE. Cassie, where could you go with two kids for two hundred pounds?

CASSIE *says nothing for a moment.*

CASSIE. Sure you'd need thousands wouldn't you? Enough to buy yourself into a different country and a different kind of house and a different kind of life altogether. Thousands. (*Shakes her head.*) But I'm going.

MARIE. Oh Cassie you don't mean it.

CASSIE *just looks at her.*

MARIE. That would kill your Mummy.

CASSIE. I could leave her the children, Teresa turns to her before she turns to me and Brian's getting all the washing and polishing and wee cups of ice cream to keep him smiling that Martin ever got.

MARIE. But you couldn't leave your children. No . . . You couldn't leave your children.

CASSIE. Why not, Marie? Why not? Amn't I just a black hole of sins already? Why not?

MARIE. But . . . you *couldn't*. It'd eat you up missing them.

CASSIE. I'm getting chewed and swallowed and eaten alive by all that I'm wanting and can't have whatever I do. It'd be cheaper to leave them, easier . . . you're just across the road.

MARIE. But . . . Cassie.

CASSIE (*sighs*). No. I can't leave the children.

MARIE. You wouldn't want to.

CASSIE. Oh Marie . . . (*Sighs again.*) Here's our taxi. Let's get those wains back to their own beds.

They exit. DEIRDRE enters, looking over her shoulder. She is clutching a few bags, handbags and a carrier. She starts to empty them out, searching methodically for valuables which she pockets swiftly, pausing to try a lipstick on the back of her hand before hurling it disdainfully away. She rummages in the carrier bag, pulling out a couple of cans of beer and a knife, a switch blade. She stares at it wonderingly, then flicks out the blade. She grins. She looks back in the bag. She pulls out a swathe of material, a remnant, fifteen yards of shiny, peach polyester. DEIRDRE stares at it then flicks the roll so it unravels at her feet. She looks at the broad, smooth stretch of material then starts to slash at it, ripping it, trampling it till she's breathless. She stops, panting.

Lights down.

Scene Four

MARIE's house, later that night. CASSIE is slouched in a chair. NORA slightly more upright in another. They have fresh drinks in their hands.

CASSIE. So the thing of it is, I wouldn't know how to do it.

NORA. Where's Marie?

CASSIE. She's feeding the birds.

NORA. What?! It's pitch black out there.

CASSIE. She's a flock of owls come in special.

NORA. Is she alright?

CASSIE. Was she ever? No, she's worried she'll not be out of her bed to give the wee sparrows their crusts first thing; you wouldn't want them to go hungry would you?

MARIE *comes in carrying an empty plate.*

NORA. What've you been doing Marie?

MARIE. Just . . . (*Embarrassed.*) I was just throwing some scraps out for the birds there.

CASSIE. She wouldn't tread on a spider if she found it in her shoe.

MARIE. You'll take a sandwich? (*Crossing to the kitchen.*)

NORA. If you're making one Marie, thank you, I'll be needing to get to my bed soon. What time is it?

MARIE. After four.

NORA. What a night. He promised me that remnant, it was as good as money down.

CASSIE. She wouldn't squash a caterpillar if she found it in her salad and here's me talking about murder.

MARIE (*pausing in sandwich-making*). What?

NORA. She's just talking rubbish, Marie. Months I've been planning how to make over that front room. Months.

CASSIE. First I thought of ground glass, but how do you grind it? Put it in a tea towel and hit it with a rolling pin, under your heel on the stone step? However you did it the bits were so big he'd never think it was gravy granules.

NORA. She'd have you believing her, wouldn't she Marie?

CASSIE. Then I thought, stab him. Chop the vegetables, slice the bread, cut the bastard's throat . . . but there's a mountain of fry-ups and beer and other flab to get your knife through and who knows if he's a heart to be stabbed in at all?

MARIE. Pickle with your cheese, Cassie?

CASSIE. Thanks. So then I hit upon the perfect method: wait till he's drunk, dead drunk, blind drunk, drunk so he weeps for his Mummy and wets the bed . . . and I wouldn't have long waiting . . . take a pillow, put it on his face and sit on it. It might not kill him but at least it'd stop him snoring.

MARIE (*handing it to her*). Here's your sandwich.

CASSIE. He farts as well. Thanks.

NORA. Listen to her and wasn't she desperate to marry the man?

CASSIE. I was desperate to marry David Essex as well. My brains hadn't grown in yet.

NORA. And him with his own business and good money coming in. There's plenty would've been glad to be in your shoes, Cassie.

CASSIE (*kicking her own shoes off*). They can have them, anytime they like.

NORA. I don't know what you thought marriage would be, but you should've learned by your age. You've a job to do bringing up that family and making a decent home for you and your man, so get on with it.

CASSIE. I'll start crocheting a new house for us tomorrow.

NORA. And he never lifted a finger to her, Marie. Not once.

CASSIE. Oh I should've thanked him for that should I? Thank you Joe for not taking the poker to me every Saturday.

NORA. Well you should know what it could've been like. You of all people should've been able to see when you were well off.

CASSIE. What that's supposed to mean?

MARIE. Does anyone want some fruit loaf?

NORA. As if you didn't know.

MARIE. I'll get some crisps out, we can have crisps with our drinks.

CASSIE. No, I don't know.

NORA. Because you don't want to know, you never did.

MARIE *pauses on her way back to the kitchen, looking nervously from one to the other.*

NORA. Not even when you saw it with your own eyes.

CASSIE *doesn't say anything.*

NORA. I would say to him, 'Would you hit your own wife in front of your own wains?' Sure I never got any answer at all but bruises. Sean was never much for conversation.

CASSIE *(low voice).* That hardly ever happened.

NORA. That happened every time he had enough drink in him.

CASSIE. You should've left him alone.

NORA. Oh right, I shouldn't have thrown myself in the way of his fists like that.

CASSIE. I couldn't sleep for you nagging on and on at him, that stupid wee shrill complaining, complaining, on and on.

NORA. She'd come down in the morning, Marie, and find me crying on the floor with the bruises going black on my face and all she'd say was, 'Have you been upsetting my Daddy again?' Go and fix herself a cup of tea.

CASSIE. He never beat you that bad. You'd all of us terrified with your squealing and carrying on.

NORA. Eight years old, Marie, and all I saw on her face was hatred, of me. Of *me*. There's something wrong with this girl's heart.

CASSIE. He was the gentlest man! The gentlest man if you'd just given him peace!

NORA. It was down to my Martin to stand up for his own Mother; he'd come to me, crying worse than I was, 'I'll get big soon Mummy,' he'd say, 'I'll beat him back for you.'

CASSIE. And didn't he get big enough to up and kill him! Your precious Martin put my Daddy in his grave!

NORA. That's a black-faced lie!

CASSIE. Him with his heart! He hadn't the strength left to get out of the bath himself but I never saw you lift him!

NORA. I couldn't get near him for his own wee girl combing his hair and singing him songs when she should've been at the school!

CASSIE. He was fifty and he was an old man!

NORA. It was the drink that did it to him!

CASSIE. And here's his own son pushing him flat on his back like he was a dog you're saying's too old to get fed anymore!

NORA. Sean had thrown his dinner at me!

CASSIE. He missed!

NORA. He would've killed me if he could!

MARIE. You'll wake the children.

NORA and CASSIE fall silent. MARIE goes to the kitchen, opens some crisps, puts them in a bowl, brings them out and sets them down. The other two women stare at their drinks.

CASSIE. I never hated you.

NORA scrubs one fierce hand over her eyes but gives no sign she's heard.

CASSIE. I just wanted you to make it happen different.

NORA. Well you'll need to go to some other place where they make the world different, Cassie.

CASSIE. Well so I will.

NORA. You do that.

CASSIE. I will. I'm leaving.

NORA. Though it seems to me there's not a place in the world that is different.

CASSIE. Well I'll write and tell you.

NORA. Oh she's got her flight booked, Marie.

CASSIE. Tell her, Marie.

MARIE. It's not for me to tell her, Cassie.

CASSIE. Mummy, I've two hundred pounds saved and I'm getting out.

NORA. Oh.

No one says anything else for a second.

So you've got yourself a flat?

CASSIE. No. I'm leaving Belfast.

NORA. What?

CASSIE. I'm getting on a ferry and I'm getting out.

NORA. What are you saying to me, Cassie?

CASSIE. How many ways do you want me to say it!

Pause.

NORA. Well, where are you going!?

CASSIE. I'll see where I get to. I'm telling you though I'm not going to be one of those that go out on one boat and come home on the next with their luck all spent. I'm leaving, Mummy.

NORA. And what about your children?

CASSIE. They'll be better off out of here.

NORA. Are you going to just tear them out by the roots and drag them along after you?

CASSIE. No . . . I . . .

NORA. To live God knows where on two hundred pound?

CASSIE. I'll send for them . . . (*Catching* MARIE's *eye*.) Oh don't look at me Marie.

NORA. Oh don't come it with your tall tales again, Cassie. Two hundred pounds indeed.

CASSIE. Oh is it proof you're wanting? Here then.

CASSIE *gets up and goes to Michael's picture.*

MARIE. Cassie what are you doing?

CASSIE *feels behind it, stops then starts running her hand frantically over the back of the picture.*

MARIE. What are you doing to Michael!?

CASSIE *pulls it off the wall and looks at the back of it. She stares at it for a minute then turns to* MARIE.

CASSIE. Where is it?

MARIE. What?

CASSIE. My money. Where'd you put it Marie?

MARIE. I never touched a penny of yours, Cassie!

CASSIE. You were the only one knew I had it.

MARIE. I never knew you'd hidden it up the back of Michael!

CASSIE. I had to put it through here; have you seen the way she dusts? (*Points at* NORA.)

MARIE. Well I never touched your money, Cassie.

CASSIE. Oh Jesus, someone's lifted it.

CASSIE collapses back into her chair, still clutching Michael's picture.

They've taken my money off me!

CASSIE bows her head. She seems to be about to cry. NORA *and* MARIE *look at each other.* NORA *crosses to her.*

NORA. Cassie?

CASSIE shakes her head. NORA *hesitates a moment.*

NORA. Och you're not crying, are you?

CASSIE just looks at her.

NORA. Well, what age are you to be making up daydreams and spoiling your face crying for them. Come on, now.

NORA pats briskly at CASSIE's shoulder, CASSIE *knocks her hand away.*

NORA. Well you're not going anywhere, Cassie Ryan. That's clear as daylight.

CASSIE (*quiet*). I'm going anyway, money or no money.

NORA. But your home's here! Your family's here!

CASSIE. Yes. It is.

They stare at each other for a few seconds.

NORA. And what I feel goes for nothing, does it?

CASSIE. What do you feel, Mummy? For me? What have you got left?

NORA turns away from her, shaking. MARIE *takes a step towards her but before she can get there* NORA *turns, struggling to look bright.*

NORA. Well . . . thanks for the sandwich Marie, but we'll not be troubling you further; you must be desperate for your bed.

CASSIE (*still staring at* NORA). Can I get another drink, Marie?

MARIE *hesitates again, looking between them.*

NORA (*pleading*). Cassie . . .

CASSIE. Good night, Mummy.

CASSIE *looks away from her.* NORA *draws herself up.*

NORA. Oh you'll be telling me a different tale in the morning! There's no end to your wild tales, Cassie! There's no end to them, Marie!

NORA *snatches up her drink and takes an angry gulp.*

And I'd it all to do. I'd it all to put up with! Are you hearing me?

CASSIE *doesn't look at her.*

NORA *takes another gulp.*

He's lost my remnant, Marie. He's lost it. I'd all the money saved, as good as paid. It's gone he says, gone. I'll never find a colour like that again. Months I'd been dreaming of the glow that would give my front room. Months. And he's lost it. I'll never have it the way I want it now. Never. (NORA *is getting tearful in her turn.*) My lovely wee room. It could be lovely, couldn't it Marie?

MARIE. You'll get it right Nora.

NORA. Well where will I ever find a colour like that again? Tell me that? (*Waits for a response.*) Cassie? I'm asking you!

CASSIE *looks up at her.*

CASSIE. Good night, Mummy.

NORA *stares at her for a moment, then she nods.*

NORA. Well I'm going up the town tomorrow. I'm just going to go up the town and buy a piece of what I want. I'll get credit. I'll give them a false address and I'll get credit and I'll have my loose covers. And if you don't want to come and help choose them, Cassie, you needn't sit on them.

NORA *exits.*

MARIE *puts the gin bottle down in front of* CASSIE. CASSIE *helps herself to another drink.*

MARIE (*quiet*). It'll tear the heart out of her, Cassie.

CASSIE. Mummy's heart is made of steel. She had to grow it that way.

MARIE *reaches over and takes Michael's picture. She goes and rehangs it carefully.*

CASSIE. There's a waitress up that club will be walking round without her hair tomorrow if I can find her.

MARIE. You don't know it was her. There's people in and out of here all the time.

CASSIE. Who else would it be?

MARIE. Well . . . if she's thieving round the club there'll be others sort her out before you do.

MARIE *steps back to admire the picture.*

CASSIE. How do you stand it here, Marie?

MARIE. Sure where else would I go?

CASSIE. How do you keep that smile on your face?

MARIE. Super-glue.

CASSIE. There's not one piece of bitterness in you, is there?

MARIE. Oh Cassie.

CASSIE. You see, you're good. And I'm just wicked.

MARIE. Aye you're a bold woman altogether.

CASSIE. Is it hard being good?

MARIE. I took lessons.

CASSIE. Well, tell me what you've got to smile about Marie, because I'm sure I can't see it.

MARIE. I've a lot to be thankful of. I've my kids, a job, a nice wee house and I can still pay for it.

CASSIE. You've two wee boys growing out of their clothes faster than you can get them new ones, a part-time job licking envelopes for a wage that wouldn't keep a budgie and three red bills on your mantelpiece there.

MARIE. That's what's great about a Saturday out with you Cassie, you just know how to look at the bright side of things, don't you?

CASSIE. Well just tell me how you can keep filling that kettle and making folk tea without pouring it over their head?

MARIE. Ah well you see, I'm a mug.

CASSIE. I think you are.

MARIE. I didn't marry Joe, but.

CASSIE. No. You did not. That mug was me.

MARIE. See Cassie, I've had better times with Michael than a lot of women get in their whole lives with a man.

CASSIE. And that keeps you going?

MARIE. It's a warming kind of thought.

CASSIE (*holds out her arms to Michael's picture. Sings*). Thanks . . . for the memories.

MARIE. Oh Cassie.

CASSIE. That doesn't work, Marie. I've tried to keep myself warm that way. Find some man with good hands and a warm skin and wrap him round you to keep the rain off; you'll be damp in the end anyway.

MARIE. Cassie, don't talk like that; you know you've not done half the wild things you make out.

CASSIE. Not a quarter of what I've wanted to Marie, but enough to know it doesn't work. Grabbing onto some man because he smells like excitement, he smells like escape. They can't take you anywhere except into the back seat of their car. They're all the same.

MARIE. If that's what you think of them that'll be all you'll find.

CASSIE *gets up to stand, looking at Michael.*

CASSIE. They are *all* the same, Marie.

MARIE. No.

CASSIE. *No*, not *Michael*. (*Sarcastic*.) Wasn't he just the perfect man, the perfect saint of a man.

MARIE. He was no saint.

CASSIE. He was not.

MARIE. I never said he was a saint.

CASSIE. Not much perfect about him.

MARIE. We cared about each other! We were honest with each other!

CASSIE. Honest!?

MARIE. We were. He was a good man!

CASSIE. Good!? He was a lying worm like every one of them!

Pause.

MARIE. I think you should go home, Cassie.

CASSIE. So he told you all about it did he? All the times he made a fool of you to your face?

MARIE. Just go now.

CASSIE. I don't believe you could have kept that smile on your face Marie, not if he was honestly telling you what he was up to.

MARIE. Cassie . . .

CASSIE. Making a fool of you with all those women.

Pause.

MARIE. I heard the stories. Of course I heard them.

CASSIE. Did you, though?

MARIE. He was a great-looking man. He was away a lot. There were bound to be stories.

CASSIE. There were books of them, Marie.

MARIE. But if there'd been any truth in them Michael would've told me himself.

CASSIE. Oh *Marie*!

MARIE. That's trust Cassie!

CASSIE. That's *stupidity*, Marie. You haven't the sense of a hen with its head off!

MARIE. Michael would no more lie to me than you would, Cassie.

CASSIE. Well we both did! That's what I'm telling you Marie! We were both lying to you for years!

MARIE *freezes where she is.*

CASSIE. Ah Jesus . . .

She moves to take another swig of her drink. MARIE *doesn't move.*

CASSIE *can't look at her.*

CASSIE. He started it but I followed it through. That was before Joe was lifted. Even the smell of *him* was bringing my dinner up on me. I felt like I was trapped in this little black box and it was falling in on me. Michael was a window. Just a bit of excitement you know? He was exciting, Michael . . . Marie?

MARIE *hasn't moved.*

CASSIE. I'm going to tell you this, Marie. I'm tired of keeping it from you. I'm tired of keeping the smile on your face.

I knew it was bad. I knew lying to you was worse. I wanted to tell you . . . but I've been telling you for four years and you wouldn't hear me. Are you hearing me now Marie?

MARIE *still hasn't moved.*

CASSIE. We'd just go out in his car, that old blue one you had before my Daddy won it. Sometimes we wouldn't do anything you know? Just sit. Talk. He was great crack Michael.

I didn't think it was so bad. I always knew he loved you. He always loved you, Marie. And he did always tell you the truth, but there's only so much of the truth anyone wants to hear. That's what he gave you Marie, what he gave everyone, enough of the truth to keep us all charmed.

MARIE *has still not moved, her eyes fixed on* CASSIE's *face.*

CASSIE. So. There you are. That's the truth. Now you can tear the face off me.

Still nothing.

Marie?

No response.

(*Sighs.*) I'll put the kettle on.

MARIE (*whisper*). Get out.

CASSIE *stops.*

MARIE. GET OUT OF MY HOUSE!

CASSIE *hesitates, she takes a step towards* MARIE. MARIE *steps back.*

CASSIE (*urgent*). Well, what did you expect? Sure what man would tell you that kind of truth? He'd be crazy to talk about it. What woman would stand for that? If he told you, he'd have to change. They'd sooner leave than they would change, Marie . . . You didn't want him to leave.

Pause. MARIE *just stares at her.*

MARIE (*whisper*). Hell isn't deep enough for you, Cassie Ryan.

CASSIE *flinches. She turns to pick her coat up.*

CASSIE. Sure we'll . . . we'll talk about it another time.

MARIE. No.

CASSIE. We're both thinking through drink tonight but . . .

MARIE *grabs crisps, drinks, everything she can lay her hands on. She pelts* CASSIE *with them, moving closer and closer.* CASSIE *tries frantically to protect herself.*

CASSIE. Jesus! Jesus, Marie! No!

MARIE *is on top of her, a heavy plate raised to smash down.* CASSIE *stares up at her, terrified.* MARIE *lowers her arm. Turns away.*

MARIE. Just get out.

CASSIE *straightens up, shaking, and edges out the door.*

MARIE *stands for another frozen moment then she screams, a great howl of pain and loss.*
A child starts to cry offstage. MARIE *lowers her head, hugging herself, rocking herself. The child goes on crying. After a moment* MARIE *raises her head.*

MARIE (*eyes shut, still rocking*). Your Daddy was a good man and a brave man and he did the best he could and he's in heaven watching out for you . . . And that's what keeps us all together, keeps me going, keeps me . . .

She can't go on. After a second she gets up and goes to the child.

DEIRDRE *enters and goes and sits in the chair* CASSIE *has vacated. She is still wearing her waitressing clothes but her face is bare of make-up, her hair limp again. She is nursing one arm as if it hurts her. She sits looking up at Michael. She takes out the knife and flicks out the blade. Experimentally she pushes it into the back of the chair. She tries another couple of slow stabs then leaves the knife there, its handle sticking out. She pushes at it, pushing it further in, wiggling the blade, her expression intent. Offstage the crying stops. After a moment* MARIE *comes back into the room. She stops dead when she sees* DEIRDRE. DEIRDRE *turns quickly, leaving the knife where it is.*

MARIE. What do you want?

DEIRDRE. I brought your money back.

She pulls CASSIE's *roll of bills out of her pocket and lays it on the table.*

DEIRDRE. There's a fiver gone on chips and drinks.

MARIE *comes further into the room, watching* DEIRDRE *like she's a dog deciding whether to bite or not.*

MARIE. What happened to your arm?

DEIRDRE. Just these fellas up the club. They wanted me to go in their car. It's just bruised.

MARIE *looks at her for a moment.*

MARIE. You've followed me, you've watched me and you've stolen from me.

DEIRDRE. Yeah.

MARIE. What more do you want?

DEIRDRE *points to the picture of Michael.*

DEIRDRE. Him.

MARIE *crosses slowly to look at Michael then she rips him off the wall and throws the picture at* DEIRDRE.

MARIE. Take him.

DEIRDRE *clutches the picture awkwardly. Bemused.*

MARIE. What good do you think he'll be to you?

DEIRDRE. He was my Daddy.

MARIE. What?

DEIRDRE. He was. He was my Daddy.

MARIE closes her eyes for a moment.

MARIE. Why did you think he was?

DEIRDRE. My Mum told me.

MARIE. Oh.

She opens her eyes and looks at Michael.

DEIRDRE. She said my Dad was a bad man, and for years I thought my Daddy was a hood, then she told me he was a bad man because he left her, left her flat with me on the way and I thought that didn't make him so bad because didn't I want to leave her too? So I started asking.

No one will tell you the truth to your face. But I heard his name, so I went looking for him.

MARIE. And did you find him?

DEIRDRE. I used to follow him about. That's how I saw him with her.

MARIE. Cassie.

DEIRDRE. Aye.

MARIE. You saw them together?

DEIRDRE. In his car. She was wearing a bright red dress with no back to it, that made me stare first you know because I couldn't imagine how she could stand it being so cold, even in his car. Then they moved and I saw his face so I had to stay then, I had to stay and watch. I saw his face and I saw hers just before he kissed her . . . Just before he did she looked like my Granny, old and tired and like she didn't care about anything at all anymore . . .

I stopped following him after that. I thought if he was with her he'd never come back to me and my Mum. Then I heard he was dead . . .

Pause.

DEIRDRE. I didn't know where to look for him then. I'm cold.

MARIE doesn't respond.

DEIRDRE. Can I get a cup of tea or something?

MARIE. No.

DEIRDRE. Oh. (*She looks at Michael, then puts him down.*) That's just a picture.

MARIE. Yes.

DEIRDRE. I thought . . . you know . . . I thought if I came and watched . . . maybe I wouldn't lose him altogether.

MARIE. And was he still here?

DEIRDRE. No. But I kept looking.

Pause.

Now I've told you everything. Now you've to tell me.

MARIE. You can ask anyone. They all know stories about Michael. There's no end to the stories about Michael.

DEIRDRE. But you know the truth.

MARIE. Oh, it's truth you're wanting?

DEIRDRE. They said he was with the Provos.

MARIE. He was wild when he was young.

DEIRDRE. They said he was a hero?

MARIE. Maybe he was.

DEIRDRE. What did he do?

MARIE. He went away to do it. I stayed here and cleaned the floor and when he came in I'd put his tea in front of him. Do you want to know what he had for his tea? I could tell you that.

DEIRDRE *doesn't move.*

DEIRDRE. I brought your money back. So you've to tell me.

MARIE. But I've no story, haven't they told you? I know nothing at all. That's the only story I'm fit to tell you, about nothing at all . . . Except being brave and coping great and never complaining and holding the home together . . . Is that the story you're wanting?

DEIRDRE *says nothing.*

Oh but they think I don't know how to be bitter, they think I never learned. I'm just a wee girl with a smile that feeds the birds.

So is this the truth you wanted to rob me of? Is this what you wanted to hear? Go you back now, go you back to your own Mother. She can tell you how bad he was, how he lied to her; that's a better story, that's a story that'll keep you safe from any man with a gentle smile and warm hands. Go you back to your own place!

DEIRDRE. She'll have locked me out.

MARIE. So go back to the street.

MARIE turns away. DEIRDRE doesn't stir.

DEIRDRE (*quiet*). She's not sure. She's never been sure, if he was.

MARIE. So he only cheated on me with the best, well, that's a great comfort to me isn't it? Have you been chasing a herd of Daddies then?

DEIRDRE. But you'd know. I know you'd look at me and you'd be sure.

MARIE doesn't turn. DEIRDRE gets up and clumsily pulls off her top, drags off the jeans. There are bruises all over her back. She goes to MARIE and pushes the clothes in front of her.

DEIRDRE. Here, that's you got everything back.

MARIE turns, startled then starts to laugh, hysterically. DEIRDRE hurls the clothes at her. She snatches the knife out of the chair and waves the blade at MARIE. She advances on her slowly.

DEIRDRE. I want the truth out of you. I mean it.

MARIE backs off a step.

DEIRDRE. Tell me!

Suddenly MARIE flies at her.

MARIE. Tell you! I'll tell you!

She wrenches the knife and the picture off the startled DEIRDRE and smashes and slashes Michael's picture with swift, efficient destructiveness. She looks down at the pieces at her feet for a long moment. She drops the knife on top of them. Her breathing slows. She goes to the kitchen area and comes back with a half-filled rubbish sack and some newspaper. She kneels down and starts to clear up the pieces of the picture.

MARIE (*quiet*). Watch your feet on that glass there.

She wraps the glass and the shredded picture in newspaper. She wraps the knife as well. She drops both in the rubbish sack and takes it back to the kitchen. DEIRDRE has barely moved through all of this, watching MARIE fearfully. MARIE returns from the kitchen, wiping her hands.

MARIE (*still quiet*). There. (*She looks at* DEIRDRE.) Those are some bruises you've got.

MARIE reaches out and touches DEIRDRE's shoulder. DEIRDRE flinches, then allows the touch. MARIE turns her gently. She looks at her bruised body. MARIE touches DEIRDRE's back.

MARIE. Who did this to you?

DEIRDRE. Just the fella she's got living with her just now.

MARIE (*stroking DEIRDRE's back*). They took the lying head off Michael, didn't you know? Didn't they tell you that story?

DEIRDRE (*quiet*). Yes.

She pulls away from MARIE.

MARIE seems to focus on her again.

MARIE. Ah God forgive me . . . (*She sways momentarily. Runs her hands over her face.*) You should go home. It's late.

DEIRDRE *doesn't move.*

MARIE. Here.

She offers the clothes again, DEIRDRE *shakes her head again.* MARIE *takes a rug off the back of the sofa and drapes it over her.*

MARIE. Well whoever your Daddy was, it's a pity he didn't give you the sense to look after yourself. Are you hungry just now?

DEIRDRE *shakes her head.* MARIE *goes and sits closer to her.*

MARIE (*gentler*). The thing about Daddys, all the Daddys, is they up and leave you; they go out with their friends, they go inside, they die, they leave you. You'll always have it all to do so there's no good wishing on them.

Half the time I don't think they want to go. Sure half the time all they want is something better for us all, for them, for us.

They don't want to be raging and screaming and hurting more than they can ever forget in the booze or the crack or the men beating men. I don't think they know what they want at all or how to get it if they did. So they leave and we've it all to do but we're missing each other even when we're together and so it goes on and so it goes on and so it always will go on, till we learn some way to change . . . because this place is no different to anywhere else.

I never told him that. It wasn't that I lied. I just didn't tell all the truth that was in me. Sure, what good would telling that kind of truth do you? You'd be crazy to talk about it wouldn't you? What man would listen to that? If he heard you he'd have to change. Maybe he'd sooner leave. I didn't want him to leave. I loved him. I can't throw that away even now. I loved him. You see I'm just a mug, Deirdre. Cassie was right. I knew who you were the first time I saw you. I knew.

What age are you?

DEIRDRE. I'm sixteen.

MARIE *sucks in her breath.*

MARIE. I was married sixteen years.

DEIRDRE. I know.

Pause.

MARIE. Sometimes . . . sometimes when he came home he'd cry, from tiredness, because his heart was sick in him. He'd cry and I'd comfort him.

DEIRDRE *pushes at the money on the table for a minute.*

DEIRDRE. I'll get the other fiver to you.

MARIE. It doesn't matter.

DEIRDRE. It's your money.

MARIE. It's Cassie's now. It'll go back to her. She needs it to dream with. (*Shakes her head.*) She'll not use it for much else. You're shivering.

DEIRDRE. I've cold blood. That's what they say . . . I'm away now. (*She gets up.*)

MARIE. You can't go out like that.

DEIRDRE *pulls the blanket round her; she looks at* MARIE.

MARIE. Your Daddy . . . Your Daddy was a man, like any other.
If he knew you were alive he never told me. And he's dead now
. . . You've got his eyes.

They look at each other for a minute. DEIRDRE *nods.*

DEIRDRE. I'll be away up the road then.

MARIE. Not at this hour, it's nearly morning. I'll get the
breakfast started. Come on you'll be hungry soon.

MARIE *moves back to the kitchen. Starts getting out food.*

MARIE. You can give me a hand if you like.

DEIRDRE *hesitates, then goes to join her.* MARIE *hands her a loaf.*

MARIE. Slice the top crust off that bread but keep it.

DEIRDRE. What for?

MARIE. For the birds. Did you ever feed the birds, Deirdre?

DEIRDRE. No.

MARIE. I like the common wee birds, the pigeons and the
starlings and the sparrows, it's easy enough to build a great wee
nest when you've a whole forest to fly in, but you'd need to be
something special to build one round the Falls. Someone
should feed them.

You make crumbs of that. I'll put the kettle on.

Fade lights.

INFIDELITIES ■ RICHARD ZAJDLIC

RICHARD ZAJDLIC was born in Rochford, Essex in 1962, one of twins. After graduating in English Literature at Southampton University he became a founder-member of Ratskins Theatre Company working as writer, actor and director.

He is the co-author (with Richard Crowe) of *Cock & Bull Story* (published by Methuen 1988) which has received productions as far abroad as Scandinavia and New Zealand. As an actor he has worked in theatre (throughout the U.K. and also Canada) television and film. His writing work includes a script for Thames T.V.'s *The Bill* and a radio play *Harry Abbot*.

Infidelities was the winner of the 1990 West London Playwriting Competition. It was his first solo stage play.

To Jean

Characters: (Five Actors)

JENNY	Actor 1
HARRIS	Actor 2
LINDA	Actor 3
TANNER	Actor 4
BRIAN	Actor 5
SQUADDIE	Actor 4
BARMAID/MAN	Actor 3 or 4
SECRETARY	Actor 3
MAIREAD	Actor 1
CAITLIN	Actor 3
GUNMAN	Actor 4

Setting:

Belize. England. Ireland.

Infidelities was first staged at the Tabard Theatre, London on 25 July 1990 with the following cast:

JENNY	Jilly Bond
BRIAN	Adam Magnani
LINDA	Elizabeth Moynihan
HARRIS / TANNER	Mike Goodenough

Designed by Johanna Fox
Lighting by Simon Clark

The revised script was subsequently performed as a rehearsed reading at Watermans Art Centre on 11 January 1991. The cast was as follows:

JENNY	Kirsten Hughes
BRIAN	Richard Zajdlic
LINDA	Helen Pearson
HARRIS	Kieron Jecchinis
TANNER	Richard Crowe

Directed by Robert Schofield

ACT ONE

Scene One

Belize. Night-time in the jungle. The actors start to whisper their phrases – first one, then another, until all five are talking at once.

JENNY (*ACTOR 1*). Is she? Isn't she? Ask her. Tell her. Slut. Dirty slut. You've married a slut. (*Laugh.*)

HARRIS (*ACTOR 2*). What's she like, Bri? Your wife? The camp slag? What's she like? Good stuff? Hot stuff? I'll have her. We'll all have her. When we get home. (*Laugh.*)

LINDA (*ACTOR 3*). Listen. Listen. Listen to them laughing. She's laughing at you. Listen! Stop her. Hit her. Hurt her. Teach her. Bitch. Bloody bitch. (*Laugh.*)

TANNER (*ACTOR 4*). Let me use her, Bri. Bruise her, Bri. Suck and abuse her. Word is your wife's easy. Sleazy. Just some whore who can please me. (*Laugh.*)

BRIAN (*ACTOR 5*). Stop it. Stop it. For Christ's sake, stop it! Please. Leave me alone. Please. Stop it. (*Shouts.*) Jesus bloody Christ!

The whispers stop.

BRIAN (*quiet*). Jesus bloody Christ.

Pause. BRIAN *inserts a blank cassette into a tape recorder. He presses play/record.*

Belize. 15th June. 11.30pm. (*Pause.*) Jenny?

Split stage: JENNY *is at home. England. Daytime. She is listening to* BRIAN'*s tape and pretending to have a conversation with him.*

JENNY. Yes? (*Pause.*) What?

BRIAN. How's it going?

JENNY. How d'you think?

BRIAN. I mean, looking after yourself. Having fun and that.

JENNY. Sort of. You too?

BRIAN. Seems ages since we last spoke. I mean . . . I'm missing you, Jen.

JENNY. Bloody liar.

BRIAN. You missing me?

JENNY (*laughs*). Ha!

BRIAN. Please say yes . . . Jen . . .

JENNY (*surprised*). Yes. Of course I am.

BRIAN *switches the tape recorder off.*

BRIAN. Christ, I'm no good at this! Come on. You useless bastard. Ask her. Tell her. She's your wife, isn't she? (*Laughs.*) Yeah. She's your wife, isn't she.

BRIAN *switches the tape recorder back on.*

BRIAN. I don't know what to say.

JENNY. You useless bastard. Get on with it. How's Belize?

BRIAN. Belize is still the same stinking cesspit it's always been. It's still hot. Christ, it's hot. Even the flies are sunburnt. (*Laughs.*) Boom-boom.

JENNY. You said that last time.

BRIAN. I said that last time, didn't I? Not boring you, am I?

JENNY (*snoring*). Zzzz . . .

BRIAN. I got my hand bandaged up at the moment. Got stabbed by a tree out on patrol.

JENNY. A tree?

BRIAN. Harris flicked a snake at me. I dived out of the way. Put me hand on this tree and its two-inch long needles went 'Shong!' – straight through me hand.

JENNY. Ow!

BRIAN. Harris laughed so much he went and sat on one.

'Shong!' Straight up his jacksy. He's walking about like he's shat himself.

They both laugh.

BRIAN. Yeah. You gotta watch your step out here, you know. Everything's after you. The snakes, ants, scorpions – all the nasties. Keep out. That's what they're saying. You don't belong here. This is our place. Well, that's fine by me. I'd be on the next plane home if I could.

JENNY. Yeah. If.

BRIAN. But then that's not up to me, is it? I'm just private nobody in Her Majesty's bleeding Army. Doing my time in Belize. Doing what I'm told. Bastards. (*Pause.*) I dunno. Maybe you're right. Maybe I should get out –

JENNY *switches her tape recorder off.*

JENNY. Oh, you shit! (*Mocking.*) 'Maybe you're right.' But you're not going to do anything about it, are you? You never do, you bloody wimp. Wimp!

JENNY *takes out a cigarette, lights it. She fast forwards the tape, stops it. She takes a drag on her cigarette and then switches the tape recorder back on.*

BRIAN. And I turned round and went 'Bollocks!' (*Laughs.*) Funny, eh?

JENNY. Yeah. Hilarious.

BRIAN. Cheers for your last tape.

JENNY. 'S okay.

BRIAN. It was good to hear all the news from home. Long time, tho'. Over a month. What happened?

JENNY. I don't know. Sorry.

BRIAN. I really missed that. Time here. Goes so slow.

JENNY. Snap.

BRIAN. Just night after night in the N.A.A.F.I. Watching the same old videos.

JENNY. Try sitting at home. Watching T.V.

BRIAN. Still, I expect it's no different for you. Sitting at home. Watching T.V. an' that. Or d'you get out much? I don't mind. You get out. Have a good time.

JENNY. Huh! What with?

BRIAN. I mean, me and the lads, we go out. Now and again. Ol' Raul's Rose Garden. That sort of bar come pick-up joint, remember?

JENNY. I remember.

BRIAN. Some of the lads, Harris for one, they'll go with anyone. Harris says his missus wouldn't mind. Says she don't expect him to be a monk while he's away. I didn't reckon much on that. What if, right, I goes to him. What if your missus got up to a bit of that back home. He just laughed and said she should be so lucky.

JENNY. Charming.

BRIAN. Christ, there's so many girls here you have to fight 'em off, but I wouldn't touch 'em with a barge-pole.

JENNY. What are you getting at, Bri?

BRIAN. Christ, listen to me. What's he getting at? I bet that's what you're thinking. Don't he trust me? 'Course I do. It's just that . . . I'm missing you, Jen. Fed up of never seeing you. Touching you. All I get here is sewers and shit. Kids selling themselves for fifty pee. I don't even notice it anymore.

JENNY. So what's new?

BRIAN. How's the giving-up-smoking going? 'S pretty much the whole six months now, isn't it? I keep trying but . . . I'm proud of you, though. When I get back, I'm gonna treat you, okay? Something really special. And a meal. First night back we'll go for a meal. Get dressed up. What d'you think?

JENNY. Sounds great.

BRIAN. Wherever you want. It's your treat. You decide.

JENNY. The Moulin Rouge.

BRIAN. Anywhere but the Moulin Rouge. I can't stand that place.

JENNY. My treat, you said!

BRIAN. Anyway, it's up to you, okay?

JENNY. Thanks.

BRIAN. Let's see. What else?

JENNY. I love you, Jen?

BRIAN. Nah. Oh, yeah. You missed a cracker last night.

JENNY. Oh, I should've just popped over –

BRIAN. Colin McClane's stag night.

JENNY. Who?

BRIAN. Yeah, I couldn't believe it either. Little fat Col. Michelin man married. Some Belizian bird working her ticket to England, I reckon.

JENNY. Unromantic pig.

BRIAN. Course, the C.O. tried to talk him out of it. I mean, she don't even speak English! So he can't talk to her. Can't communicate or nothing. They just hold hands and smile at each other a lot.

JENNY. Lucky them.

BRIAN. Yeah, he's mad, innhe?

JENNY. Yeah.

BRIAN. Wait 'til she gets to good old English weather. That'll teach her. It's a 110 degrees here – you can fry an egg on a stone. What's it like there?

JENNY. ⎰ Raining.

BRIAN. ⎱ Raining, probably. Look, I better sign off now. Got nothing to say really. Just wanted to make sure you hadn't forgotten me.

JENNY. Huh! You wish.

BRIAN. But I'll be back soon enough. I'm missing you. Have I said that?

JENNY. Keep saying it.

BRIAN. Only three more weeks now. Then I'm home. And I hope to God I never have to come back. Belize. It's the worst place in the world. Central American paradise? Hell on earth, more like. Three more weeks, then I'm home. It'll be alright

then. Not long now. Take care of yourself, Jen. See you soon.
Jen, I . . . Bye.

BRIAN exits. JENNY switches off the tape recorder.

JENNY. Take care of yourself, Jen. See you soon. Jen, I . . . love
you? Want to shag you silly over the back of the sofa? Want to,
finally, at long last have babies with you? Huh. You wish.

Scene Two

JENNY's house: JENNY sitting quietly. The doorbell/buzzer sounds.
JENNY jumps, startled.

JENNY. Christ.

The doorbell sounds again.

Little bastards.

The doorbell sounds again. It rings a third time and stays pressed.

Right.

She opens the door.

Just sod off, will you!

LINDA (*entering*). Sod off yourself, you cheeky cow.

JENNY. Linda! Sorry, I –

LINDA. Get in, will you! It's pouring–

JENNY. It's these kids. They keep ringing. I didn't think.

LINDA. Not your forte, is it.

JENNY. What are you doing here, anyway?

LINDA. Oh , that's nice. I'm doing you a favour, that's what.
John phoned. They're going to be late. About an hour or so, he
thinks.

JENNY. Oh. Right.

LINDA. He called me a few minutes ago. Been trying for ages, he
said. Sure. And I'm Mel Gibson's love-toy.

JENNY. 'Least you got a call.

LINDA. Some problem of logistics they have to sort out at the barracks, apparently.

JENNY. Logistics?

LINDA. Oh, I don't know. Like as not he's got his fat nose in a pint at *The Harrow*. Savouring his last moments of freedom. Plucking up his courage to meet me.

JENNY. Yes.

LINDA. He always said the real war was living with me. That's why he became a soldier, he said. If he hadn't been trained to fight he'd never have lasted. Well, six months in Belize should've toughened him up.

JENNY. Bri hated it. He said in one of his tapes –

LINDA. Tapes?

JENNY. Yeah, you know, cassettes. Telling me what he's doing. What it's like.

LINDA. Bloody gorgeous, John says.

JENNY. It's lovely to hear his voice. If you close your eyes, you can imagine he's right next to you. Holding you close.

LINDA *sticks her fingers down her throat and pretends to throw up.*

JENNY (*laughing*). Oh, piss off! It's nice. It is! It was Bri's idea anyway. The tapes. Makes us feel less lonely in a way.

LINDA. John never feels lonely. Only when he's at home.

JENNY. That's horrible.

LINDA. I'm a horrible person.

JENNY. No, you're not. Not all the time.

LINDA. Ooh, you ⎱ bitch!

JENNY. ⎰ Bitch!

They laugh.

JENNY. Didn't John write?

LINDA. Twice. Both times telling me what a great time he was having and how he didn't want to come home. Bastard.

JENNY. You love it really. Make me a coffee, you.

LINDA. What did your last slave die of?

JENNY. Not doing what she was told.

LINDA. White, no sugar?

JENNY. Two sugar.

LINDA. Uh-Uh. Diet.

JENNY. I don't care. I want two sugars.

LINDA. I thought you wanted to be slim and beautiful for the big day.

JENNY. Big day. Big deal.

LINDA (*with relish*). Big sex session!

JENNY. I wonder if they'll have changed at all?

LINDA. John won't have. Same socks as the day he set off.

JENNY. No. Changed. Different. That scares me sometimes.

LINDA. What?

JENNY. That when Bri comes back, all those new things he's done, people he's met – I get scared that he'll come back changed and that what we had won't be the same anymore.

LINDA. Don't be stupid.

JENNY. I'm not.

LINDA. It's been six months. It's bound to be a bit awkward at first.

JENNY. Linda?

LINDA. Yes? (*Pause.*) What?

JENNY. I'm nervous.

LINDA. It's okay.

JENNY. I don't know why. I don't know what I'm going to say.

LINDA. You won't be doing much talking!

JENNY. I wish he wasn't in the Army. When he's away, I get so lonely. I sit here, wondering what he's doing. Wondering if he's thinking about me. If he's missing me.

LINDA. Tell him that.

JENNY. You know, last time, when he came back from Cyprus. It was like we had to get to know each other all over again. Like strangers almost. And really shy. We both were. So shy we . . .

LINDA. What?

JENNY. We didn't even make love at first. We just fell asleep holding hands. When we woke up that way the first morning, I don't know why but I cried. Bri thought something was wrong but there was nothing wrong. I just cried.

Pause.

LINDA. I envy you.

JENNY. Why?

LINDA. I don't know.

JENNY. I do. It's because you're a lot shallower than I am.

LINDA. You bitch!

They laugh.

LINDA. You make the coffee, scumbag.

JENNY. Where are the girls?

LINDA. Round at their grandma's. For the rest of the day and night. So John's got no excuses. We can do it where we like and be as loud as we like. I quite fancy the kitchen table myself.

JENNY. Excuses?

LINDA. Oh, yeah. I mean, he used to be like a man possessed. I never even had time to say hello before I was dragged upstairs. Mind you, that was it, no action replays. If you missed it the first time . . . but now, I have to drag him! Tell him how big he is. How wonderful. Yawn.

JENNY. You told me you loved it.

LINDA. I do. It's getting him started though. After that, well, when you're into it you can think about who you like, can't you? (*Laughs.*) And believe you me, I'm not thinking about him.

JENNY. No?

LINDA. No. Are you joking? What's exciting about your husband? Well, do you? Think about Bri?

JENNY. Yes.

LINDA. Always?

JENNY *thinks, then grins and shakes her head. They both laugh.*

Scene Three

Army depot. England. Trucks unloading, departing, etc . . .

SQUADDIE (*ACTOR 4 laughing*). Get on with it, will yer!

HARRIS. So this bloke says, 'You're in my wardrobe, in my bedroom, with my wife! What the hell d'you think you're doing? And the milkman goes –'

BRIAN. Give it a rest, can't yer?

HARRIS. 'Ere, shut up. (*Using audience.*) He ain't heard this one.

BRIAN. Well, he's the only sod who ain't.

HARRIS. 'S just a joke, Bri. 'S nothing personal.

SQUADDIE (*ACTOR 4*). Come on, Harris –

HARRIS. Bit touchy, innhe?

SQUADDIE (*ACTOR 4*). Harris! What's he frigging say?

HARRIS. Who?

SQUADDIE. The frigging milkman!

HARRIS. Oh yeah. So this bloke opens the wardrobe door, finds his missus getting her extra pinta, starts having a real go. And the milkman says, 'Oh, that's right. Pick on the smallest bloke in here.'

HARRIS, SQUADDIE *and other soldiers laugh.* HARRIS *does so hysterically.*

BRIAN. I don't get it.

HARRIS. Pick on the smallest bloke in here. 'Cos there's an ol' army of blokes in there with her. Not just the milkman.

BRIAN. Oh.

HARRIS. You ain't laughing.

BRIAN. It ain't funny.

HARRIS. It is a bit.

BRIAN. Gimme a break, Harris. Alright?

HARRIS. What's the matter now?

BRIAN. Nothing. You just piss me off sometimes, that's all.

HARRIS. Oh dear. Hark at His Highness. Well, what about this, then? I could rework the end. Make it a bit more topical. Same as before, right? Only this time the milkman says, – 'I'm sorry, Brian. It may be your wife we're all screwing but you'll still have to get to the back of the queue.'

BRIAN *attacks, wrestling him to the ground.*

HARRIS. Joke! 'S a joke! Help!

SQUADDIE *separates them.*

SQUADDIE. Alright. That's enough of that. Leave it. Come on, we all wanna get home.

HARRIS. I don't. You seen my wife?

General laughter, including BRIAN.

BRIAN. Prat.

HARRIS. Yeah, come on Bri. This one's our lorry. Shift yer arse.

BRIAN. What's the rush?

HARRIS. I wanna get home really, don't I? Surprise the missus.

BRIAN. Catch her at it, you mean.

HARRIS. Oi! 'S have a bit of respect. My old lady knows how to behave. She'll be desperate to have me back.

BRIAN. Desperate's the word.

HARRIS. When I came back from Cyprus me and Sue stayed in bed for a week.

ALL. Oh, yeah!

HARRIS. We did! A whole week. Bloody starving by the end of it, mind.

General laughter.

Scene Four

JENNY's *house: same day.*

JENNY. Sue Harris? When was this?

LINDA. Last night. Barged in bold as anything. Said she wanted to borrow some sugar.

JENNY. Oh, yeah!

LINDA. I won't stop, she said. Seeing as you've got company.

JENNY. Nosy cow.

LINDA. Susan Harris, I said. You can stop what you're thinking right now, you gossiping old slag.

JENNY. Linda, you didn't!

LINDA. This bloke, I said, is my brother Tom. And besides, we haven't screwed each other for years!

They laugh.

JENNY. Oh, no. So she'll be round here today. Checking up on me.

LINDA. Well, give her a boot up the arse and send her packing.

JENNY (*laughs*). I can't, can I? Not with her husband.

LINDA. Eh?

JENNY (*mocking*). Bri's 'best mate', isn't he?

LINDA *shrieks with laughter.*

LINDA. Men are such wankers! (*Sniffing.*) 'Ere, you been smoking?

JENNY. No. Why?

LINDA. Smells a bit whiffy, that's all.

JENNY. I can't smell anything.

LINDA (*smelling her armpit*). Maybe it's me, then.

JENNY. Well, I didn't like to say. No, six months more or less. No smoking. No drinking. Lots of exercise –

LINDA (*laughs*). Ha!

JENNY. More than you. My body is now in perfect shape to create new life.

LINDA. It's no good if Brian isn't doing the same. After all, he's making the other half. Isn't he?

JENNY. Yes! He's trying to give up smoking but –

LINDA. No willpower, men. None of 'em. Mind you, I'm amazed you've talked him into the idea –

JENNY. Yes.

LINDA. Oh. I see.

JENNY. It's difficult in a letter. Or tape. I mean . . . Now he's back, well, we'll be able to talk about it. Properly. I mean, he does want kids. He just doesn't want them yet.

LINDA. I can see why you're so optimistic.

JENNY. I am. I don't know why but I am. It just feels right somehow. D'you know what I mean?

LINDA. Haven't a bloody clue. Now shut up and get me some whiskey for this – give it some flavour.

JENNY. Bloody alkie.

LINDA. And proud of it.

Scene Five

Army depot: same day. BRIAN *and* HARRIS *are shifting a large crate.*

HARRIS. Cor . . . bloody norra . . . I'm gonna shit meself . . .

BRIAN. 'S the last one . . . shift it . . .

HARRIS. I can't hold it . . . Bri . . .

BRIAN. Don't drop it! . . . Nearly there . . .

HARRIS. I've ruptured meself . . .

They dump it on the truck and collapse.

BRIAN. Thank Christ for that.

HARRIS. Me back's gone. That's it. I'm paralysed.

BRIAN. England's finest – look at us!

HARRIS. Oh, tell me that's it. There's no more, is there?

BRIAN. Better not be. I never want to see another of those
bloody boxes. Packing, unpacking bloody boxes.

HARRIS. Wanna fag?

BRIAN. I'm trying to give 'em up.

HARRIS. Me too. Here.

BRIAN. Ta.

HARRIS. Well, that was an impressive show of resistance.

They lie back, pulling on their cigarettes. Pause.

BRIAN. Peaceful, innit?

HARRIS *burps. Pause.*

BRIAN. Good to be back though, innit?

HARRIS. Yeah. Better here than Belize.

BRIAN. Or Belfast.

HARRIS *grunts in agreement. Pause.*

BRIAN. You got that letter?

HARRIS. Letter?

BRIAN. Come on. One your Sue wrote.

HARRIS. Somewhere.

BRIAN. Let's see.

HARRIS. What now?

BRIAN. Yeah, now. Let's see.

HARRIS. Well, I don't know if I got it.

BRIAN. You just said –

HARRIS. On me. I don't know if I got it on me. Like I said . . .
it's probably all bullshit.

BRIAN. Yeah.

HARRIS. My Sue. She likes a bit of gossip, you know.

BRIAN. Sure.

HARRIS. Only happy when she's stabbing her mates in the back –

BRIAN. That's alright, then.

HARRIS. Wish I'd never told yer now.

BRIAN. Bit late for that, innit!

HARRIS. Yeah. Sorry.

BRIAN. It weren't just your Sue. I've heard the same from others.

HARRIS. She just thought it a bit strange, that's all. You know, that T.V. repair bloke popping round that many times to your Jenny.

BRIAN. How many times?

HARRIS. She never said how many. Just some. You gonna say anything to her? Are yer? Bri?

BRIAN. Yeah. For starters, I'm gonna tell her to go round your house and rip your bloody Sue's tongue out, alright!

HARRIS. Suits me. Wish I'd thought of it before now.

BRIAN. My Jen's had a bit of trouble with something and she's got it fixed –

HARRIS. Alright, alright –

BRIAN. Sure?

HARRIS. 'S how I see it, Bri.

BRIAN. Well, make sure your Sue sees it that way, an all!

HARRIS. Yeah. 'Course. Sorry mate.

BRIAN. What's Tanner doing anyway? Bloody Families Officer. He's meant to check up on this sort of stuff. Stop it happening.

HARRIS. Look, I'm sorry about what I said. 'S just a joke, alright?

BRIAN. Forget it.

HARRIS. An' that's just what you should do an' all. Forget it. Look, they all do it. 'Spect my Sue's had a cuddle or two while I been away. Or three, the dirty cow. Where you going?

BRIAN. Nowhere.

HARRIS. Walking off ain't gonna solve anything.

BRIAN. Maybe it just makes me feel better.

HARRIS. You're mad –

BRIAN. Bloody right! Mad as hell. And is she gonna know it. When the time's right. When I'm sure.

HARRIS. 'S gossip. Rumours. A laugh.

BRIAN. A laugh!

HARRIS. Don't make a prat of yourself, Bri –

BRIAN. She'll get her chance –

HARRIS. Hark at Jesus bloody Christ here. What about all them tarts in Cyprus? An' Belize, eh? Ol' Raul's Rose Garden –

BRIAN. That weren't nothing.

HARRIS. Says you.

BRIAN. Bought and paid for. Nothing else. No complications. No ties. No feeling.

HARRIS. No guilt?

BRIAN. None!

HARRIS (*laughing*). Tell Jenny all about them, did ya? Well, did ya?

BRIAN (*walking off*). Piss off! What do you know?

HARRIS. I know a bloody hypocrite when I see one!

Scene Six

Split stage: BRIAN, *outside the house, smoking.* JENNY, *inside, getting ready.*

BRIAN. Once more unto the breach, dear Bri. On your own now, mate. Don't lose your rag, finish your fag and get yourself in. Nice and easy. Nice and calm. Just trust her. She's your wife, isn't she?

JENNY. Late as usual. You were like this when we were going out. Arranged to meet at eight and you'd arrive at ten past. Said you'd phone at nine – it'd be half past, or the next day, or not

at all. As if that meant something. As if that made you more
. . . I dunno . . . more of a prat, I suppose.

BRIAN. Harris says that being told your wife's unfaithful is like
being told someone's just pissed in your beer. Even if it ain't
true – it just don't taste the same anymore.

JENNY. Christ, I need a fag. What am I so nervous about? I
know what it's going to be like. Same as last time. Same as
every bloody time. 'S like bumping into a man you had a one-
night stand with. Yes, you've done 'it' but what do you say to
each other now? It's like trying to get to know a six-foot
vibrator.

BRIAN. Relax, will you. Nice and easy. Don't barge in with 'How
long have you been nobbing the T.V. repair man then?' Just
talk about it. Have a laugh about it.

JENNY. And for Christ's sake don't charge in with, 'Bri, I want to
have a baby.' Talk about it. Joke about it. He might like the
idea. I mean, he's not going to start knocking you around, is
he?

BRIAN. But if it's true. If she's been screwing behind my back. If
she's been laughing at me all this while. If she's the tart they
say she is –

JENNY (*checking make-up*). I look like a tart. Oh, sod it. We all look
the same on our backs.

BRIAN. Then is she gonna pay. If that's the truth, if she's been
whoring on me, Christ! I'll make her pay alright.

JENNY. Oh, smile, for God's sake. This is a happy day. He's
home. Everything's going to be fine.

BRIAN. You won't know what's hit you, Jenny my love. You
won't bloody know what's hit you!

JENNY. Just fine.

Scene Seven

House interior. JENNY *making last-minute alterations to her appearance.
The doorbell sounds.*

JENNY. Oh, God. Here we go. Keep calm. Nice. And. Calm.

She opens the door.

BRIAN. Hello, Jen. Remember me?

JENNY *hugs him. He sort of hugs her back.*

JENNY. Bri!

BRIAN. How about that? You do.

JENNY. Only just. That tan. I wouldn't have recognised you.

BRIAN. No. Bit hot out there.

Pause.

I missed you, Jen.

JENNY. Me too.

Pause. They move awkwardly to each other and hug.

BRIAN (*breaking away*). Well, let us in then.

JENNY. Oh, yes. Sorry.

BRIAN. What's the house like this time? Changed round again?

JENNY. Some. I moved the sitting room to the back. Hope you like it. Well, you'll soon get used to it. Could move it back if –

BRIAN. Be fine. Just as long as the loo's in the same place. I don't want to get up in the middle of the night and shit in the laundry basket.

JENNY (*laughs*). The loo's where it's always been. Come here. Kiss.

They kiss, not very passionately, and BRIAN breaks away again.

BRIAN. Sitting room at the back?

JENNY. Yes. Through here. I didn't fancy the video being on view to anyone who looked in.

BRIAN. Video?

JENNY. Yes. Oh, yes. I got one in. Didn't I tell you?

BRIAN. No.

JENNY. Oh. Oh, well. Nice surprise, then.

BRIAN. Yeah.

JENNY. Being on my own so much. Nothing to do. Thought I'd get some films in. Thought it'd be cheaper than going out.

BRIAN. Yes.

JENNY. Not that I had anywhere to go.

BRIAN. No.

JENNY. Come here.

He does so. She holds him.

JENNY. Kiss.

He gives her a peck.

JENNY. I'm not your granny. Give me a proper one.

They kiss 'properly'. Again BRIAN *breaks it.*

JENNY. What?

BRIAN. Nothing.

JENNY. Good.

She goes to kiss him again.

Don't do that.

BRIAN. What?

JENNY. You feel like you're pushing me away.

BRIAN. No, I'm not.

JENNY. Not that repulsive, am I?

BRIAN (*laughs*). No.

JENNY. Well, show a bit of bloody enthusiasm, then.

BRIAN. Look . . .

JENNY. What?

BRIAN. Sorry.

JENNY (*laughs*). 'S alright. Come on . . . Let's go to bed.

She takes him by the hand and tries to lead him. He pulls slightly.

JENNY. What's the matter?

BRIAN. Nothing.

JENNY. Don't you fancy me?

BRIAN. Yeah. 'Course.

JENNY. Well, come on then. What?

BRIAN. Nothing . . . it's just, well, you're not on the Pill anymore, are you?

JENNY. No. I came off it when you went away. No point staying on. You know I hate taking it –

BRIAN. Yeah, I know, but . . .

JENNY. What? (*Pause.*) You're killing the mood here slightly, Bri.

BRIAN. I ain't got any johnnies.

JENNY. What?

BRIAN. I forgot to get some. I forgot you were off the Pill.

JENNY. Oh.

BRIAN. So I . . . sorry.

  Pause.

JENNY. Does it matter?

BRIAN. Eh?

JENNY. Does it matter? I mean, why don't we . . . (*Laughs.*) do it anyway? Eh?

BRIAN (*he knows what she means*). Oh.

JENNY. Be nice, eh? Bri? Let's risk it. Why not? Please.

BRIAN. Look, I'll get some tomorrow.

JENNY. Tomorrow!

BRIAN. Tonight.

JENNY. Oh.

BRIAN. Look, I just got back. Don't start hitting me with families and stuff. I just got in through the door.

JENNY. Sorry.

BRIAN. Let's get a bit settled first, eh?

JENNY. Yeah.

BRIAN. Then we can chat about it, yeah?

JENNY *nods. Pause. They stand awkwardly for a moment.*

BRIAN. I feel like a twat.

JENNY. Well, I've just offered you mine and you didn't want it.

BRIAN (*laughs*). I know, but . . .

JENNY. Oh, forget it.

She moves away from him and sits down. Pause.

BRIAN. Sorry about being late.

JENNY. That's alright.

BRIAN. We had a lot of shifting to do. Boxes an' that.

JENNY. Yeah. Linda said.

BRIAN. She alright?

JENNY. Linda?

BRIAN. Yeah.

JENNY. Great.

BRIAN. See much of her?

JENNY. Every day.

BRIAN. Oh.

JENNY. She's been great. Kept me going really. You know, when I was down and that.

BRIAN. Yeah. Good.

Pause.

What's up with this cushion?

JENNY. Eh?

BRIAN. This green one.

JENNY. Oh, that. I cuddle it at night.

BRIAN. It's been chewed up at the corners.

JENNY. I know. Sorry.

BRIAN. Army'll go mad. The Families Officer seen this?

JENNY. No. It's ours, anyway. I can chew my own things up.

BRIAN. Dogs do that.

JENNY. Thanks very much.

BRIAN. No, I didn't mean that. I just thought it funny. You know, chewing a cushion.

JENNY. I told you. I've missed you.

BRIAN. The F.O. not seen it then?

JENNY. No. Though he's been round often enough.

BRIAN. Yeah?

JENNY. Checking up all the time. Where I'm going. Who was that round last week? I don't like him, Bri. He's . . .

BRIAN. He's what?

JENNY. It's just stupid.

BRIAN. What?

JENNY. I mean, he's meant to be helping us out, right?

BRIAN. Well, yeah.

JENNY. Yeah. Giving us advice. And if we've got any problems, any trouble, helping us out. But it's not like that.

BRIAN. Why not?

JENNY. Because he's the one causing the bloody problems in the first place! My husband's never home and I cry myself to sleep wanting him back. That's my biggest problem Mr Tanner and what the bloody hell are you going to do about that!

BRIAN. He's trying to help.

JENNY. Help! Snidey little creep.

BRIAN. Snidey?

JENNY. Things he says.

BRIAN. Like what?

JENNY. Oh, I don't know. Like –

BRIAN. Where are you going at night and hasn't the T.V. repair man been round a lot lately.

JENNY (*laughs*). Yes, that's right. Yes, it's not only the house. It's the personal bit. Poking into your private life. Being checked up on. By him. It's horrible.

BRIAN. Yeah.

Pause.

So when d'you get this video, then?

JENNY. Eh?

BRIAN. The video. When did all this happen?

JENNY. About three months ago – you sure I didn't tell you?

BRIAN. Work okay?

JENNY. Eventually.

BRIAN. How d'you mean?

JENNY. It's been a pain in the backside ever since it arrived. Faulty this, faulty that – the repair man practically lived here.

BRIAN. Yeah?

JENNY. If I hadn't been so set on the idea I wouldn't have bothered – sent it back.

BRIAN. So why didn't you?

JENNY (*surprised*). Because I wanted one.

BRIAN. Well, can we afford one?

JENNY. So what if we can't! You give me something else to take my mind off the fact that you aren't around for ten months of the bloody year and I'll send it back! Okay!

BRIAN. Okay! Alright.

JENNY. Jesus, if that's a big problem –

BRIAN. It's not a problem.

JENNY. Good.

Pause.

BRIAN. Working now, then?

JENNY. Yes. Do you want to try it? I've got –

BRIAN. So who was this geezer who sorted it out?

JENNY. Terry?

BRIAN. I dunno. Was that his name?

JENNY. Yes, Terry. Mr Fixit.

BRIAN. Good bloke?

JENNY (*laughs*). Drop-dead gorgeous bloke. And patient. Very, very patient. Yeah, he was great –

BRIAN. How long did it take then?

JENNY. What?

BRIAN. The video. You said he practically lived here.

JENNY. Couple of weeks. On and off. He –

BRIAN. Same bloke every time?

JENNY. Yes. Why?

BRIAN. Didn't they have anyone else they could send?

JENNY. I don't know. I suppose –

BRIAN. Or was it just a complete bloody coincidence that it was this same bloke, this 'Terry', every day of the sodding week!

JENNY. It wasn't every day.

BRIAN. Sue Harris reckons it was.

JENNY. Sue Harris?

BRIAN. Mary Fraser. Clare James. They all think so an' all.

JENNY. Think what!

BRIAN. You want me to spell it out? Come on, Jenny. I know.

JENNY. Know what?

BRIAN. You're not that stupid.

Pause. JENNY *begins to laugh.*

BRIAN. What's funny? What's so bleeding funny!

JENNY. You're having an affair with the T.V. repair man. That's what you're trying to say, isn't it, Bri. Are you having an affair with . . .

She carries on laughing. Genuine laughter.

BRIAN. Don't laugh at me, girl. I said, don't laugh at me!

He grabs her violently. The ferocity of his attack shocks them both. He lets her go, but is still on the verge of hitting her.

BRIAN. I don't think it's funny. I've had weeks of people thinking it's funny. All the lads. Cracking jokes. Jeering. The nudges, the winks or even worse, even bloody worse is the sympathy. All the lads sympathising 'cos I'm married to the camp slag.

JENNY. Don't call me that. Don't you ever call me that!

BRIAN. It's true, isn't it? The F.O. He knows. He knows the score.

JENNY. Oh, he knows the score alright –

BRIAN. That's why he's been round here so often. Haven't you realised that? He's been checking up on you. Everyone's told him what you've been up to – he's trying to put a stop to it.

JENNY. Stop to it?

BRIAN. Yeah, that's right –

JENNY. Stop to what? My fling with the T.V. repair man? Yes, well, I couldn't last, could I? Six months without a man in my bed? Oh, no, you didn't expect me to be a nun, did you? I made sure he was young tho' and had your colour hair and eyes so I could pass it off as yours if I got pregnant –

BRIAN. Shut up! Just –

JENNY. That's how careful I was. Not bad for a slag, is it? Not bad for the camp slag!

BRIAN. So it's true, then?

JENNY. No! No, it's not true, you stupid man. You stupid, stupid man. No, it's not. No.

She starts to laugh again.

BRIAN. I said don't laugh at me!

JENNY (*calming down*). I'm not. I'm not. I'm sorry.

BRIAN. Look at me. Jenny, I said look at –

JENNY. Will you shut up ordering me about! Stop laughing. Look at me. I said. I said. I've said No. No, I'm not sleeping

with the T.V. repair man or anyone else for that matter. And if
you'd rather believe a poisonous old slag like Sue Harris . . .

BRIAN. It was just her letters.

JENNY. What letters?

BRIAN. She sent letters. To Harris in Belize. All about this bloke –

JENNY. And straight off you believed her?

BRIAN. No –

JENNY. Well, thanks a lot.

BRIAN. No, I –

JENNY. That's pathetic.

BRIAN. Look, it weren't like that. I never meant to say it like that.

JENNY. Oh, right. How did you mean to say it, Bri?

BRIAN. I was gonna have a laugh about it. Tell you what they
been saying and have a laugh about it.

JENNY. I laughed. I thought it was funny, didn't I? What's the
matter? D'you lose your sense of humour at the vital moment?

BRIAN. They been taking the piss outa me for weeks! Do you
know what they say about you now?

JENNY. Do you think I care?

BRIAN. I do! I care. They're my mates.

JENNY. 'Mates!'

BRIAN. And like it or not I'm stuck with them. I have to go
around with them. I have to trust 'em 'cos if I don't I'm dead.
And that ain't toy bloody soldiers that's the truth. They stick us
in Ireland again an' we ain't rock solid together then we're
nothing. We're dead.

JENNY. I don't see the difference.

BRIAN. Eh?

JENNY. If you don't trust me. If we're not 'rock solid' – then
where the hell are we?

BRIAN. I ain't talking about us. I'm talking about the Army.

JENNY. It's the same thing!

BRIAN. It's not.

JENNY. It is to me! Not to you, no. All your little boxes. This box is Jenny. This is the Army. That's one part of my life, this is another. You can't split up your life like that, Bri.

BRIAN. I don't.

JENNY. You do. Bri, you do. I'm boxed in, shut off from every other part of you, feeling like I don't know you. Every time you come back I've got to get to know you all over again. I want more than one little box, Bri. . .

Oh, say something for Christ's sake.

BRIAN. What?

JENNY. Oh, Jesus, I don't know. Tell me I'm wrong. Tell me to shut up, you stupid cow. Tell me you love me.

BRIAN. You know I do.

JENNY. How do I? I know a part of you – I think a part of you, might, love me, but so what? So what when I don't know what the rest of you feels.

BRIAN. Rest of me? What? I don't understand. You know how I feel. Alright. Ask me. If you want to know, ask.

JENNY. Jesus God.

BRIAN. Ask me a question. Go on. And I'll tell you how I feel.

JENNY. I don't want to ask questions. I don't want to probe and pry and nag and wrench things out of you. I want you to share them. I want you to want to share them. With me. What are you so scared of?

BRIAN. Any question. Just ask –

JENNY. Are you listening to me!

BRIAN. Yes! What do you want me –

JENNY (mocking). 'To say'. God, sometimes, Bri I could smash your brains in.

BRIAN. If I had any.

JENNY. Yeah.

Pause.

Okay. I'll ask you a question.

BRIAN. Yeah?

JENNY. And you'll tell me the truth?

BRIAN. 'Course.

JENNY. The real and honest truth?

BRIAN. Go on, then.

JENNY. Have you ever been unfaithful to me?

BRIAN. Eh?

JENNY. You heard.

BRIAN. Have I ever been unfaithful to you?

JENNY. Sorry to spring it on you like this but I've often wondered. Oh, I trust you, of course. Especially now, after all this moral outrage. I mean, if you've been screwing left, right and centre all the time you've been away, it would be a bit hypocritical to get all steamed up if I do the same, wouldn't it? But now I've set your mind at rest on that score maybe you could do the same for me.

It's only one word, Bri. Either way, it's only one sodding word! Have you ever been unfaithful to me?

BRIAN. No.

JENNY. Liar!

BRIAN. I'm not –

JENNY. You rotten, stinking liar. Liar! LIAR!

She hits him repeatedly.

BRIAN. Alright! Alright! That's enough! Yes. Yes, I've been unfaithful. Yes, I'm a bloody hypocrite. Okay? Happy now? You asked. You bloody asked. You started this. Jesus!

JENNY. Where are you going?

BRIAN. Out.

JENNY. Where to?

BRIAN. I've had enough of this.

JENNY. Don't go. You can't go now.

BRIAN. Can't I?

JENNY. There's no point. What is the point of walking away?

BRIAN. None.

JENNY. Then stay. Talk.

BRIAN. Later.

JENNY (*holding him*). Now!

BRIAN *shrugs her off.*

JENNY. Where are you going?

BRIAN. Down the boozer – see my mates. They'll all be there. All sick of the sight of their loved ones an' all.

JENNY. You're going to her, aren't you?

BRIAN. Her?

JENNY. Your woman –

BRIAN. Her is a tart. A prostitute. Her is in Belize. There's a million hers. They ain't even got a name – that's how important her is!

He leaves.

JENNY (*calling*). Bri!

Scene Eight

Pub interior: 'The Harrow'. BRIAN *is sitting, brooding.* HARRIS *is bringing the drinks over.*

HARRIS. There you go, Bri.

BRIAN. Cheers.

HARRIS. So she didn't admit it?

BRIAN. No.

HARRIS. They never do. You have to catch 'em with their pants round their ankles and they'll still try and bluff their way out of it.

BRIAN. Leave it, eh?

Pause.

HARRIS *(laughs)*. Got her back, tho'.

BRIAN. How d'you mean?

HARRIS. The tarts an' that. Cyprus, Belize – must have given her something to think about. *(Laughs.)* Thinking she was so smart and all the time we're giving it wayhay! Bonking in Belize.

BRIAN. I thought she knew. I thought it was agreed. Silent, like. But agreed.

HARRIS. Then why d'you deny it?

BRIAN. I dunno. I just . . . it's like, when I came back from Cyprus – an' I'd got a dose, hadn't I?

HARRIS. Ol' Canteen Carol. I told you to keep away from her.

BRIAN. Take a week to clear up the M.O. said. I was doing my nut. Thought Jenny was bound to want to make lo – have a screw as soon as we got back.

HARRIS. So what d'you do?

BRIAN. Well, I couldn't do nothing, could I? We sort of hugged and kissed a bit and then just fell asleep holding hands

HARRIS. Ah! Inn that sweet.

BRIAN. Next morning she started crying and I thought, 'she knows'. She kept saying nothing was wrong but I knew she'd guessed.

HARRIS. So she never said nothing?

BRIAN. No. Seemed as happy as anything so I thought, well, it obviously don't bother her.

HARRIS. Sounds fair enough to me.

BRIAN. Yeah.

The pub bell sounds for time.

BARMAID/MAN *(ACTOR 3 or 4)*. Time, gentleman please! You as well, Harris. Let's have those glasses.

HARRIS. 'Ere, drink up. I got a load of cans back at my place. We'll put a bluey on and drown ourselves in beer, eh?

BRIAN. No. Another time, maybe.

HARRIS. Aw, let her stew for a bit. She'll come round. It's always the same. My Sue don't say a word to me first week back. After that I can't shut her up. (*Pause.*) I really enjoy that first week.

BRIAN. No, I'm going back.

HARRIS. Why? What for? Don't say you love her. I've just eaten.

BRIAN. Got nothing else, have I?

HARRIS. You got my sofa and a six-pack. Settle down with that for the night. You can't screw it but then it won't yak in your ear all night either.

BRIAN. See ya.

HARRIS. She won't thank you for it.

BRIAN. No.

HARRIS. How's your (*He whistles.*) this time? Alright?

BRIAN. Night.

BRIAN *leaves.*

HARRIS. Prat.

(*To* BARMAID.) Right then, Bessie. You fat-bosomed beauty. How about one for the road?

or: (*To* BARMAN.) Right then, Norman. You red-hot sex machine. How about one for the road?

ACT TWO

Scene One

Exterior. Busy road in town. JENNY *and* LINDA *enter carrying heavy loads of shopping. It is one week later.*

LINDA. Oh, my god!

JENNY. Come on –

LINDA. I've dislocated my shoulder.

JENNY. Stupid. You'd be in agony if you'd done that.

LINDA. I am in agony. This is agony.

JENNY. Let's get the bus, eh?

LINDA. Wimp! (*She collapses.*) Your house is closest. I want tea and cake.

JENNY. Only if you shove it down quick. I've got the Families Officer coming round at one-thirty.

LINDA. Again?

JENNY. Why am I so lucky?

LINDA. Maybe he fancies you?

JENNY. Maybe you've got a dirty mind.

LINDA. Is there any other kind?

They laugh.

JENNY. So, I've got to give the place a good scrub before he comes. You know what it's like – If there's as much as a smudge on the wall.

LINDA. Sore point. My kids are going to cost me a fortune. 'Oh

that's a new scratch isn't it, Mrs Cartwright?' Smug bastard.
'Oh, that's a kick in the balls isn't it, Mr Tanner?'

JENNY *laughs*.

JENNY. He'd probably enjoy it.

LINDA. Too right. Little pervert. Always trying to leer down my
blouse. Christ knows why – he's got bigger tits than I have.

JENNY (*laughs*). Come on. Bus.

The bus arrives. They get on, show their passes and sit down.

LINDA. And he keeps questioning me too. Have I been a
naughty girl?

JENNY. You?

LINDA. Don't sound so surprised.

JENNY. No, I –

LINDA. Apparently, I've been very friendly with the milkman
lately.

JENNY. ⎫ Thank you Susan Harris.
LINDA. ⎭ Thank you Susan Harris.

They laugh.

JENNY. Scrotty bitch.

LINDA. Chance'd be a fine thing.

JENNY. Yes.

LINDA. I mean it. A little love affair while John's away.
Wonderful.

JENNY. Don't be daft.

LINDA. Well, why not? Look what they get up to out there.

JENNY. Yes.

LINDA. Oh, Jen. I'm sorry.

JENNY. That's alright.

LINDA. I didn't think.

JENNY. It's okay. Really. Like you said. They all do it.

LINDA. Yes.

JENNY. I mean, it's natural, isn't it? After all, he's ten thousand miles away. Who's going to know about it?

LINDA. Half the bloody Army.

JENNY. But not you. Or me. And when he leaves he's never going to see her again. They've got the time and the opportunity. And the money.

LINDA. So do we.

JENNY. What?

LINDA. Have the time and opportunity. You'd probably need the money as well, of course.

JENNY. I would not!

LINDA (*laughing*). That's better. Oh, come on, let's do it. Next chance we have. The next man who gets on this bus.

JENNY. Supposing he's horrible?

LINDA. I'm not picky.

JENNY. I am.

LINDA. Oh, you're too bloody careful, you are.

JENNY. And you're all talk. All talk, no action.

LINDA. That's all you know.

JENNY. What?

LINDA. Surprised you, didn't it?

JENNY. I don't believe you.

LINDA. Alright. I'm lying.

JENNY. Who?

LINDA. Who what?

JENNY. It's someone really awful, isn't it? That's why you won't say.

LINDA. Not that awful –

JENNY. Then you have! Oh, who? Who? Tell me–

LINDA. I can't –

JENNY. You can. You can. You must. Oh, please –

LINDA. Shh! For God's sake.

JENNY. Sorry. Sorry. Who?

LINDA. Uh-uh. If I tell you then you've got to tell me.

JENNY. Tell you what?

LINDA. Who you had a mad, passionate affair with while Bri was in Belize?

JENNY. What?

LINDA. I'm joking –

JENNY. Oh, not you as well, Jesus!

LINDA. It was a joke.

JENNY. Very funny.

LINDA. Sorry. Your face.

JENNY. I've thought about it, you know. Now and again.

LINDA (*getting up*). I should hope so too. Our stop. Come on.

They get off the bus and start to walk.

So you've thought about it, have you?

JENNY. Vaguely.

LINDA. Well, I wouldn't bother.

JENNY. So why did you?

LINDA. Me? Oh, I was getting my own back. On John. Same as Brian, see. They're all the same, Jenny. Little boys. Off screwing in secret whenever they can, or whenever they're able in John's case which can't have been often. Not as often as me anyway. And doesn't he know it.

JENNY. He knows?

LINDA. Of course. What was the point of having an affair if I couldn't taunt him with it? Where's the revenge in that?

JENNY. That's horrible.

LINDA. I told you. I'm a horrible person.

JENNY. Why are you telling me this? I don't want to know this.

LINDA. I'm telling you so that you don't go off and do

something bloody stupid just to get your own back on Brian.
It's not worth it. Not if you've got something worth saving and
you have. Swallow your pride, Jenny. Forget what he's –

JENNY. No!

LINDA. Look –

JENNY. Not forget. I won't. Can't. Not ever. All I can do is try
and make it . . . not matter. That's all. Until the next time, of
course.

LINDA. Don't you trust him?

JENNY (*laughs*). Trust him!

LINDA. I thought he'd promised. No more 'tarts'.

JENNY. He has. So?

LINDA. So, don't 'tit for tat'. You do it, he'll do it and you'll do
it back until what you're fighting for's not even there anymore –

JENNY. Have you finished?

LINDA (*pause*). Yes.

JENNY. Good, because I've got to go.

She moves off. LINDA *stops her.*

LINDA. Jenny? How are things with you two?

JENNY. Alright.

LINDA. Good.

JENNY. I'm lying.

LINDA. I know.

JENNY. Better than they were though. (*Laughs.*) Which isn't saying
much.

LINDA. He's only been back a week.

JENNY *nods.*

LINDA. Is it really bad?

JENNY *shakes her head. Tries a smile, fails.*

JENNY. It's like . . .

LINDA. What?

JENNY. It's like last night. We went to bed and did 'it'. Then he rolled off me – and we just lay there. All night. Awake. All night. Not saying a word. He went at six and it was then that I could roll over and go to sleep. (*Pause.*) Do you still envy me?

LINDA hugs her.

LINDA. Do you want me to come in?

JENNY. No. Thanks, but I –

LINDA. 'S okay. Shall I pop round later?

JENNY. Please.

LINDA. Go on. Go and tidy your house. (*Going.*) And don't you dare spread any lies about me to that man, d'you hear?

JENNY. Would I?

LINDA (*calling*). Yes, you bloody would, you old cow!

They leave in opposite directions.

Scene Two

JENNY's house: JENNY *enters carrying her shopping. She dumps it on the floor.*

JENNY. Bri? You in?

Centre-stage is a note and a tape recorder. JENNY *picks them up. She reads the note, then sits down and looks at the recorder. Pause. She switches the recorder on.*

BRIAN (*on tape*). Jenny. It's me.

JENNY. Hello, you.

BRIAN. I don't really know how to say this . . . so I'm just going to say it.

JENNY. Okay.

BRIAN. I'm moving back to the barracks . . . I mean, look, it ain't working, is it?

Pause.

JENNY. No.

Pause.

BRIAN. It ain't working. Not for you, or me. It'll only be for a bit. I just need some time on my own, that's all. Sort myself out.

JENNY. I see.

BRIAN. I been waiting for you. Tell you face to face. Where you been anyway! Thought you were always in in the mornings?

JENNY. No. Not always.

BRIAN. I'm sorry, Jen. Look, I'll see you. We'll talk. Work something out. Okay?

Pause.

JENNY. Okay.

Pause.

BRIAN. Don't worry. I mean, it's not over or anything. I just need some time, you know. Bye.

JENNY. Bye.

Scene Three

Families Officer TANNER's *office:* TANNER *is seated behind his desk.* SECRETARY *enters (ACTOR 3).*

TANNER. Yes, Barbara? What is it?

SECRETARY. A Mrs Collins to see you, sir.

TANNER. Ah, yes. Good. Show her in, would you?

The SECRETARY *leaves, then re-enters with* JENNY. TANNER *stands.*

TANNER. Mrs Collins.

He offers her his hand which she refuses to take. He ignores the snub by gesturing with his arm to a vacant seat.

TANNER. Would you . . . Thank you, Barbara.

The SECRETARY *leaves.* JENNY *and* TANNER *sit.*

TANNER. Well. How are you?

JENNY. Oh, let's cut all this crap and get on with it, shall we? You know how I bloody well am. My husband's been in barracks nearly two months now and I'm sick to death of these bloody 'chats' we keep having. I don't want to see you, Mr Tanner. I want to see Bri!

TANNER. Yes, of course. But, unfortunately, Brian does not want to –

JENNY. 'See me.' I know. Well, what about what I want?

TANNER. Mrs Collins. Believe me. I know how you must feel.

JENNY. Oh, don't flatter yourself!

TANNER. Yes, but these things do take time.

JENNY. Time! I haven't any bloody time left! In just over a month, as you've so kindly informed me, if we haven't 'settled our differences', I'm out on my bloody ear! I mean, does he know that? Have you told him that?

TANNER. Brian is aware of the situation you're facing, yes.

JENNY. Bastard!

Pause.

TANNER. I could, of course, compel Brian to meet you –

JENNY. Then why don't –

TANNER. But in my experience that would prove to be a totally counter-productive measure. Brian must decide to see you of his own accord. Forcing him to do so before he is ready will merely stiffen his resolve in making the split a permanent one. Divorce, Mrs Collins. Is that what you want?

JENNY. No.

TANNER. Then please. You must try to be patient.

JENNY. I'm trying to be patient but I'm running out of time! I've got one month.

TANNER. Less than that, I'm afraid. Brian's regiment leaves for Northern Ireland in . . . (*Checks his papers.*) two weeks and three days.

JENNY. But you said –

TANNER. They've brought the date forward since then. I'm sorry. There's nothing I can do.

JENNY. But by the time he comes back I'll be gone. Kicked out.

TANNER. Oh, hardly kicked –

JENNY. What do you call a court eviction order then!

TANNER. Mrs Collins, please. I'm sure it won't come to that. I'm full of hope that a reconciliation can be achieved before then.

JENNY. Oh, well, that makes me feel a whole lot better. Now that you're 'full of hope!'

TANNER. I think I may safely say from my meetings with Brian that he, like your good self, is striving to make the marriage work.

JENNY. Then why won't he see me? How can we solve anything if he won't talk to me? Jesus bloody Christ! What can I do? What the bloody hell can I do?

TANNER. For the moment Mrs Collins, regretfully, you must do as your husband does. If you will not talk to each other then you must talk to me. And I shall relay the pertinent facts.

JENNY. Right. Well, relay this!

Scene Four

TANNER's *office*.

BRIAN. I didn't hit her much. Once, twice, I dunno. What's she been saying? What's she said?

TANNER *doesn't answer. Pause.*

BRIAN. I just don't trust myself with her anymore. Sometimes, when we were together, arguing, I didn't know what I was gonna do. I just didn't know.

TANNER. I think you should see her –

BRIAN. No.

TANNER. Talk to her –

BRIAN. We've done all that! We've talked and talked and nothing come out of it. We just end up shouting, fighting –

TANNER. You won't be alone with her. I'll be there, riding shotgun, as it were. (*Harder.*) I want this thing settled, Collins.

BRIAN. It is settled!

TANNER. Sir.

BRIAN. Sir. It is settled, sir. I've settled it. I want a divorce.

TANNER. Brian. She's pregnant.

BRIAN. What?

TANNER. Pregnant. Tomorrow at three, then?

Scene Five

TANNER's office: TANNER *is seated behind his desk.* JENNY *and* BRIAN *are seated at opposite ends of the table.*

TANNER. Well, now. Who's going to begin? Mrs Collins? Jenny? Brian? (*Harder.*) You have something to say, I'm sure.

Despite TANNER's *stare,* BRIAN *shakes his head.*

TANNER. I'll start then, shall I? We cannot continue like this. The time for sullen silences has gone. It is your marriage, not mine, and the responsibility for its success or failure lies ultimately with you. A daunting thought. But no matter how impossible the task ahead appears, I will say this – Always remember that by being here today, by just sitting at this table, each of you has declared a tremendous commitment to the other. A commitment to trying again. To making your marriage work. And that is the seed of success.

Pause. He waits for them to speak. They don't.

TANNER. I have explained to Brian, Jenny, about the fact of your pregnancy –

BRIAN. Is it mine, though!

JENNY. You shit!

TANNER. I feel sure that Brian will want to apologise for that remark.

Pause, while TANNER *waits. It was not a request.*

BRIAN. I'm sorry.

TANNER. Jenny?

JENNY *does not answer. She gets up and moves to the far side of the room.* TANNER *gestures to* BRIAN *to go to her.* BRIAN *gets up and moves slowly across to his wife. He goes to put his hands on her shoulders, hesitates.*

BRIAN. Jen?

He tries again, touching her as he would a sharp blade.

BRIAN. Jen, I –

She shifts slightly at his touch. Pause. BRIAN *turns and walks angrily across the room as if to leave.*

TANNER. I haven't dismissed you, Collins!

BRIAN *stops at the door. He remains there, back turned.*

TANNER. Sit down, Brian.

BRIAN *turns and sits.*

TANNER. Mrs Collins? Jenny, would you be seated, please?

JENNY *turns to face him. She does not sit down. Pause.*

TANNER. When are you leaving for Northern Ireland, Brian?

BRIAN *stares blankly, nonplussed by the change of tack.*

TANNER. Belfast. How long before you leave?

BRIAN. Two weeks and two days. Sir.

TANNER. You've been before?

BRIAN. Just the once, yeah.

TANNER. So you've tested the water, as it were.

BRIAN. Yes, sir.

TANNER. You were wounded, I believe? Shot.

BRIAN. Nah. Just a flesh wound. Looked worse than it was, sir.

Doing a rummage search. House to house. It was stupid. I got careless.

TANNER. Mind not on the job?

BRIAN. No, sir.

TANNER. You can't afford to get careless in Northern Ireland. You've got to keep your mind on the job twenty-four hours a day. Every day.

BRIAN. Yes, sir.

TANNER. Otherwise you'll be flying home in a body bag. I love the Union Jack, Collins, but I don't want to see it draped over your coffin, do I?

BRIAN. No, sir.

TANNER. Still. As long as your mind's on the job there'll be no fear of that, will there? As long as your mind's on the job you'll be fine. Won't you?

BRIAN. Yes, sir. *(Pause.)* I'll be fine.

Pause.

JENNY. You really are a bastard, aren't you, Mr Tanner? A smug, superior bastard. Don't you dare sit there and lay that shit on me. This isn't my fault. It's yours. You're the problem. You and that little boys' club you call the Army. Don't talk about my marriage as though it's nothing to do with you, it's everything! Everything. Sitting there like some public school boy with a carrot up his bum – you've got no idea, have you? No bloody idea at all. You prick.

Pause.

TANNER. Sit down, Mrs Collins. Would you?

Pause. JENNY *crosses to* BRIAN.

JENNY. The baby. It is yours.

BRIAN. I know. I'm sorry.

JENNY. Come with me. Come home.

BRIAN *shakes his head.*

JENNY. Why? Why not?

BRIAN. I'm scared. Scared I'll hurt you.

JENNY. You won't hurt me. Come on.

He gets up. They sort of hold each other.

JENNY. 'S only two weeks. I can stand it if you can.

BRIAN. Yeah. Two weeks. And then what?

JENNY. I don't know. Just come back in one piece, alright?

BRIAN. Yeah. Ireland. Christ.

JENNY. And you thought this was bad. Wait 'til you see what a real war's like.

Scene Six

Riot on the streets of Belfast: an explosion of noise, lights, action.

HARRIS. Petrol bomb! Look out!

BRIAN. Jesus!

HARRIS (*laughing*). Come on, you Irish bastards. Come on.

BRIAN. Harris. Stay close.

HARRIS. Come on – you little shits!

BRIAN. Hold the line –

HARRIS. We don't have to take this. Let's charge 'em –

BRIAN. Hold the bloody line!

HARRIS. Break a few heads –

BRIAN. Harris!

HARRIS (*laughing*). Real soldiering this, innit? Beats poxing about Belize looking out for Russians.

BRIAN. Watch out!

HARRIS. Heads!

BRIAN. Lunatics. Bloody animals, that's what they are.

HARRIS. Ain't sodding about, are they?

BRIAN. Oughta be in cages –

HARRIS. Could be worse, mind.

BRIAN. How's that?

HARRIS. Could be at home with the wife!

BRIAN. Yeah.

They laugh.

HARRIS. } Look out!

BRIAN. } Look out!

Scene Seven

JENNY*'s house: she is recording a cassette to* BRIAN.

JENNY. Monday 18th. 11.30am. Hello. Me again. How's things? I'm . . . I'm . . .

She switches off.

I'm bored! Bored, bored, bored, bored, bored!

She switches on.

I'm fine. Everything's fine back here. Still helping out at the Nursery. We're taking them all to the Zoo next week. A day out at last – my God!

She switches off.

My God. All those bored animals in cages. Watching them. Watching me. Lucky them. Who'd pay to see my life?

She switches on.

So that'll be good. (*Pause.*) I'm having sex with the T.V. repair man at the moment.

She laughs, switching it off.

No. Can't say that. Can't say anything really.

She switches on.

Dear Bri. I have nothing whatsoever to say to you. Love Jenny.

She switches off. She lights a cigarette, remembers the baby and stubs it out irritatedly. She switches the recorder on.

JENNY. Jenny's tape. 11.40am. Dear Bri. How are the Irish tarts?
Keeping you warm nights? Oh no, I forgot. You're not going to
do that anymore, are you? Me neither. No more T.V. repair
men for me. Got myself quite nicely out of that one, didn't I?
Made you feel a right bastard while I came out smelling of
roses. Good for me. Good old Jenny Collins – liar and
adulteress extraordinaire. You see Bri, you were right. I have
been having an affair. It doesn't matter who, tho' it's certainly
not the T.V. repair man. Oh, don't worry, it's over now. It
didn't last long . . . it wasn't what I expected either. It made
me feel even lonelier – isn't that peculiar? I still feel detached,
distant from everyone, though the two weeks we had together
helped. Thawed me out, I suppose. Tho' it was better when we
didn't talk. I felt closer then. The silence was . . . comforting.
Talking was bad. All brick walls and boxes. The silence isn't
comforting anymore. I get scared now. I want you to talk to me
now. Phone, letters, tape, anything. I hold your jumpers at
night, did you know that?

She is crying. She switches off.

Don't stop. Don't for Christ's sake, stop.

She switches on.

I. Am. So. Unhappy. Bri. I am so unhappy with you. With me.
My life. D'you ever wonder what happens when you go away?
Nothing. Life just stops for me. All I do is go through the
motions, waiting for you to come back so I can start again. I
want more than that. There's more than that for me. Wasting
my life. The sheer bloody waste!

When I look at myself, what I've become, I get so angry. And
yes, I do blame you Bri. Unreasonable, I know, but I think I'd
be a very different person if I hadn't met you. Not better. Not
necessarily better. But different. And I resent that.

Even now, what I'm saying, what I'm trying to say. Selfish cow,
I'm thinking – me, me, me, me, me! Wrapped in my own
self-pitying little world. Get out, then. Do it. Be different. I've
tried that haven't I? I've tried him. I don't want him. I want
you. I want more of you.

D'you know, sometimes I say things to you, really nasty things.
Things I know will hurt just to get a reaction. Just to get inside
you and start us talking, fighting, loving again. We drift on so
easily, you and me. Not noticing things. Things like we aren't

working anymore. All the talk, endless drivel, it's just echoes. Echoes from a long time ago. From when it all meant something.

There's a part of you I can't reach anymore. That you've shut off, held back, 'this part's mine so hands off'. Can't you see that's why we fail? Why you're so lonely, why I'm so empty. You've built a barrier between us and all that makes me do is draw up one of my own and believe me Bri, that hurts.

We're married. We're partners, not opponents. We've got a child – son, daughter, whatever it is I spew out my belly it's ours. And it's relying on us to work this out. You've got to choose, Bri. Sooner or later you have to decide. You can't run off to your precious Army for ever and we'll still be here long after they've chewed you up and spat you out. Your future is me. Believe that, Bri. We belong. Don't you feel that? To each other. And we have to change if we want it to work. Don't shake your head. Don't tell me you can't change, that it's just the way you are and always will be, that's crap! You're not the man I married. And I'm a million miles away from the girl you fell in love with. We're different people now and we've got to make allowances for that. Compromise. This mindless trench warfare that says I'm damned if I'm giving any more of me away first. It's stupid! We can't give up. We can't just walk away. Where to? We owe our baby more than that. I love you, Bri. (*Laughs.*) D'you know, once upon a time that used to mean, I love you, Bri. Now all it really means is help.

She switches off. Presses rewind. Pause.

Help me.

The tape stops. She presses record again.

Monday 18th. 12 o'clock. Hello. Me again. How's things? I'm fine. Everything's fine back here. Just fine.

Scene Eight

Northern Ireland: Army barracks. A drunken celebration.

SQUADDIE (*ACTOR 4*). Aw, turn it in, Harris.

HARRIS. No, listen. There's this Lord of the Manor, right? Just off on a crusade. And he goes to his beautiful and desirable wife, 'Yeah, 'course I trust yer. It's me bleeding servants I ain't too sure about'.

SQUADDIE (*ACTOR 4*). We've heard it!

HARRIS. 'Ere, shut up. So he puts this razor-sharp chastity belt on her. Anyone tries to shag her and 'Shong!' – end of Percy python.

SQUADDIE. } Someone give him a beer.

BRIAN.   Shut, up, Harris.

HARRIS. Off he goes, right. Kills a few wogs. Comes back. Inspects all his servants. Lines 'em up, cacks down. And all of 'em, every one – cockless.

SQUADDIE. No –

HARRIS. All except one. The Lord claps him on the back. Well done, he goes. Tell me. How did you manage to resist temptation? And the servant goes (*As though tongue cut off.*) mmmmmmmmmm . . .

They all laugh except BRIAN.

BRIAN. Jesus. Bloody kids.

HARRIS. Come on, Bri. Lighten up. 'Ere, have a beer.

BRIAN. No, ta.

HARRIS. Come on. We're celebrating. Couple more weeks and we're home.

BRIAN. Yeah.

HARRIS. Well, don't look too happy about it.

BRIAN. No. I am. 'S great.

SQUADDIE. Bet he's first on anyone's party list.

BRIAN. Look –

HARRIS. 'S like being with Hitler at a barmitzvah.

They all laugh except BRIAN.

BRIAN. I just ain't in the mood. Sorry.

Pause.

HARRIS. Letter from Jenny?

BRIAN. Yeah.

HARRIS. Bad news?

BRIAN. No. Usual, you know.

HARRIS. Not still worrying about her, are yer? What she's been up to an' that?

BRIAN. No.

HARRIS. I got one from my Sue last week. Suppose I oughta read it really.

BRIAN. Come by broomstick, did it?

HARRIS. Oi! Less of that. Be worth your while to read it an' all. That'll tell you soon enough if your Jenny's misbehaving –

BRIAN *grabs* HARRIS, *choking him.*

BRIAN. I'll tell you what's worth my while, Harris. It's not listening to any more of your slimy crap, that's what!

HARRIS. You're choking me –

BRIAN. You split my head in two in Belize. All them lies and rumours about my Jenny. Going on and on about it 'til I go back and kill any chance we had of making it work.

HARRIS. I can't breathe –

BRIAN. That's 'cos I'm trying to kill you, Harris. So you don't ever open your stupid trap again.

HARRIS. Get him off. Someone –

SQUADDIE. Bri, leave him!

BRIAN *lets go and pushes* HARRIS *away.*

HARRIS. Blimey, alright. Joke's over. Just calm down, eh? Who's rattled your cage?

BRIAN. Shut up, Harris. And listen. All of yer. I don't wanna hear nothing about my Jenny from now on in, alright? Nothing. My 'mates'. All having a laugh about my slag of a wife. 'S great having mates, innit? The lads. All of us out beering and whoring and taking the piss. I'm sick of it. How long can we keep it up, eh?

HARRIS. Forever!

Everyone, except BRIAN laughs. Dies down.

BRIAN. Yeah. Nice one, Harris. Pity it ain't true. The Army can do it forever, but not you. That don't help you, Harris. Sooner or later you'll go home to your Sue and what then?

HARRIS. She'll have left me!

Everyone, except BRIAN, laughs. Dies down.

BRIAN. Easy, innit. Comforting. All the lads. Good feeling, innit. You as brave as that in bed with your wife? You as hard as that when your kid's got flu? Or when you're alone in your pit and wondering what's going to happen when you're too old to fight anymore? Here we stand, scared to a man. Wanting to repay every hurt – real or imagined. Stupid. My Jenny's not a slag. She's my wife. And I don't care what you think but I'll tell you this. She's never been unfaithful to me. That's the truth. I know that now. She'd never do that. You can say what you like but I trust her. Like I should have done all along.

BRIAN walks off. Pause. The others laugh.

HARRIS. He trusts her!

SQUADDIE. Like he should have done all along!

Scene Nine

JENNY's house: evening. Fleetwood Mac's 'Big Love' is playing. LINDA is half-cut. JENNY is fiddling with the tape recorder.

LINDA. What's this?

JENNY. Fleetwood Mac.

LINDA. Showing your age, love.

JENNY. You pissed?

LINDA *(draining her glass)*. Not yet.

She pours another drink.

LINDA. Want one?

JENNY. More than anything.

LINDA. That's my girl!

JENNY (*gesturing baby*). Better not though.

LINDA. Oh, come on. Get it started at an early age.

JENNY. And have it turn out like you?

LINDA. Boring.

JENNY. And proud of it.

LINDA. What are you doing?

JENNY. Bloody recorder. I've got a tape from Bri and it won't play.

LINDA. Give it a thump.

JENNY. Leave off, you. Choose another record.

LINDA. Don't know why you're bothering.

JENNY. He might have something interesting to say.

LINDA. Not likely though, is it?

JENNY. I live in hope.

LINDA. Be weeks old, anyhow. They'll be home in a few days – he can tell you then.

JENNY *thumps the recorder.*

LINDA. Harder than that. (*Looking at the records.*) This all you got?

JENNY. There's a few upstairs but that's all the good stuff.

LINDA. 'Abba' is good?

JENNY. That's Bri's.

LINDA. Liar.

JENNY. Alright, it's mine.

LINDA (*laughs*). I knew it!

JENNY. I didn't buy it. I didn't! Was a birthday present from David – years ago.

LINDA. Who?

JENNY. You know. The one with the ears. David ⎱ Lacey.

LINDA (*shrieking*).   Lacey!

  LINDA *laughs*.

JENNY (*laughing*). Oh, piss off. He proposed to me, you know.

LINDA (*stops laughing*). Did he?

JENNY. On a moonlit beach. Very romantic it was. Better than bloody Bri.

LINDA. Spain, wasn't it?

JENNY. Yeah.

LINDA. That's romantic.

JENNY. What? Both drunk on a moped driving the wrong side of the road? He was sick later. All over the floor of the villa.

LINDA. I wonder what he's doing now?

JENNY. Bri?

LINDA. No. David Lacey.

JENNY. I dunno. Same as he was. Accountancy, I think.

LINDA. I think we should phone him. Get him round here and sexually abuse him.

JENNY (*laughing*). He must have moved by now. He can't still be living with his mother.

LINDA. But, maybe he is.

JENNY. No. Don't even think it.

LINDA. Where's your diary? You keep all your old numbers in there.

JENNY. I've forgotten.

LINDA. It's in the bedroom, isn't it?

JENNY. No.

LINDA (*going*). That means it is! It is!

JENNY (*chasing her*). Linda! No!

Scene Ten

Northern Ireland: pub interior.

BRIAN. Come on, Harris! Get the beers in!

HARRIS (*arriving*). Ain't you had enough?

BRIAN. Where you been?

HARRIS. Fifties. I need fifties. Quick, how many you got?

BRIAN. Couple, I think. Where's my beer?

HARRIS. Come on, come on.

BRIAN. Alright! What's the rush?

HARRIS. I've pulled.

BRIAN (*laughs*). Do what?

HARRIS. I've pulled. Couple of crackers in the corner by the Juke Box. See 'em?

BRIAN. No. Get some beer, you slag.

HARRIS. Oh, drink mine for Christ's sake.

BRIAN. I already have.

HARRIS. That all you got?

BRIAN. What d'you want 'em for?

HARRIS. The Juke Box. Marvin Gaye. He heard it through the grapefruit or something. Makes 'em go all funny inside, they reckon.

BRIAN (*laughs*). Harris, behave. They can't be much more than sixteen.

HARRIS. 'S all legal then, innit? Come on –

BRIAN. Nah, sod off.

HARRIS. Wassa matter? Don't you fancy 'em?

BRIAN. Fancy 'em? I don't even know 'em.

HARRIS. Well, take it from me – they got triffic personalities, alright?

He pulls BRIAN, *who resists.*

HARRIS. Oh, come on. We're leaving in three days. Who's gonna know?

BRIAN. I'll know. I promised Jen. No more tarts.

HARRIS. Tarts? These ain't tarts. No money's changing hands. 'S chemistry, innit? 'S human nature. I got an hard-on the size of a baseball bat and their knickers are just dripping for a bit of English rough.

BRIAN. No. I promised Jen.

HARRIS. Oh, don't give me that crap!

HARRIS *moves away. Pause. He returns.*

HARRIS. Okay, look. I'm full of shit. Those Mick girls ain't gonna shag us. No way. They've just come in to cock-tease as many free drinks as they can get. An' we're their boys, Bri! Where's the harm, eh? All I want is a snog and a grope – something to wank over when we get back to barracks. That's all. Your Jen wouldn't mind that. 'S window shopping, innit. I mean, you're allowed to look, ain't yer?

BRIAN (*laughs, sort of convinced*). Yeah.

HARRIS. So what d'you say? Just for a laugh. Come on, mate. They're gorgeous.

BRIAN. I can't.

HARRIS. You owe me, Bri. I stuck by you – right down the line. You'd be copping a real heavy time if it weren't for me. All that crap about Jenny –

BRIAN. Alright!

HARRIS. Attaboy.

BRIAN. I ain't gonna do nothing, mind.

HARRIS. Yeah, I know.

BRIAN. It's just for a laugh.

HARRIS. Let's go.

BRIAN. Mine's the one on the right.

HARRIS (*laughs*). Deal!

Scene Eleven

JENNY'*s house: the same evening.*

LINDA *(flicking through diary).* Right then.

JENNY. We can't do this. I just don't believe we're doing this.

LINDA. Lacey. Lacey.

JENNY. I'm not talking to him.

LINDA. Shh!

JENNY. I'm just saying – don't give me that phone. You give me that phone and you're a dead woman.

LINDA. 962 – 7040.

JENNY. I mean it. Don't give me that phone.

LINDA *(dialling).* 9, 6, 2 . . .

JENNY. Linda, we can't. We can't do it, we can't.

LINDA. 7, 0, 4, 0.

JENNY. Linda!

LINDA. It's ringing.

Pause. The tension is killing them.

He's not in.

JENNY. Thank Christ –

LINDA *(whispering).* No, he is, he is,' he is . . . Hello? Is that David Lacey? . . . Hello, this is Linda . . . You won't remember me, but I'm a friend of Jenny's . . . Jenny Sullivan – you used to . . . Oh, you do!

LINDA *beckons* JENNY *to come closer. No chance.*

LINDA. Well, we thought we'd have an evening phoning round old friends, you know. Seeing how everyone's doing . . . Yes, Jenny's with me now. It was her idea, actually. D'you want me to pass you over? . . . Yes, she'd love to.

A furious silent battle follows which JENNY *loses.*

JENNY. Hello? . . . David, Jenny, Hi – how are you? . . . Good . . . Yes, things pretty 'fab' here too.

She pulls a face at LINDA – *'fab'?*

JENNY. What? . . . Oh, yes, married. Aren't we all? . . . Oh, well, still time . . .

LINDA *laughs.* JENNY *pulls a face – 'help!'*

JENNY. Yes . . . How's your mum? . . . Oh, she's dead –

LINDA *bursts out laughing.* JENNY *tries to shut her up.* LINDA *cannot stop however and it is so infectious that* JENNY *is soon desperately trying to remain coherent.* LINDA *is eating her jumper trying to be quiet.*

JENNY. Oh, that's a shame, I'm sorry . . . It was sudden, was it? . . . and she didn't suffer much, oh, that's good . . . yes, she was a lovely lady, yes . . . Look, David . . . I'm sorry . . . could I phone you back? . . . Yes something's . . . five minutes . . . sorry . . .

She puts the phone down and they collapse with laughter.

JENNY. You tart!

Scene Twelve

Northern Ireland: pub interior. Same evening.

BRIAN. 'Ere we go. Two pints –

HARRIS. Bloody hell, I'm pissed.

BRIAN. An' two gin an' tonics, with ice and lemon. Where are the girls?

HARRIS. Piss break. Taking their time an' all. I've been twice since they've gone.

BRIAN. Oh, shit.

HARRIS. What?

BRIAN. 'S the old bog routine, innit. 'Back in five minutes' and you never see 'em again.

HARRIS. What, these two! No chance. She's just had her tongue down my earhole for the last five minutes. Cleaned it out nice, too.

They laugh.

HARRIS. What's them gins? Doubles?

BRIAN. Triples.

They laugh.

BRIAN. Be flat on their backs soon.

HARRIS. Yeah! I'll drink to that!

They laugh. MAIREAD *and* CAITLIN *enter (*ACTORS 1 *and* 3 *as the two Irish girls).*

MAIREAD. What's the big joke, then?

HARRIS. You'll know when I take me pants down.

They all laugh.

MAIREAD. Are you pissed?

BRIAN. Nope. We're paralytic.

They all laugh.

HARRIS. So what's the plan then, girls?

CAITLIN. We're going home to our beds.

HARRIS. Triffic. We'll join yer.

CAITLIN. You will not!

MAIREAD. They wouldn't be much use anyhow – not in that state.

The two girls laugh.

HARRIS. Oh! A challenge! (*To* MAIREAD.) 'Ere, I got no problem on that score, Cattling.

MAIREAD. It's Caitlin.

HARRIS. Katey-Lynn.

CAITLIN. And it's my name. She's Mairead.

BRIAN *and the two girls laugh.*

BRIAN (*laughing*). You thick prat.

HARRIS. Mairead. Mairead. I have never, never, ever had a problem on that score.

CAITLIN (*standing*). Are you ready, Mairead?

HARRIS. Except once.

BRIAN. Oh, don't go. Still early.

HARRIS. Once, I couldn't do it. Just the once, mind.

CAITLIN (*to* MAIREAD). I want to go.

HARRIS. Nah, wait. Hold up. I'm telling a story, ain't I?

CAITLIN (*to* BRIAN). It's been fun. Thanks.

HARRIS. 'Ere, Bri, tell her. Hold on. Listen.

MAIREAD (*to* CAITLIN). Sit down. Yer man's telling a story
here.

CAITLIN *sits.* HARRIS *carries on oblivious.*

HARRIS. I was pissed, right. Well gone. And I was with this bird
called Alice.

BRIAN (*laughing*). Oh, no – not Alice.

HARRIS. Horrible, she was.

BRIAN. Gruesome.

HARRIS. Face like a bag of spanners. Now, I'll go with anyone
me.

MAIREAD. Oh, thanks a lot!

HARRIS. Oh, no. No, I never –

BRIAN (*laughing*). Get on with it. (*To* CAITLIN.) This is great.

HARRIS. So there I was – plastered out me brain. Up in this
bedroom with this girl Alice. But I wasn't doing much
horizontal hokey-cokeying if you know what I mean. Bit of a
problem tacklewise.

BRIAN. He ain't called Mr Floppy for nothing.

BRIAN *and the two girls laugh.*

HARRIS. 'Ere, shut up. Listen. So I was about to knock it on the
head, go and get another beer, when she goes, Alice right, she
goes, 'Well, shall I give you a blow-job, then?'

They all laugh.

An' I thought. Well, yeah. Alright, then.

They all laugh.

Well, you would, wouldn't yer? So, I'm sitting on the bed, an' Alice is kneeling in front of me. She gets hold of me todger and goes –

He mimes a blowing action on an imaginary phallus. Everybody explodes with laughter, particularly the men.

HARRIS. Shall I give you a blow-job!

He mimes it again and laughs hysterically.

Laugh? I thought me trousers'd never dry. 'Don't tell anyone will you?' she goes.

Everyone is still laughing. MAIREAD *is the first to stop.*

MAIREAD. You're a cruel bastard, aren't you?

HARRIS (*drying his eyes*). Oh, I had to, though.

MAIREAD (*to* CAITLIN). Come on. Let's go.

She leans forward and gives HARRIS *a quick peck on the lips.*

MAIREAD. Bye.

HARRIS. Oh, gissa better one than that.

She looks at him for a second, then bends down and kisses him fully. CAITLIN *and* BRIAN *watch awkwardly.*

CAITLIN. Bye then.

BRIAN. Yeah.

BRIAN *goes to kiss her. She moves away.* MAIREAD *breaks away from* HARRIS.

MAIREAD. Better?

HARRIS. Cor, not half! Come here –

She moves back, slapping his hands away.

MAIREAD. Think you could handle me?

HARRIS. I been trying to all night, but you won't let me.

She laughs and waves goodbye. The two girls start to go.

HARRIS. 'Ere, hold up. We'll walk you home.

BRIAN. Yeah. 'S no trouble.

MAIREAD (*going*). I'm saving myself for Mr Right.

HARRIS. But I'm here! Oi, Caitlin!

BRIAN. Mairead.

HARRIS. Mairead. I'm here!

MAIREAD (*offstage*). Bye.

They've gone. Pause.

HARRIS. Bollocks.

BRIAN. Yeah.

HARRIS. Thought I was in there.

BRIAN. Me too.

HARRIS. I bet she goes like a train.

MAIREAD (*returning*). I do. Now, are you coming or not?

She exits. BRIAN *and* HARRIS *look at each other, then race out after her.*

Scene Thirteen

Northern Ireland: the wasteland behind the pub. Ten minutes later. Night-time. No street lights.

HARRIS. Gor, it's a bit dark, innit?

MAIREAD. Oh, yer man's scared of the dark, Caitlin.

HARRIS. Yeah. You'll have to hold me hand.

MAIREAD (*squealing*). That's not your hand!

HARRIS. Oh. Ain't it?

BRIAN. Freezing, innit?

HARRIS. Yeah, come on girls. Warm us up a bit.

HARRIS grabs MAIREAD and they start to kiss. BRIAN and CAITLIN stand awkwardly.

CAITLIN. Well?

BRIAN. What?

CAITLIN. Don't you fancy me?

BRIAN. Yeah. Course.

CAITLIN. Well, come on then. (*Pause.*) Are you scared of me?

BRIAN (*laughs*). No. Course, I ain't.

CAITLIN. I'm not going to hurt you.

BRIAN. I know.

CAITLIN. I thought you Army boys had seen it all before?

BRIAN. We have.

CAITLIN. Are you married? That it? Got a wife and kids at home?

BRIAN. No.

CAITLIN. You a virgin? A virgin soldier?

BRIAN (*laughs*). Don't be daft.

CAITLIN. Gay?

BRIAN. No!

CAITLIN. Well, come on then. Prove it.

He moves across to her. They kiss, BRIAN *getting more and more enthusiastic. An I.R.A.* GUNMAN (*ACTOR 4*) *steps out of the shadows behind* BRIAN. *The girl pushes* BRIAN *away.*

BRIAN. What's wrong?

CAITLIN. Nothing. I need a piss. Wait there.

She goes.

BRIAN. Oh, bloody – (*Laughs.*) Hurry up.

The GUNMAN *shoots* BRIAN *in the back.* HARRIS *breaks away from his girl and finds himself face to face with the* I.R.A. MAN. HARRIS's *girl (ACTOR 1) moves out of the way.*

HARRIS. What – Bri? Bri!

GUNMAN (*ACTOR 4*). English bastard.

HARRIS. Oh, Jesus, no. (*To* MAIREAD). You whore!

The GUNMAN *shoots him twice.* HARRIS *falls to the ground. The* GUNMAN *walks over to him and shoots him in the head from point-*

blank range. MAIREAD *goes to the* GUNMAN *and gestures to* BRIAN.

MAIREAD. Make sure.

CAITLIN. He's dead.

MAIREAD. Make sure!

The GUNMAN *walks over to* BRIAN *who tries to get up.*

BRIAN. Jen, I –

The GUNMAN *shoots him twice, the last from point-blank range.* MAIREAD *and the* GUNMAN *exit.* CAITLIN *looks at* BRIAN's *body for a moment before she too walks quietly away.*

Scene Fourteen

JENNY's *house: later that same evening.* LINDA *has gone.* JENNY *is still fiddling with the tape recorder.*

JENNY. Ohh! Bloody thing!

She shakes the recorder, then thumps it, hard. It starts working.

Oh! Thanks, Linda.

Pause.

Hello, Bri.

(*Production Note:* BRIAN's *tape can be pre-recorded or delivered by the actor onstage in whatever manner so desired.*)

BRIAN. Hello, Jen.

JENNY. I'm alright.

BRIAN. How are you?

JENNY. Yes, I'm having fun an' that.

BRIAN. Having fun an' that?

JENNY (*laughing*). God, you're so predictable!

BRIAN. Things okay this end. Not dead yet. (*Laughs.*) Touch wood. This'll probably be my last tape. Only three weeks left now. Won't be worth sending another before we get home.

JENNY. Home.

BRIAN. Christ, I'm looking forward to that.

JENNY. Me too.

BRIAN. An' I thought Belize was bad. Here it's cold, wet and lonely – and the nasties are people, not animals. Kids, women, everyone's after yer. Keep out. That's what they're saying. This is our place. You don't belong. Well, that's fine by me 'cos I don't belong. Not here or in the Army. I belong at home. With you.

JENNY. You feeling alright?

BRIAN. Jen. I'm buying myself out.

JENNY. What?

BRIAN. 'S gonna take a while but I've made up me mind.

JENNY (*laughs*). What?

BRIAN. 'S for the best, innit?

JENNY (*laughs*). Yes. Yes, it is.

BRIAN. Know what changed my mind?

JENNY. ⎫ No, what?

BRIAN. ⎬ Getting smacked on the head with a clock. Should've happened a long time ago – geddit?

JENNY. Boom-boom.

BRIAN. See, there was this mini-riot down the Falls. A load of proddy boys got pissed up and decided to win the war single-handed.

Stupid berks. 'Course, as soon as we piled in to rescue 'em the whole place went berserk.

Pause.

You never seen such hate.

Pause.

People chucking all sorts. Harris got flattened by a T.V. set and I got me jaw knocked up round me ears by an antique clock – now there's class for you!

JENNY (*laughs*). I'm impressed.

BRIAN. I got sat against this wall. Waiting for me head to clear.
There was quite a few of us there. Proddies, squaddies and this
one Catholic geezer – all of us hurt in the riot. All of us
fighting like buggery a minute ago an' now, all sitting there. All
quiet and peaceable, like. Talking, joking – it was weird. But
what I remember most was the graffiti on the wall behind us.
Scrawled in big, white letters, it said: 'Is there life before
death?'

Pause. BRIAN *laughs.*

Stupid. Just some smart-arse comment on a brick wall in
Belfast. But it got me. 'Is there life before death?' An' I thought
then. Out. Get out. Make it work. And that's just what I'm
gonna do. What we're gonna do, Jen. Make it work. (*Laughs.*)
Got nothing else to say, really. I'm that excited. I'm that bloody
excited.

He laughs again. JENNY *joins in.*

Jen. Jen, I love you. An' I been missing you bad. But not
anymore. Not any bloody more. Three more weeks. Then I'm
home. Not long now. It'll be alright, then. You'll see. Take care
of yourself, Jen. Take care of our baby. See you soon.

JENNY. See you soon.

BRIAN. Big kisses and dirty thoughts. Always.

JENNY. Always.